JAN   2018

The HATRED of LITERATURE

The HATRED of
LITERATURE

WILLIAM MARX

Translated by NICHOLAS ELLIOTT

The BELKNAP PRESS of HARVARD UNIVERSITY PRESS

CAMBRIDGE, MASSACHUSETTS | LONDON, ENGLAND | 2018

FIRST PRINTING

This book was originally published in French as
La haine de la littérature © 2015 by Les Éditions de Minuit,
7, rue Bernard-Palissy, 74006 Paris.

Library of Congress Cataloging-in-Publication Data
Names: Marx, William, 1966– author. | Elliott, Nicholas, translator.
Title: The hatred of literature / William Marx ; translated by
    Nicholas Elliott.
Other titles: Haine de la littérature. English
Description: Cambridge, Massachusetts : The Belknap Press of
    Harvard University Press, 2018. | "This book was originally
    published in French as La haine de la littérature © 2015 by
    Les Éditions de Minuit, 7, rue Bernard-Palissy, 74006 Paris." |
    Includes bibliographical references and index.
Identifiers: LCCN 2017019208 | ISBN 9780674976122 (alk. paper)
Subjects: LCSH: Censorship—History. | Prohibited books—
    History. | Literature and morals—History. | Literature—History
    and criticism.
Classification: LCC PN45 .M387313 2018 | DDC 801/.9—dc23
LC record available at https://lccn.loc.gov/2017019208

The hatred of literature! The hatred of literature!

—GUSTAVE FLAUBERT

Where does this hatred of literature come from? Is it envy or stupidity?
Both, probably, with a strong dose of hypocrisy on top.

—GUSTAVE FLAUBERT, letter to Princess Mathilde,
July 2, 1867

They copied everything they stumbled upon....
Specimens of every style, agricultural, medical, theological, classic,
romantic, periphrases.
Parallels: crimes of the people—of kings—benefits of religion, crimes of
religion.
Beauties. Make a universal history of beauties.
Dictionary of accepted ideas. Catalogue of fashionable ideas.

—GUSTAVE FLAUBERT, notes for *Bouvard and Pécuchet*

Contents

The HATRED of LITERATURE

Introduction
Literature and Anti-literature

LITERATURE IS A SOURCE OF SCANDAL. It always has been. This is what defines it.

Reader, be warned: if you do not want to be scandalized, throw out this book before it is too late. Otherwise, welcome. But be aware that the scandal will not always be where you expect it.

ANTI-LITERATURE is the term used for any discourse that is opposed to literature and defines it through the process of opposing it. *Literature*, then, is any discourse to which anti-literature is opposed. There is no literature without anti-literature.

Let's explore this circle.

WHAT IS LITERATURE? Too many things: no object that has remained identical through the centuries can claim this beautiful name. The reality is so diverse, the name so flatly constant. Yet we use it, without much concern, to refer to texts dating back three thousand years in the Western world. (Mesopotamia and Egypt would take us further back in time; they could easily be included in this vast and flexible denomination.)

This book also uses the word *literature*, for lack of another currently available term and out of linguistic convenience, with the understanding that it does not imply a univocal reality.

What could possibly allow us to group together three thousand years of poetry, fiction, and theater, Homer and Beckett, Aeschylus and Bolaño, Dante and Mishima? In logical terms, nothing at all—except for the fact that this discourse has been kept apart from all others and has met with constant opposition. It has been a permanent opponent—public enemy no. 1—the thing we most love to scorn, attack, and belittle.

Literature is always the weakest, most suspect discourse, the one that is always on the verge of going out of fashion and being left behind. Other discourses have a positive identity, which, although sometimes questioned, is always asserted: philosophy seeks wisdom, science the truth of nature, theology the knowledge of God, etc. Only literature lacks its own objects. It had some once, but they were stolen.

—Surely you're exaggerating! Other discourses have faced constant attacks, starting with philosophy. Socrates was the first martyr, don't forget, and many others followed.

—Yes, but Socrates attacked Homer, and Homer hadn't attacked anyone.[1]

Philosophy was born by clashing with the discourse that came before it, denying it any claim to authority, truth, or morality. In so doing, it implicitly defined some of the most salient features of *literature*.

In Archaic Greece, poetry was the discourse of the Muses: words of truth, inspired by the Muses. At the time, there were only two fundamentally reliable discourses: that of the law, and that of the Muses. Any other discourse aspiring to a place of honor had to position itself in relation to these two. This is exactly what Plato did in *The Republic*, by inventing new laws and exiling the poets—two closely related acts. It is no accident that condemnations of poetry run as a leitmotif through Plato's dialogue.

What followed is well known: the poets wound up naked and poor, and this asceticism became their fate. Or, to put it another way, *literature* is what remains when everything else has been removed.

Which is not to say that writers have not taken a stab at criticizing discourses: Aristophanes attacked philosophers, Molière reviled physicians, Flaubert assailed the positive sciences, and, more recently, Jean-Charles Massera and Michel Houellebecq have taken on the dominant ideologies. But this critical discourse is not foundational.

Literature can also occasionally lash out at itself: there are no fiercer or more justified attacks than those by writers, from *Don Quixote* to Witold Gombrowicz, from Paul Valéry to the surrealists. These attacks, during certain periods of crisis, have to do with championing a different kind of literature, pushing literature to evolve, or inventing another ideal.

I discussed these internal attacks at length in my book *L'Adieu à la littérature* (Farewell to literature). In the present book, the attacks in question come from the outside, and the farewell is spoken without a trace of nostalgia.[2]

IN THE OPPOSITION to other art forms—music, painting, sculpture—something different is at stake. In this case the front is clearly defined: the opposition does not encroach upon its opponent's territory or turn its own weapons against it. Anti-music has no interest in musical notes, just as the anti-painter has little use for brushes and easels.[3]

Here, on the other hand, confusion reigns: anti-literary discourse and literature share a medium, the medium of language, and the result is a fratricidal struggle to occupy the territory and symbolically mark it—an effort that must constantly be renewed. The first battles do not prevent later incursions or provocations, and hostilities are resumed ad infinitum.

REPEATED THEFTS, attacks at every opportunity, and verbal, rather than physical, assaults: since Plato—and even a little earlier, if one includes Heraclitus and Xenophanes of Colophon—the aggressors have had a field day. The wildest, most absurd, and most ridiculous arguments have been used to denounce literature.[4]

Sometimes these discourses provide an implicit description of the literature of their time: they outline its ambitions, its powers, and its failures; they express expectations for literature, which naturally are never met; and, paradoxically, they enable a deeper understanding of the very literature they attack, as well as its ideological context.

But most of the time, as with every kind of madness, repetition rules; the same arguments are brought up over and over again. Plato already uses nearly all of them.

For anti-literature is anything but a reasonable discourse: it is a foundational scene that everyone wants to reenact at one point or another, to gain status or simply to exist. Literature serves as an ideal target, a punching bag, a foil—a springboard.

Anti-literary discourses do not always strive for the death of their opponent: they are often satisfied to squash it so they can take their turn at enjoying existence. If there had been no literature, anti-literature would eventually have invented it.

THE STORY of anti-literature follows the Macbeth model: told by an idiot, full of sound and fury, and meaning nothing. Rather than drawing up a useless chronological list of these repetitive discourses, this book discusses the four principal suits brought against literature:

—in the name of authority (to put other authorities in the place of literature)
—in the name of truth (literature is worthless compared with science)
—in the name of morality (literature is destructive of every kind of norm)
—in the name of society (writers are forbidden to hold rank in society or to speak in its name)

These four trials are difficult to separate: certain arguments about truth are also relevant to the moral question and are related to the refusal of authority. Nonetheless, they outline four principal fronts, four primal scenes that are reenacted in different contexts, under various terms, with varying levels of talent.

I will consider only the most general discourses, excluding those that exclusively target certain writers and literary movements, as well as individual acts of censorship and criticism of specific genres—the novel, fiction, theater—which were widespread from the sixteenth to the eighteenth centuries.[5] However, I mention some of these specific arguments when they are relevant to the general polemic.

These four trials have been constantly repeated, through eternal return and with slight variations, legal quibbling, and controversy, amid a flurry of lawyers, prosecutors, and lowly court clerks. Reader, you are entering a gallery of grotesques: a philologist dozing on his golden chair, a failed chemist giving a blockbuster lecture, a Dominican priest fulminating from the pulpit, a Protestant minister in the grips of an Oedipal crisis. You will encounter along the way a king, an emperor, a president of France, and a handful of government ministers. And even a few heroes and white knights of the literary cause.

AND YET THERE was a time before the trials. A mythical time, mythologized by anti-literature itself, in far-off Greece, where poets had specific powers and appeared as servants of transcendence, bearers of a prodigious discourse that inspired respect: a discourse of authority and truth; a literature before anti-literature, from which the entire chain of subsequent reactions was determined, and without knowledge of which the four trials-to-come would be incomprehensible. Words from elsewhere. Magical, sacred words.

These words are the focus of the brief but necessary historical overture that follows.

Call the defendant.

Words from Elsewhere

An ordinary scene in the Trojan War. What Teucer saw. Deictic, train, scissors. What Helen saw. The Odyssey as meta-epic. The Muse. Of flowers and mammoths. The shamanic aoidos. Tales of possession. Dancing on Mount Parnassus. Verse and trance. In praise of the autodidact.

THE SCENE is *The Iliad*. In the tenth year of the Trojan War. Men have been fighting under the eyes of the gods for a long time—probably *because* of the gods, who intervene here and there, in a haphazard way, tipping the scales sometimes to one side, sometimes to the other. Now the Argives are tired and the Trojans have the advantage: hurried along by valiant Hector, the army of the Achaeans (another name for the Argives) is retreating to its seaside camp in indescribable chaos. Suddenly the Achaeans find themselves trapped between the moat and the wall, which were supposed to protect them but may now serve as their grave. Though nothing offers better protection than a gravestone—it shelters you from the living—it remains a last resort. People generally prefer to try something else. It is a critical moment, as they say: Hector has sworn that if the Trojans succeed in penetrating the camp, his army will burn its ships, and the Danaäns (another name for the Achaeans) will be condemned to die on enemy soil. This would mark the end of the Trojan War and the defeat of Agamemnon's army—we're not there yet, but we might as well enjoy some anticipatory shivers.

Meanwhile, heads are sliced off, brains spurt into the air, spears slide through teeth and rip through necks, and other heartwarming deeds take place. Luckily, Agamemnon sees the danger. He crisscrosses the camp haranguing his troops, and presto, they are back in action, further revived because Zeus has just punctuated Agamemnon's speech with a miracle: an eagle drops a fawn close to the altar of the father of the gods. A rather unusual sign, admittedly, but people have returned to the battlefield for less. So here are all the beautiful heroes again, in a parade worthy of Offenbach: the indomitable Diomedes, of course; then the two Atreides, Agamemnon and Menelaus; the no less inseparable two Ajaxes (the greater and the lesser); Idomeneus and his second-in-command Meriones; Eurypylus, son of Euaemon; and finally, Teucer, son of Telamon. Teucer is a bastard, but he works wonders: he grabs his bow and slays every Trojan in sight, one after the other—a fine slaughter, really. Agamemnon, a connoisseur of the business of killing, comes to congratulate and encourage him: if you continue like this, he essentially tells him, when Ilion (another name for Troy) has fallen, you will be able to choose between a tripod (in bronze, it goes without saying—i.e., a tremendous amount of money), double horsepower (in other words, a two-horse chariot), or a woman to put in your bed (no explanation necessary).

History does not tell us which of these valuable gifts Teucer would have chosen (a difficult decision: in quantity of legs, the two quadrupeds clearly surpass the tripod and the biped, but there are probably other parameters to consider). We do not know whether he was grumpy that day or simply had gotten out of bed on the wrong side; what is indisputable is that he was offended. Word for word, this is his answer to Agamemnon:

> Son of Atreus, most lordly: must you then drive me who am eager
> myself, as it is? Never, so far as the strength is in me,
> have I stopped, since we began driving the Trojans back upon Ilion;
> since then have I been lurking here with my bow, to strike down
> fighters. And by this I have shot eight long-flanged arrows,
> and all of them were driven into the bodies of young men,
> fighters . . . .

One can easily understand Teucer's state of mind: a hero worthy of the name does not like to be told to do what he is already doing perfectly well, and on his own initiative. As for offering him gifts, isn't it offensive to assume that he is acting out of self-interest when it is only glory that is driving him? In short, Teucer's reply is utterly appropriate to this Homeric world in which warriors on the battlefield constantly challenge one another. But that's not all. Teucer also adds—listen carefully, it's important: "yet still I am not able to hit this mad dog."[1]

Suddenly everything shifts, and we find ourselves entering a new world. Who is "this mad dog"? There is no likely person indicated in the preceding lines, yet there is also nothing to suggest one should take the expression literally and believe that a real mad dog is casually wandering around the battlefield. Only men, horses, and gods have a right to be on the field—and that's complicated enough as it is. In fact, one needs to go back eighty-three lines to identify the animal in a reference to Hector, the son of King Priam, who is carrying out a horrible massacre and leading the Trojans to victory. It must certainly be Hector whom Teucer wants to hit, in order to reverse the course of the battle.

Eighty-three lines is long, very long. In fact, it is too long for the audience members listening to Homer (or the *aoidos,* it doesn't matter which one), who do not have the poem's text in hand and cannot immediately consult it. In practice, therefore, the demonstrative *this,* in *this mad dog,* cannot refer to the last mention of Hector in line 216 of book 8. It does not refer to anything that is literally in the text of *The Iliad* (in grammatical terms, it is not an anaphora). Instead, it fulfills an entirely different function: it indicates someone or something that Teucer (for he is the one speaking) sees on the battlefield and points out to Agamemnon. Someone or something that Agamemnon can therefore also see by turning his head, but whom the audience members, comfortably seated listening to the *aoidos,* cannot see with their own eyes—no matter which way they turn. The epic poem's audience can only be surprised by the use of this demonstrative that refers to nothing in the previous lines. This is exactly the effect that Homer is looking for.

Merely by using the word *this* (*touton,* in Greek, standing out at the beginning of the line), Teucer summons the audience of *The Iliad* to the battlefield: forced to put themselves in the hero's place, they suddenly discover right before their eyes a reality that is entirely different from the one surrounding them. In an instant, the devastated landscape of the plain of Troy a few centuries earlier opens out before them: there's a mêlée, the ground strewn with bodies, and here is the figure of Hector silhouetted on the horizon, relentlessly carving his way through the Achaeans. The abruptness of this demonstrative without a textual referent would have been practically unprecedented in Homeric times. Today its effect is probably blunted, so blasé are we after close to three thousand years of development of the verbal arts, which use or have used devices far more effective and sophisticated—in the same way that Diomedes's javelin would be no match for a nuclear missile. But we must put ourselves in the state of mind of someone listening to Homer. All things being relative, this deictic demonstrative would have had the intensity of the Lumière brothers' film of a train arriving at the station in La Ciotat, sending the first cinematograph audience running in fear, or the suggestive power of the first films made in 3D. This little word singlehandedly creates the illusion of seeing Hector, practically in the flesh, no less present than Grace Kelly's desperate hand coming off the screen to grab a pair of scissors in *Dial M for Murder*—except that in Homer's case, we do not need stereoscopic glasses.[2]

Fully aware of the *coup de force* he has carried out, Homer is careful not to overwhelm his audience and to ensure that surprise does not hamper their involvement with the narrative. In the very next line, he explains the meaning of *this mad dog:* "He spoke, and let fly another shaft from the bowstring, straight for Hector, and all his heart was straining to hit him."[3] It's about time: the slightly distracted listener finally understands who Teucer was talking about. Homer is not as provocative as Paul Valéry, whose audacious use of a single demonstrative plunges his reader into uncertainty for the whole length of a poem. (Some would even accuse him of mystification, furious that they had been unable to decipher the nature of "this" famous "quiet roof, where dove-sails saunter by" in *Le Cimetière marin* [*The Graveyard by the Sea*]).[4]

It is not the first time that Homer uses this technique. In book 3, while watching the battle from atop the ramparts of Troy, old King Priam asks Helen a question:

> So you could tell me the name of this man who is so tremendous;
> who is this Achaian man of power and stature?
> Though in truth there are others taller by a head than he is,
> yet these eyes have never yet looked on a man so splendid
> nor so lordly as this: such a man might well be royal.

Helen answers him, of course, but one has to wait eight lines for her to satisfy the old man's curiosity and finally name the splendid Achaian: it is none other than "Atreus's son Agamemnon, widely powerful, at the same time a good king and a strong spearfighter."[5] The uncertainty of the audience, as well as that of Priam, therefore lasts longer than in book 8. Yet the uncertainty is also less acute: though he is not named, Agamemnon is described. Those in the audience know no more than the king of Troy. Like him, they wait for a reply. Book 8 puts an end to this fine equivalence between the audience's knowledge and that of the characters: both Teucer and Agamemnon know who "this mad dog" is before the audience does. Line 299 briefly opens a window onto another world: by means of this linguistic expression of a hallucinatory or shamanic vision, another reality suddenly appears about which the audience lacks information—a reality greater than the words that refer to it, conjured by words but not limited to them.

Even Teucer's words come from this other world, having been uttered through fictional lips that refer to an elsewhere that is inaccessible other than through language. Such is the transcendence of the *aoidos*'s song: it is not him speaking, but another—in this case,

Teucer, dead so many centuries ago. In *The Odyssey,* Odysseus himself expresses surprise at this mysterious power, saying to Demodocus:

> . . . you sing the Achaians'
> venture, all they did and had done to them, all the sufferings
> of these Achaians, as if you had been there yourself or heard it
> from one who was.[6]

This passage displays the meta-epic, nearly reflexive aspect of *The Odyssey,* in which Homer—whoever may bear that name—wonders about the definition of his art and the conditions under which it is exercised. (Let's take this opportunity to ask whether one can really say there ever was a golden age of the epic if the second great Homeric poem already proposes its critique and deconstruction. Setting the epic down in writing was in and of itself a betrayal of the rhapsode's trade: *The Iliad* betrays *The Iliad.* In other words, the transcribed poem as we know it disfigures the infinite modulation of the rhapsodic songs about the Trojan War by setting them in stone. The period of decline had already come. This statement comes with a corollary, however: if decline has always existed, then it is only a myth.)

As it happens, neither Demodocus nor Homer ever visited Troy. If both are able to know with extreme accuracy what the war was like, to describe its slightest incident, to speak for Agamemnon and Teucer, and to create the impression that they can see in detail the horrible chaos of a battlefield several centuries earlier, it can only be because that power came from a god. The Muse, or perhaps Apollo, has either instructed them or speaks through them—it comes down to the same thing. Odysseus says as much about Demodocus:

> "Demodokos, above all mortals beside I prize you.
> Surely the Muse, Zeus's daughter or else Apollo has taught you
> . . .
> If you can tell me the course of all these things as they happened,

I will speak of you before all mankind, and tell them
how freely the goddess gave you the magical gift of singing."
He spoke, and the singer, stirred by the goddess, began, and showed
them
his song.[7]

Thus, Demodocus begins his poem in the same way as Homer, who plainly admits in the first lines of *The Iliad* that his song belongs not to him, but to the Muse.

LONG BEFORE RIMBAUD, the poet was an other—except that this metamorphosis was in no way a metaphor glossed to dullness: it was experienced as a reality.[8] And why not? All things considered, there is a change of identity as soon as language serves a function unrelated to the immediate action or to a simple description of surrounding reality, as soon as one is no longer speaking in one's own name but borrowing someone else's words. If you stop to think about it, recounting an event distant in time or space or reporting another person's words is not self-evident. To bring forward an absent reality, to be able to modify one's own self, is a privilege no less than a danger: it is one quick step from here to misunderstanding, even scandal. Poetry and fiction were bound to eventually take that step.

There is a big leap from, "I'm off to find us a mammoth for lunch" to "Daddy said: 'I'm off to find us a mammoth for lunch.'" In the latter statement, the speaker is retrospectively repeating someone else's words, rather than speaking directly in the here and now. The leap is even greater to, "And the Great Goddess said: 'Let us create mammoths so that humans can have lunch'" (for these linguistic developments took place in the far distant past, long before Homer, perhaps in the era of the great goddess mothers—that is, if they themselves are not a myth invented in modern times). In this last statement, one imagines the words of a fictional and distant creature in the context of a vision of the world that structures the visible and the invisible, the past, the present, and the future.[9] The practice of reported speech involves a twist applied to language, an act of violence against ordinary utterance, in so far as the first person no longer refers to someone speaking *hic et nunc,* but to a being distant in time and space, dead or imaginary. As soon as the deixis no longer corresponds to the lexis, language functions like a shamanic mask: it alters the speaker and makes an absent being appear instead. At the same time, a strange veil falls over the environment shared by the speaker and listener, and another world appears indistinctly, brought forth in its entirety by the absent being who is suddenly present.

"I say: a flower!" writes Mallarmé, "and, out of the oblivion into which my voice consigns any real shape, as something other than petals known to man, there rises, harmoniously and gently, the ideal flower itself, the one that is absent from all earthly bouquets."[10] In the late nineteenth century, the poet of the *Coup de dés* desperately sought to restore to language the evocative power it must originally have had. For that is also what is meant by "[giving] a purer sense to the words of the tribe": restoring a power that Archaic poets still had at their disposal, with which they could play without fearing to exhaust its spells.[11]

The *aoidos* was a shaman—or at least wanted to be, and presented himself as such—and Mallarmé, the poet of the rue de Rome, was trying to become one too. Yet the Muses were never seen roaming his bourgeois Paris neighborhood: they would certainly have attracted attention wandering around in a pack. They might even have been mistaken for cheap hussies in revealing outfits.

TODAY the Muses are met with indifference at best, or with a mocking smile. Unless they are beautiful teases with vaguely libidinous artists hanging off their arms ("Let me introduce you to my muse," one artiste says in a whisper either flattering or ironic, wearily gesturing to his female companion—or to the glass in which the last drop of his dry martini quivers), they are to be locked up in a closet with other poetic relics. Who would want to bring them back out? Ronsard did not believe in the Muses anymore, only using them as cold allegories of poetry. Horace and Virgil were hardly more enthusiastic.

Homer's case is entirely different: the Muse that opens *The Iliad* and *The Odyssey* is no joke. In fact, she does better than open the books: she sings them. "Sing, goddess, the anger of Peleus's son Achilleus," "Tell me, Muse, of the man of many ways": the *aoidos* can only sing what the source of divine inspiration sings in him and through him.[12] One could provide a more literal translation of the first verse of *The Odyssey:* "Tell *in* me, Muse . . ." Let the Greek words speak for themselves: *moi ennepe.* The Muse speaks *in* the poet, who lends her his mouth. Medium, shaman, whirling dervish: any of the comparisons made today accurately conveys the supernatural origin of this song in which the human being serves only as a go-between.

The poet's knowledge is only borrowed, particularly when it's a question of listing all the combatants on the plain of Troy. I refer to the famous catalog of ships in the second book of *The Iliad:* three hundred interminable lines naming all the Greek leaders, followed by a less expansive enumeration of the Trojan leaders. Now, before launching into this perilous anthology piece, the *aoidos* again invokes the Muses:

> For you, who are goddesses, are there, and you know all things,
> and we have heard only the rumor of it and know nothing.
> Who then of those who were the chief men and the lords of the
>   Danaäns?
> I could not tell over the multitude of them nor name them,
> not if I had ten tongues and ten mouths, not if I had
> a voice never to be broken and a heart of bronze within me,
> not unless the Muses of Olympia, daughters
> of Zeus of the aegis, remembered all those who came beneath Ilion.[13]

Homer's knowledge, like Demodocus's, comes from elsewhere: both men allow us to hear a voice that is not theirs. They are inspired or possessed.

A few decades later, Hesiod says the same thing: not content with opening his *Theogony* with the usual invocation of the Muses, he puts them first in the long series of divine genealogies that make up the poem. Before even mentioning the origins of the world, he begins to sing the birth of the Muses, daughters of Zeus and Memory (Mnemosyne): the first one hundred and fifteen lines are devoted to the Muses. This they ordered the poet to do through an irrevocable decree, and the order is logical, given that without the Muses there would be no poem and no origin of the world, either: the Muses are the source of every truth, as well as "lies identical to the truth," as Hesiod adds in a cutting remark that may be meant for Homer. It is through them that the poet can "name what will be and what has been," and from them that the poet's knowledge and authority derive legitimacy.[14]

Many of the most ancient surviving Greek poems begin with an invocation to the Muses or to Calliope, the principal Muse: "Muse, sing a hymn to Hermes," "Muse, tell me of the feats of Aphrodite, shining with so much gold," "Muse, sing a hymn to Artemis," "Harmonious Muse, sing a hymn to the mother of all the gods and all men," "Muse, speak to me of the son of Hermes."[15] Muse here, Muse there, Muse everywhere . . . Yet the Muse never explicitly takes the floor; it is the invocation itself that imperceptibly develops into the evocation of the requested hero:

> Sing, goddess, the anger of Peleus' son Achilleus
> and its devastation, which put pains thousandfold upon the Achaians,
> hurled in their multitudes to the house of Hades strong souls
> of heroes, but gave their bodies to be the delicate feasting
> of dogs, of all birds, and the will of Zeus was accomplished
> since that time when first there stood in division of conflict
> Atreus' son the lord of men and brilliant Achilleus.[16]

This is the beginning of *The Iliad*. The entire thread of the story unspools from the initial call to the Muse, through successive additions to the opening sentence, without ever marking a break between the voice of the poet and that of the goddess, which take each other's place through the snowball effect of the invocation. Is it not significant that the Homeric *I* most often appears only to invoke the *you* of the goddess, as if the two persons remained inseparable?[17] Such is the linguistic formula of that particular type of possession known as poetic inspiration.[18]

The Iliad presents itself both as a single long prayer to the Muse and as an actual song sung by the Muse. Here, one must forget the modern claim that no clause can have two concurrent speakers: what is true of the ordinary use of language cannot be applied to the poetic liturgy of the Muse.[19] One is reminded of the character in H. P. Lovecraft's fantastic tales whose voice alters when he is possessed by the demon.[20] The same is true of all the hymns to the Muse mentioned above. This Greek poetry is literally a godsend—at least it presents itself as such.

THE MUSES WERE FAR more than beautiful young women who charm poets, as they are portrayed in seventeenth-century paintings. They were also not abstract allegories, cold emblems of the roles they were each assigned by tradition, mere mannequins to which accessories could be attached: there would be no Euterpe without her flute, as we know, or Melpomene without a tragic mask. Urania didn't have an easy life, either, with her armillary sphere and compass, so cumbersome when it's time to go to bed.

This division of labor did not occur until late in the history of the Muses. There are not nine Muses because there are nine arts. On the contrary: there are nine arts because there are nine Muses. There are nine Muses because the Parcae (Fates), Furies, Hours, and Graces all come in threes, and nine is the natural outgrowth of three (furthermore, there may originally only have been three, venerated in a sanctuary on Mount Helicon).[21] There are nine Muses because the memory of the world rests on them; since they are charged with enumerating the world, they must have all the numbers available to them. There are nine Muses because they themselves are the daughters of Memory, and Zeus made love to this Titaness nine nights in a row. There are nine Muses because, as everyone knows, children embody the memory of the most intimate and fleeting moments in their parents' lives. There are nine Muses because the responsibility to remember falls to children. There are nine Muses because it takes at least nine of them to celebrate the victory of the gods of Olympus over the Titans, which inspired their first song. There are nine Muses because it takes nine to tirelessly twirl on Mount Parnassus in a perpetual dance. There are nine Muses because multiplicity and polyphony are the principles of poetry. There are nine Muses because there is a tenth one: Apollo. Or more precisely: Apollo Musagetes, literally, "the leader of the Muses," the one who leads their songs and their dances.

But careful: this is no night out at the disco. On Mount Parnassus, dance has a liturgical function; it is the great rite of the advent of the presence, of the appearance of the divinity, which can also be found in Phrygia with the Corybantes or Crete with the Curetes. The Curetes danced without respite, loudly banging their weapons together to drown out little Zeus's wailing with the crashing of bronze and thus to prevent his father, Cronus, from becoming aware of the infant's existence. What more needs to be said about the power of the dance than that it ensured the survival of the most powerful of the gods? According to some sources, there were also nine Curetes, and they shared the Muses' gift of clairvoyance and prophecy.

It is no coincidence that Mount Parnassus dominates the site of Delphi: while the Muses dance up high on the mountain, the Pythia vaticinates on her tripod. Apollo Musagetes is the god both of music and of oracles. These two activities only appear separate to us profane moderns, for whom truth is separate from beauty and science from music and poetry. Yet the authority of Apollonian speech manifests itself first in its particular form, which allows the divine to be present here below.

Plutarch tells us that the oracles of the Pythia were originally given in verse:

Accordingly, the God [namely Apollo] did not begrudge to the art of prophecy adornment and pleasing grace, nor did he drive away from here [i.e., from Delphi] the honored Muse of the tripod, but introduced her rather by awakening and welcoming poetic natures.[22]

However, Plutarch considerably reduces the role of verse: according to him, rhythm and poetry are only adornments gratuitously added to truthful content, at best useful for mnemotechnic purposes. This is how Plutarch justifies the fact that in his time, the turn of the second century CE, it was no longer necessary for the Pythia to express herself in verse.

Here, Plutarch is guilty of excessive rationalization: he is forgetting verse's ritual quality in Archaic Greece. Five or six centuries earlier, song, dance, music, and poetry had not yet become simple adornments of the rite; they *made up* the rite, which, along with sacrifice, was one of the doors through which divinity entered this world. After centuries of church organs and hymns having been pushed into the background, as mere liturgical ornaments which the mass could easily do without, it's time to get rid of our modern habits: throughout its history, Christianity has constantly intellectualized most of the pagan and even Christian observances that related to the body, and turned them at best into mere supplements to the liturgy. In many ways, fans of techno parties and Wagner aficionados who dress to the nines to flock to Bayreuth in search of ecstasy are rediscovering a physiology of trance and transcendence that modern religions have often tended to neglect, if not scorn.

In another section of the text quoted above, Plutarch recalls that in the Archaic period "history and philosophy" were themselves expressed through verse and music. Far from being incompatible with a discourse of truth, poetry was its distinguishing feature; what was formulated in verse necessarily fell under a superior order, unrelated to the usages of ordinary language. It was not merely the seal of truth; it brought the truth out with the help of Apollo and the Muses, who only agreed to reveal it once the yoke of a determined rhythm and cadence had been imposed.

> Honor of mankind, Sacred LANGUAGE,
> Ordered and prophetic speech,
> Chains of beauty that enwind
> The god bewildered in the flesh,
> Illumination, and largess!
> Now a wisdom makes utterance,
> And rings out in that sovereign voice
> Which when it rings can only know
> It is no longer anyone's
> So much as the woods' and the waters' voice![23]

By a finely-wrought coincidence, these lines by Valéry present the curious twentieth-century resurrection of a poetics of possession not so far removed from that of most Archaic Antiquity, where the voice of truth necessarily comes from elsewhere, from high above or deep inside, without becoming identified with the poet's voice, which only serves as a medium.

This is how one should interpret the famous lines of *The Odyssey* in which the *aoidos* Phemius, at great risk of being slaughtered by Odysseus during the killing of the suitors, tries to plead his case to the vengeful hero: "I am an *autodidact*," he exclaims (*autodidaktos* in Greek), "and the god has inspired in me the song ways of every kind."[24] In this case, *autodidact* cannot mean "a self-taught person," in the modern sense of the word, nor even "a person who has not had a teacher," as it is sometimes translated: this clause would be in flagrant contradiction with the reference to divine inspiration that immediately follows. The word simply indicates that the *aoidos* did not seek his knowledge where it is usually found, that is in learning (*mathêsis*), listening (*akroasis*), or inquiry (*historia*), but that this knowledge appears in him spontaneously, in a manner both natural and miraculous, irreducible to human reason. Ultimately, Phemius is saying, "I am innately all-knowing" and "My knowledge arises spontaneously." Marvelous knowledge, indeed, for it is sufficient to give Odysseus justification to spare the *aoidos,* which he does without hesitation. But it is also a terribly fragile knowledge in that it is not put to the test of truth and does not know the conditions under which it was produced.

Through the mere presence of characters like the *aoidoi* Phemius and Demodocus, *The Odyssey* initiates an examination of the art of the rhapsodic song, and of poetry in general, that is absent in *The Iliad.* While the author of the earlier epic poem seemed to practice a happy art, free of doubt and criticism, the author of the poem of Odysseus— regardless of whether or not he also wrote the poem of Achilles— insists on justifying here and there, in subtle ways, the importance of his role and the value of his words.

One should frankly also ask whether Homer himself believed in the Muse. It is not at all certain that he did. It would be reckless to see *The Iliad* and *The Odyssey* as naïve evidence of an allegedly original state of literature: they are only the oldest surviving works, the last representatives of a tradition that was already in decline or in the midst of transformation. Homer's relationship with the Muse appears to be typical of archaism, but that appearance may be illusory. At least he pretends to believe in her, in the context of an authentic theory of poetry—for Homer was, before Aristotle, the first theorist of Western literature. And why not? After all, it was inevitable that the knowledge of the *aoidos* would eventually have to become its own object: the innate knowledge that came from Apollo and the Muses could not long ignore the Apollonian injunction "Know thyself," which was inscribed on the pediment of the temple at Delphi. This set in motion a spiral of endless justification from which poetry would not emerge unscathed.

Or could it be that *The Odyssey* was already seeking to respond to external criticism now forgotten, of which the only implicit trace is this fragmented praise addressed to the mythical Phemius and Demodocus? Patience! The denigrators of poetry would soon appear in broad daylight. Then the time of anti-literature would be upon us.

First Trial
Authority

Hector emerges from a hat. Genesis of literature. The poet naked and exiled. Parable of the two kings. Xenophanes of Colophon. On authority regarding kittens and their mittens. The violence of Heraclitus. Archilochus's cow and Homer's lice. Three attempts at a definition of literature. A weapon of mass seduction. Lying, a privilege of state. The versatility of the poet. Truth is a new idea. How philosophy rewrote The Odyssey. *The first book-burning. The jealous old rhetor. A world without revelation. Chairman Plato's cultural revolution. No* Republic *in the* Republic. *Jesus and Paul versus the men of letters. The surprising rise of the Catholic novelist. Three saints to the rescue of literature. Isidore's guilty conscience. An anti-literary psalm. Is it better to burn heretics or grammarians? The holiness of barbarism. God doesn't care about grammar. Poets are pagans. How Thomas Aquinas saved literature. Anti-literature in Rome.*

POETS PRIDE THEMSELVES on being "servants of the Muses."[1] Wouldn't it be better to serve the truth? They have been reminded of this time and time again.

For indeed, the form of discourse in which the speaker claims not to be the author is certainly annoying. Making the dead speak, conjuring up absent beings, making us believe in their presence: can all this really be taken seriously? Line 299 of book 8 of *The Iliad* is like an epistemological scandal, a cheap piece of verbal sleight-of-hand: Hector appearing in the guise of a mad dog, like a rabbit pulled out of a top hat?[2] Come on! It's about time this masquerade came to an end.

—What is it called, by the way?

You could call it *literature,* and its problems are only beginning.

IN FACT, it is when literature begins to have problems that it actually begins. It does not start with Homer, with *Gilgamesh,* or with the romantic period, but with Plato driving the poets out of the city, just as God drove our first forebears out of Eden. That is literature's genesis, and this genesis is a historical fact.

As long as we lack consciousness, we do not exist. Did Adam and Eve really exist, nonchalantly strolling among the flowers and animals in earthly paradise, effortlessly speaking a language understood by all in a blissful melding with the world and its Creator? From the day they discovered that they were naked and that this nakedness brought them shame, they were conscious. They became fully human, these two who had previously been satisfied with *being*—a huge step, but one that was easy to take. All they had to do was eat the fruit from the tree of knowledge of good and evil. The tree did not need to have some hidden quality or mysterious power: any tree, plant, or rock can easily provide this knowledge, as long as it is forbidden. Any old closet, drawer, or box in a house will do the trick: what child, what Ariadne, could resist opening the seventh door in Bluebeard's castle? The nature of the forbidden object has little importance: the most ordinary object will not be the least effective—far from it. The law creates the sin, says the Apostle, since the prohibition creates covetousness, but in doing so it opens a space to consciousness, freedom, and existence.[3]

So it went with the poets: they described the world, the gods, the heroes—not on their own, as things they knew that they knew, the way I know from experience, for instance, that the sun is shining outside this window, that my hand has five fingers, and that the cat closes its eyes when I rub its head—but through the effect of an innate knowledge, a knowledge without consciousness and without proof, the knowledge that the Muses lavish upon their faithful servants.

Then came the philosopher, who, for his part, really *knew*, that is, knew that he knew or even knew that he did not know, the essential in this case being that he was not unaware of the conditions either of this knowledge or this ignorance. At the same time, he also knew that the poets did not know with real knowledge and that they produced only the appearance of knowledge. Socrates demonstrated this at length to the rhapsode Ion, who strutted about in town squares but came away from this conversation sheepish and humiliated, his arrogance defeated.

This is how the poets came to know that they were naked, like the proverbial emperor, and that they would never again be able to touch the tree of knowledge or claim to share its fruit. This is also how they learned that they were not philosophers.

And this is how they became poets.

THE FIRST LESSON OF PHILOSOPHY: whatever it is that poets do, it's not philosophy. What a lesson! The poets' cheeks are still stinging from it. But if it isn't philosophy that they're doing, what is it?

TWO KINGS LIVE UNEASILY in the same city. One king will eventually want to cut off the other king's head. In the best of cases, he will settle for driving him out, and leave it at that.

One day, the philosophers decided to take power and become kings. They built an ideal city and banned poetry and poets once and for all. They would have cut off the poets' heads if they could have, just like the rulers of Athens had sentenced Socrates to drink poison.

In the Greek city, it is always one discourse against another: every political victory is a victory for a particular discourse. Conversely, there is no discourse that is not political. The philosophers' ban on poetry is not just a particularly long-winded showdown: it is a struggle for power—or for influence over power.

* * *

IN FACT, the trial of literature did not exactly begin with Plato.[4] First, because Plato was not targeting literature as such, in the modern sense of the word, but something that would become literature—and would become it precisely because of this ban on poets. But also because Plato was not the first to draw his weapon.

The first attack of which evidence has survived was by Xenophanes of Colophon, who lived sometime between 570 and 470 BCE. We know very little about Xenophanes, outside of a few fragments. Among these fragments, one finds a peculiar drinking song—peculiar not because it fails to open with an invocation to the Muses (nothing unusual about that: the Muses were typically not invited to drinking sessions), but for its provocative conclusion, consisting of an all-out attack on the old poems inspired by the nine sisters:

> Praise the man who when he has taken drink brings noble deeds
>   to light,
> as memory and a striving for virtue bring to him.
> He deals neither with the battles of Titans nor Giants
> nor Centaurs, fictions of old,
> nor furious conflicts—for there is no use in these.
> But it is good always to hold the gods in high regard.[5]

Though the Muses are not named, this is clearly aimed at them and challenges the idea that they are a source of inspiration. The battles of the Titans were the subject of their first song, intended to celebrate the victory of the Olympians, and one does not have to search far to realize that the phrase "furious conflicts" refers to *The Iliad*. In short, the nine sisters are dismissed. Though said to be their mother, Memory (*mnêmosynê*) does not arrive through their intervention, but simply through the effect of wine—this purely material and physiological source of inspiration is as good as any other. The great poems of the tradition are qualified as "inventions," or "fictions" (*plasmata*), far removed from the truth to which Homer and Hesiod innocently referred, and equally remote from virtue. Out of consideration for the gods, the drinkers are invited to sing of real exploits and to reject the old poems, full of lies and impurities.

Elsewhere, Xenophanes expresses his criticism of poetry in even more explicit terms. "[From] the beginning all have learned according to Homer," he notes in a resigned manner. The problem, he adds, is that Homer's teaching is worthless: "Homer and Hesiod have attributed to the gods all sorts of things which are matters of reproach and censure among men, theft, adultery, and mutual deceit."[6] How can we grant authority to teachers such as these?

IN THIS HANDFUL OF FRAGMENTS, we find the principal criticisms that for centuries would endlessly be directed at poets and at literature in general: poets and literature are full of lies and immorality, immorality and lies—no matter the order, there is no escaping it. The immediate conclusion: take away any authority they have in the city, at school, over children, and so on.

Except that perhaps one needs to invert this reasoning to fully grasp its ins and outs: the essential point of this line of argument is the question of authority. You wouldn't dream of criticizing the absurdity of nursery rhymes on the grounds, for instance, that kittens do not wear mittens or that even if they did, it is unlikely that they would hang them out to dry. Yet what a lot of lies for a single little story! No one finds fault with it, though, because even children don't put much stock in these empty words.

It's a different story when it comes to Homer and Hesiod—or at least until Xenophanes, Plato, and a few others got involved in the debate. The reason it became worthwhile to attack Homer is that he was never a Mother Goose for good little Greek kids: as Xenophanes recognized, Homer was nothing less than the instructor to all of Greece, along with his colleague Hesiod. To replace the teacher, one had to begin by criticizing him.

*   *   *

XENOPHANES'S POSITION is especially interesting given that he himself did not stop using the poetic, versified language that was already the substance of the great founding poems. Like Homer and Hesiod, he used dactylic hexameter—in other words, epic verse. Verse was at that time the mark of excellent discourse, the discourse of authority, no matter its object; it served to lift language out of ordinary usage. There was no antinomy between verse and truth. Scholars were not only in the habit of versifying, but they could not do otherwise: verse was the vehicle of transcendent knowledge.

As it happens, Xenophanes does not settle for writing in verse: as we have seen, he composes drinking songs or, more accurately, banquet elegies to be recited at the ritual moment of libations, when the assembled move from food to drink. Yes, these elegies are intended to be critical, but they are elegies nonetheless: Xenophanes is fighting on practically the same field as the poets he attacks. The "noble deeds" he wants to hear songs about should, in his opinion, replace the false and immoral epics of his predecessors. He is not promoting a radically different type of discourse, but rather a new poetry, with a more legitimate foundation in truth and goodness. Or, to put it very anachronistically: an *other* literature, rather than a non-literature.

CONSEQUENTLY, Xenophanes's place in the history of philosophy remains exceedingly ambiguous. Was he an early philosopher? Was he still a poet in the traditional sense? Scholars continue to ponder these questions, and while the lack of available material makes a definitive answer unlikely, the principal difficulty may be that the separation of the two discourses was not yet complete.[7]

Half a century later, however, the appearance of Heraclitus opens a new era, in which Xenophanes does not escape the criticism leveled at the other representatives of the old school of erudite poetry: "The learning of many things does not teach understanding, else would it have taught Hesiod and Pythagoras, and again Xenophanes and Hecataeus."[8]

The discourse of knowledge (*polumathiê*), however vast, is not the discourse of intelligence (*nous*). Didactic poetry is the province of the former and is represented by Hesiod, who has little more to offer than the scholars who succeeded him. Elsewhere, Heraclitus aims a few contemptuous remarks at Hesiod: "Hesiod is most men's teacher. Men think he knew very many things, a man who did not know day or night! They are one."[9] What intelligence teaches Heraclitus—that "it is the same thing in us that is quick and dead, awake and asleep, young and old," that "God is day and night, winter and summer, satiety and hunger," and that "the way up and the way down is one and the same"—the Muses did not deign to teach to Hesiod.[10] That being the case, how can we value their teaching, which the *aoidos* and society held in such high esteem?

As for Homer, is it still necessary to talk about him? Heraclitus could not be more disparaging: "Homer should be turned out of the lists and whipped, and Archilochus likewise."[11] It is poetry itself that is targeted here, for the Greeks saw Homer and Archilochus as the most famous embodiments of poetry, the first for the epic and the second for lyricism.

We have seen how much Homer respected the Muses. Archilochus was no less sincere in his respect. As a child, he had set out to the market to sell a cow, when he encountered nine mysterious young women in the night. They made fun of him, then vanished with his cow, replacing it with a lyre: he had just met the Muses. So goes the ancient legend explaining how Archilochus simultaneously discovered poetry and satire, of which he would become the undisputed master.[12] Such familiarity with the Muses should have motivated Heraclitus to restrain himself and show some respect; but on the contrary, it made him lash out at Homer and Archilochus as if they were lowly servants, apparently without worrying that he might meet the same fate as the murderer of Archilochus, who was driven out of the sanctuary of Delphi by the Pythia for having killed a man devoted to the Muses.[13]

Heraclitus's judgment of Homeric works is characterized by contempt for the Muses and an aristocratic attitude: according to Heraclitus, these works should be considered childish things. "Men," he writes, "are deceived in their knowledge of things that are manifest, even as Homer was who was the wisest of all the Greeks. For he was even deceived by boys killing lice when they said to him: 'What we have seen and grasped, these we leave behind; whereas what we have not seen and grasped, these we carry away.'"[14]

Here is Homer, Greece's teacher, fooled by a childish riddle, failing to see through the paradox because he is once again unable to understand the unity of opposites. If the poet of the Trojan War was duped by plain old lice, how can we trust him in matters of human and divine realities?

According to Heraclitus, poetry is no better than common opinion, as held by the majority of people, in opposition to which he wants to propose a discourse closer to the truth. Not just any discourse, but the ultimate discourse: that of reason, *logos* itself.[15]

First Attempt at a Definition of Literature

With Heraclitus, a new kind of speech appears, a new discursive form: not in verse, but in prose. This is the language of *logos,* which is distinct from poetic language.

Admittedly, Heraclitus did not invent Greek prose: the credit for that is traditionally given to Cadmus of Miletus, Anaximander, or Pherecydes of Syros, who lived a few decades or even a century earlier.[16] But with Heraclitus the demand for a higher and truer discourse is developed, surpassing all the others and throwing them on the scrap heap. A discourse without compromise, so faithful to the reality of the world that it has no need for the charms of poetry and does not hesitate to go against the ordinary usages of language in order to provide a more accurate description of reality: "the Sibyl, with raving lips uttering things solemn, unadorned, and unembellished, reaches over a thousand years with her voice because of the god in her."[17]

What the Sibyl can do thanks to the god Apollo, Heraclitus claims he can accomplish thanks to intelligence and *logos,* plain and unadorned. He alone keeps watch while the others sleep.[18]

Literature is the sleep of reason.

Second Attempt

Apollo was once the god of poetry and truth. Since Heraclitus, he is only the god of poetry. So do idols fall and shatter.

Criticism of literature is always exercised in the name of another authority, whether religious, political, or philosophical. One only overthrows something in a position of power to put something else in its place:

—Is it a revolt?

—No, Sire, it is a revolution.

Naturally, there cannot be a coup d'état without a state or an authority: the appearance of anti-literature implies that literature was initially in a position of power.

Or, to be more specific, there was a power before Heraclitus, and it is to this forgotten lost power that we now give the name *literature.*

Literature is nostalgia for a fallen power.

Third Attempt

The power that rises and drives out the other is philosophy—for there was a time when the love of wisdom (*philosophia*) curiously coincided with the hatred of poetry.

However, even in Plato, the prince of philosophers—and prince of anti-literature—the attacks were aimed neither at all of poetry nor at every possibility of poetry.

It was more like a hatred of something that did not yet have a name. In seeking to define itself and position itself in the field of discourses, philosophy defined its opposite. We should be grateful to it for that.

Literature is what remains when the other discourses have completely taken over the field. It claims the smallest share.

Literature is what is attacked. Even the smallest share can still be reduced, can't it? (Read: scribblers, be happy with what you've been left—it's already more than you deserve.)

LITERATURE is what is exiled—for after Heraclitus came Plato, who has remained in the collective memory as the greatest exiler of poets in the entire history of anti-literature (on paper, it goes without saying: there is no record of Plato personally carrying out mass deportations—probably for lack of opportunity).[19]

The fact that in Ancient Greece the condemnation of poetry is expressed in the form of exile shows that the issue is eminently political. It is a question of power: in the ideal city conceived by Socrates, who will be the best suited to exercise it? Book 5 of *The Republic* provides the answer: the philosopher.

Compared with the philosopher, the poet is but a dangerous charmer:

> Now, as it seems, if a man who is able by wisdom to become every sort of thing and to imitate all things should come to our city, wishing to make a display of himself and his poems, we would fall on our knees before him as a man sacred, wonderful, and pleasing: but we would say that there is no such man among us in the city, nor is it lawful for such a man to be born there. We would send him to another city, with myrrh poured over his head, and crowned with wool.[20]

This is certainly a more courteous procedure than Heraclitus's whippings, but aside from the physical pain, the result is the same: the poet does not have the right to live in the perfect city and is sent to

the neighboring state as a pernicious agent with the ability to under-
mine the enemy.

Here we have a use for poetry undreamt of by its opponents today:
poetry as a weapon of mass seduction. But for that, one would have to
believe in its power, the way Socrates and Plato do: they do not drive
out the poets because they are useless, but because they are harmful.

Not all the poets, however—for immediately after throwing them
out in a flurry of ironic considerations, Socrates admits that a certain
kind of poetry is useful:

> We ourselves would use a more austere and less pleasing poet and
> teller of tales for the sake of benefit, one who would imitate the style
> of the decent man and would say what he says in those models that we
> set down as laws at the beginning, when we undertook to educate the
> soldiers.[21]

So there is another type of poetry: one authorized by the state, with
a place in civic and military schooling. What is at issue here is strictly
power and authority: the lies of poetry are dangerous not because
every lie is dangerous, but because every lie is dangerous when it is
not told by the state. Only the city has the right to lie, and these lies
are too valuable to be left in the hands of poets:

> Then, it's appropriate for the rulers, if for anyone at all, to lie for the
> benefit of the city in cases involving enemies or citizens, while all the
> rest must not put their hands to anything of the sort.[22]

Significantly, it is not poetry itself that is condemned, but the poets,
who are criticized for a lack of authority, in the strongest sense of the
term: they are not authorized to lie, for they are unable to vouch for
the consequences of their tales.

This accusation appears to be the negative side of the poetic
aura. Speaking through Socrates, Plato readily admits that the poet is

indisputably "sacred," "wonderful," and "pleasing" and that he charms his audience. This passage from *The Republic* repeats a description found earlier in *Ion:*

> For a poet is a light and winged and sacred thing, and is unable ever to compose until he has been inspired and put out of his senses, and his mind is no longer in him: every man, while he retains possession of that [faculty], is powerless to write verse or chant an oracle.[23]

The problem is that this divine inspiration strips the poet of both his mastery and his identity, which go hand in hand. Since he does not create by virtue of an art but by "divine privilege," he has no control over his work. In the process, he loses an essential property of human beings: reason, or intelligence (*nous*), which Heraclitus already deplored the absence of in Hesiod.[24]

As it happens, the poet's madness is coupled with another pathology that is equally dire: the loss of individuality, which, etymologically, is "dementia"—taking leave of one's own mind (*demens*). By being able to speak for several entities in succession, to embody numerous characters, and literally "to become all sorts of things" (*pantodapon gignesthai*), the poet, in a disquieting way, avoids the unity and coherence that is the lot of ordinary mortals: he is the various, the undulating, the elusive transformist, always a stranger both to others and to himself. How could a city accept such words from elsewhere, without author or authority?

If ever poetry must be present in the city, it can only be in the form of a properly *authorized* poetry.

IN THIS PLATONIC REPUBLIC that the philosopher wants to see as a solidly organized, hierarchical, monolithic whole, can there be any worse threat than alienation, a virus carried deep inside poets themselves?

In Archaic Greece, many poets lived an itinerant life, roaming from one city to the next to participate in competitions and sell their songs to audiences who had fallen under their spell, traveling here and there to deliver words that were always foreign, if only in their inspired utterance. Their mere presence would serve to invalidate the utopia of a self-sufficient republic closed in on itself and set up as a system of defense against the outside world.

One must remember this historical context in order to detect the rejection of exteriority and refusal of pernicious foreign influences behind the Platonic condemnation of the poets. It is first and foremost a question of politics: who will have power in the new city? Many answers are conceivable, but one thing is certain and not up for discussion: authority will not be shared with strangers. The territorialization of power entails the end of winged, mobile, migrant, uncontrollable speech.

TRUTH, in the modern sense of the term, was a new idea at the time: it was not necessarily thought that truth had to be unambiguous and separate from the conditions of its utterance. Was Plato himself convinced of the possibility of a real absolute, one that was unique, timeless, universal, utterable, and writable? There is reason to doubt it, if we consider that in his dialogues he hid behind the mask of Socrates or some other foreigner passing through Athens: the polyphony of conversations on the agora or on the banks of the Ilisos is every bit as good as inspiration by the Muse.[25]

One thing is certain: if there was only one truth, then the authority granted to certain kinds of speech now had to be automatically stripped from every other kind—or the latter had to be subordinated to the former. The discrimination of discourses was underway.

The banishment of the poets corresponds to both a change of political regime and an upheaval of the regime of truth. In Archaic Greece, the plural truth was taught by three kinds of teachers: the *aoidos,* the soothsayer, and the king.[26] Plato establishes a new regime, in which the philosopher plays the most important part. The poet bears the consequences of this transition from one system to another:

what could his place be in a world governed by philosopher kings who are the voice of both truth and authority? This holy alliance of knowledge and power necessarily excludes other pretenders from the regime; it is no more and no less than a coup d'état (but a virtual one, since here the play of the mind is primary).

Exit the poet, then—but not poetry. Isn't it curious that book 10 of *The Republic,* in which Plato's fiercest attacks against these shady fabricators are concentrated, is also the book that includes one of the most famous Platonic myths? This myth, the story of Er the Pamphylian, concludes *The Republic* with a description of the hereafter and the mechanism of rebirth; it is as if as soon as poetry and mythical imagination were chased out the door, they came back in through the window.

Socrates himself underlines the parallel with the Homeric songs, both at the beginning and the end of this passage, announcing first that he's not going to tell "a story of Alcinous, . . . but rather of a strong man, Er, son of Armenius, by race a Pamphylian," then concluding with the exemplary case of Odysseus in Hades, who wisely chooses to be reborn as "a private citizen who minds his own business" rather than as a hero.[27] There is also a nod to grammarians: according to Er, Ajax is the twentieth to choose a new life, just as he had been the twentieth to meet Odysseus in his evocation of the dead in Homer.[28]

This eschatological myth thus transcends the existing myths and proclaims their end. In a way, Socrates comes up with a different *Odyssey:* not that of the legendary and false tales told by Odysseus to King Alcinous, but the true story of what happens to souls after death. Or to put it more precisely, the philosopher explains that it is impossible for there to be a new *Odyssey,* given that the new life Odysseus decides on is modest, invisible, and utterly uneventful. He has come a long way from the fabrications he had indulged in on the island of the Phaiacians. Having seen the light regarding the vanity of his adventures, the dead hero chooses an antiheroic existence of silence or—at least—an existence devoid of a narrative that would sum up his life as an antihero.

Yet an anti-*Odyssey* is still an *Odyssey,* though a different kind of *Odyssey.* The exile of the poets does not necessarily entail the end of poetry. From now on there will be poetic lies of state, which Socrates emphasizes the necessity for. More importantly, there will be philosophical (read: *true*) myths, destined to replace the old and dangerous epics and tragic legends. One discourse drives out another, truth drives out falsehood, philosophy drives out the epic. Poetry as such may disappear, but its performative and truth-telling function remains, taken on by a variety of people other than poets.

Could this final myth be seen as the ultimate contradiction, or the ultimate evidence of an irony used unsparingly both by Socrates and Plato, and which Leo Strauss has shown the importance of in *The Republic* itself?[29] Fundamentally, it does not make much difference: rather than nullifying the competition between philosophy and poetry, the irony, if irony there is, underlines it. For the irony to be fully revealed, the dialogue must end with Socrates clearly engaging in the activity he had earlier condemned: the construction of myths. In this way, the equivalence between epic myth and philosophical myth is formally asserted, no matter what form it takes (substitution of one for the other or rejection of both).

Diogenes Laertius reports that in his youth, Plato "wrote poems, first dithyrambs, afterwards lyric poems and tragedies." One day, "when he was about to compete for the prize with a tragedy, he listened to Socrates in front of the theater of Dionysus." Plato, who was twenty at the time, decided to devote the rest of his life to philosophy.[30] This is the first farewell to literature on record. And also the first public burning of poetry, at the hands of the prince of philosophers. The lesson is clear: poetry and philosophy are not compatible, but this is because they contend for the same powers, the same territories—and the same people.[31]

IN PHILOSOPHY'S DEFENSE, it was not alone in attacking poetry. The assaults came from several directions at once, as if poetry itself had manifested a curious tendency to arouse aggression and hostility.

And so during the very period that Plato was writing his *Republic* (380–360 BCE), we find the rhetor Isocrates producing his own anti-poetic couplet, accusing the poets of taking advantage of the ornaments of language to cleverly hide the weakness of their thought, and encouraging the public not to fall for it. Isocrates took the opportunity to propose a little experiment in textual manipulation worthy of the Oulipo:

> If one retains the words and ideas of the most famous poems, but does away with their meter, they will appear far inferior to the opinion we now have of them.[32]

Turning poetry into prose was probably one of the traditional exercises of grammarians; it now made it possible to put the content of poems to the test and distinguish the substance from the form. The orator had to denounce the deception of versification, which adorns empty thought with frills and flounces, and show his talent by dealing with the same subjects as the poets but doing it better and in prose.

A decade later, the indictment was repeated when old Isocrates, the author of an imposing body of oratory work, bitterly reproached the Athenians for giving him less respect and recognition than they gave to Pindar for a single line describing the city as "the bulwark of Hellas": while Isocrates, over eighty years old, found himself plagued with unfair taxes, Pindar had been given not only the fine title of ambassador, but the handsome sum of ten thousand drachmas.[33] This disproportion was truly scandalous. Down with the poet!

The interesting thing here is that this assault against poetry was not launched in the name of philosophy. Or rather, yes, it is *philosophy* that Isocrates seeks to defend, for that is the term he uses, but the sense of the word is far removed from what Plato gave it and which it has basically kept to this day. By "philosophy," Isocrates refers to general culture and the oratory art that was his trade—less a search for truth and virtue conceived as bodies of knowledge than a mere

awareness and examination of opinions, along with rhetorical exper-
tise. While relations between Isocrates and Plato were never particularly friendly, they could agree on at least one thing: the rejection
of poetry, which was accused of dominating other discourses, and
which they both declared held an unjustifiable position of strength.

In the first half of the fourth century, such domination was more
likely a memory than a reality, a reminder of the practices of Archaic
Greece and its "masters of truth." But fundamentally it makes little
difference: the tactic consists of choosing an enemy, even an imaginary, weakened one, to promote one's own vision of the world. Poetry
is always a convenient target for accusations of usurped authority,
just as it can always be used to justify the existence of a rival discourse, whatever it may be—rhetoric for Isocrates, philosophy for
Plato. And it is always available for all the energies of (so-called) good
and truth to be mobilized against it, to be a black sheep or scapegoat
against which to join forces.

IT IS NOT BY CHANCE that these first attacks took place in Ancient
Greece, in Athens, rather than in Jerusalem, to mention the other center to which European civilization traditionally prides itself on tracing
its origins. Poetry would not have been subjected to these attacks
had the Greek religion been founded, like the Jewish one, on revealed
texts and an official doctrine promoted by a sacerdotal hierarchy.
As strange as it may seem to us, familiar as we are with the revealed
religions—Judaism, Christianity, Islam—there was no Pentateuch in
Ancient Greece, no equivalent to the Law and the prophets, and no
voice of divine truth. While there were oracles, they offered only isolated truths. Instead, the Greek religion consisted of an amalgam of
traditions, practices, and cults with indeterminate geographic and
cultural boundaries, open to occasionally incorporating more or less
foreign or distant gods and rites. The poets sometimes delved into all
this to create their work and introduce a semblance of order, based on
the time and place of utterance: what is known as a story. Produced

in particular by the choruses of young men charged in each city with singing the exploits of the gods and heroes, these narratives were partial and, more importantly, contradicted one another. Given the lack of a single body of revealed words that prevailed over other discourses, a poetic text was qualified to articulate not *the* truth, but *a* truth about the gods. Neither Homer nor Hesiod escaped this general polyphony. Like the others, their work was theological; like the others, they explained the world, describing what happens underground and in the sky and proposing the first theories on humankind and the divine. Yet they were more admired than all the others, and their songs practically served as a bible, though they lacked the Bible's authority and did not claim to be consistent. There was no unifying, reliable discourse.[34] According to Plato, this was the problem.

Perhaps it is not so difficult for those of us in the West at the beginning of the twenty-first century to imagine a world without divine revelation: isn't that the world we live in? A world in which magi, prophets, and sacred texts can barely be heard anymore, to the great dismay of clergies of all faiths. It is trickier, however, to conceive of a world in which, in spite of or precisely because of this absence, certain discourses are endowed with a particular aura and an authority that can make up not for the silence of the gods—for on the contrary they prove too talkative in this Hellas humming with oracles—but for their cacophony. The Muses were the great organizers of Archaic Greece, planners of the cosmos and memorialists of humans, heroes, and gods. But there remained a question to be asked openly: could they be trusted? This was the alarm raised by Plato. The Muses were probably not directly targeted—the gods wouldn't stand for it—but the blows rained down on their servants, the poets.

It is no coincidence that Plato's criticism of poetry focused on the question of the gods: the matter was too serious to be left in the hands of the poets. The horrors and absurdities they uninhibitedly reported about the Olympians indisputably proved their incompetence. It was essential to deprive the poets of the right to talk nonsense about such serious subjects, which exposed the city to great dangers, and to entrust doctrinal authority on divine matters only to those competent to deal with them: the philosophers, who stated loud and clear that their function was precisely to tell the truth about gods and humans.

THE CHARGE LEVELED at epic poetry also held for tragedy: surely the authors of tragedies were guilty of awakening harmful passions in the members of the audience. Gathering people at the theater to subject them to collective trances of terror and compassion could weaken a fighting nation, whose citizens were required to show their bravery on the battlefield. Such performances were a real public danger. If there had to be tragedy—that is, a dramatic representation of life—how could it be entrusted to mere private individuals? Equipped with these arguments, Plato sets out a simple, incontrovertible proposition in his final dialogue, *The Laws:* the city should, through its own actions, write "the most beautiful and best tragedy," for the city's constitution is already based on "a representation of the fairest and finest life." This is "tragedy of the truest kind," the only one worth seeing and hearing. Those who erect temporary stages, those "children sprung from the gentle Muses,"[35] will simply have to set up camp elsewhere.

Although *The Republic* had mentioned the possibility of a different poetry taking the place of poetry as it was, the years had radicalized the elderly Plato: now, in *The Laws,* he plans nothing less than the end of all tragedy and poetry. In a sense, to declare the constitution the best tragedy is to impose the civil code as the only authorized reading material. And why not? History offers more than one example of such practices: as a theory of cultural revolution, *The Laws* is on a par with Mao's *Little Red Book.*

In these circumstances, it is difficult not to suspect that Plato's accusations against poetry, that it is immoral and dishonest, were mere pretexts in an overall strategy to achieve power. Convict the Muse of lying and then hang her: the first thing to do is to eliminate her in order to take her place. The most important thing is authority. The totalitarian state conceived by the philosopher only has room for one doctrinal authority, in order to ensure its cohesion and stability. The rest is a question of tactics. Poets are only banished because they are a threat to the totalitarian order.

THIS EXPLAINS WHY NOTHING TODAY is more subject to misunderstanding than Plato's banishment of poets. Ironically, this is the philosophical proposition least comprehensible to our contemporaries, who do not realize that it accurately reflects their most quotidian reality.

The reason it is so difficult today to understand Socrates's aggressive attitude toward poets is that poetry and literature in general have lost all authority or retain only a minute vestige of it, when even the memory of this lost authority has been more or less permanently blotted out—except among a few literary types lost in the great flux of unanimity. Why be so angry at these harmless, insignificant beings? Because they tell tall tales? Big deal! Even a child would not be taken in by them. What a strange idea to forbid the inconsequential. It's like tilting at windmills.

This is how the thinking goes today, by which we make our first mistake: anachronism. Socrates was no Don Quixote: he knew exactly what he was doing by attacking poets, because in his time poetry was endowed with real power and an educational virtue; it was worth fighting against. Plato had enough enemies to want to avoid imaginary or unlikely ones.

The second mistake is more serious: blindness. This is the blindness of our contemporaries unable to see that they are living in the very world Plato hoped for, conceived, and willed, that is to say a society whose members only ever open a book to experience the purely gratuitous pleasures of the imagination; a world in which literature has lost nearly all power and authority and has become an empty shell merely used to pass the time by a shrinking class increasingly monopolized by many other distractions. For supposedly that is all we are talking about: enjoying ourselves. If Plato were to return and walk among us, how happy he would be to find that his plan for poets had been applied practically to the letter. Admittedly, they have not totally disappeared, but their fictions are most often read or seen only as mere fictions; their truth is at best allegorical, while in Homer it was literal. This internal exile is on a par with the banishment suggested by Socrates: less painful, perhaps less violent, but just as effective, if not more. If Plato were to return and walk among us, he would cut from *The Republic* all the passages dealing with poets, for they are now useless (both the poets and the passages): no need to write *The Republic* in the Republic.

In a way, Plato has won—perhaps not Plato directly, but his numerous epigones, who repeated his arguments over the centuries and adapted them to contemporary circumstances. The authority that poets still held in Plato's time has now passed to science. Consequently, anti-literature today no longer has the meaning it did in Plato's era, and the version practiced by Plato has become practically incomprehensible to us, despite the fact that we are his very heirs, we who have most effectively, though unwittingly, realized his program.[36] Anti-literature has outlasted the literature it attacked, using apparently similar arguments, but endowed with other values because the context is different.

DID THE PHILOSOPHERS ever take power? Their attempts in Antiquity, whether involving Pythagoras or Plato, took a disastrous turn. Then a certain vision of the world carried out its coup d'état and imposed itself for centuries, first upon an empire, then an entire continent, and finally several continents at once: this was Christianity, the first of the universal totalitarianisms that aimed to rule over every aspect of humans, both internal and external, as well as over society. In any case, it was the first to succeed. And maybe the only one.

It was inevitable that Christianity would come into conflict with literature, given Jesus's inherent preference for the ignorant and the simple-minded: "I thank thee, O Father, Lord of heaven and earth, because thou hast hid these things from the clever and intelligent, and hast revealed them unto babes."[37] Paul takes it one step further: he does not want to resort to the "cleverness of words" (*sophia logou*), for "it is written," he continues, that "'I will destroy the cleverness of the clever, and will bring to nothing the intelligence of the intelligent.' Where is the clever one? Where is the scribe (*grammateus*)? Where is the disputer of this world?"[38]

In short, a relentless war is declared. A war not only against the scribes and experts in words, but also against wise men (*sophia* combines both meanings): through the shared detestation of which they are now the object, literature and philosophy are one, four centuries after being bitter enemies in Athens. As the fable has it, the third thief is always the one to scoop the pot (if the reader will allow me this connection between Calvary and La Fontaine).

And yet Paul's discourse is so skillful. His rhetoric so effective. His poetic imagery so astounding. Despite his anti-literary profession of faith, the last of the apostles, as he liked to call himself, was also one of the most brilliant writers of Antiquity (just as Plato, the denigrator of fiction, was a marvelous inventor of myths). And he was not completely unfamiliar with literary culture: one finds the occasional allusion to Menander and Aratus.

Which only goes to show that Christianity has an ambiguous relationship with literature. As revelation and transcendence, it claims to break with the entire literary heritage that preceded it in order to put forward a radically different Word, drawing its authority exclusively from God. Yet as incarnation, it has no choice but to make do with existing forms of language and thought, on which poetry and literature have left their nearly irreducible mark. Furthermore, Christianity's historic triumph as the recognized religion of the Roman empire aggravated the internal rift by adding an unprecedented political complication: the new religion's official status required it to take on the empire's cultural heritage, which was marked by centuries of paganism, while at the same time, a specifically Christian culture and literature developed over the generations that became increasingly fit to rival pagan letters and, eventually, replace them.[39] In short, what took place in Christianity's complicated relationship with literature was nothing less than the repetition on a smaller scale of the drama (or mystery, if you prefer) of its historical existence: its survival and triumph came at the cost of its initial radicalness. The advent of holy ignorance was proclaimed, and what came along was the Catholic novelist: here we have a crude summary of two thousand years of Christian cultural history.

MANY WERE THE VOICES among the church fathers to rise up in favor of literature. In 397, Saint Jerome recommends that pagan literature should be treated like a captive woman whom one has taken for a wife after having removed all the hair from her head and body, following the elegant recommendations of the book of Deuteronomy, that is to say, after having rid her of any idolatry, error, or lust. He goes on to list the authors of the new Christian literature, of whom there were already many: by this time, there were enough to fill a library, which Jesus himself would have been surprised to see.[40] As for Augustine of Hippo, he suggests that one should deal with literature in the manner of the Hebrews who fled from Egypt and took all of its riches with them—to put them to better use, of course.[41] In the Greek world, Basil of Caesarea wrote a work entitled *Address to Young Men on the Right Use of Greek Literature.* Everywhere one looks, these good fathers and doctors of the church are trying to save ancient and pagan literature and poetry, making compromises with the original radicalness of the evangelical message.

Such unanimity seems somewhat suspect. Isn't it odd to find such eagerness to save something that should logically have been vigorously condemned? Let me venture a hypothesis: perhaps these texts represent only the visible part of the iceberg, the part that rose to the surface from an internal church debate about whether or not literature should be saved. The arguments in favor remained, and those against perforce disappeared: since anti-literature had lost the battle, accounts of it were neither preserved nor passed down, but simply tossed onto the trash heap of history. After all, those in the anti-literature camp were as a matter of principle less verbose than their opponents: while the former were loath to express their hatred in fine texts worthy of being copied by the monks of the Middle Ages, the defenders of poetry went down in history thanks to their beautiful words. If it is true that the opponents of literature chose not to leave a written record, this would explain why the dust of oblivion has settled over the Christian battlefield of literature versus anti-literature.

What remains of it, however, is still enough to fully gauge the violence of the conflict and the force of the arguments used. Here, one should quote the entire chapter of Isidore of Seville's *Sentences* devoted to the "books of the pagans," which condemns those "who took more pleasure in pondering the words of the pagans, due to the exaggerations and embellishments of their speech, than Holy Scripture, with its language full of humility":

> If externally the words of the pagans shine with the brilliance of eloquence, they remain empty of wisdom and virtue internally, while the sacred words, which externally display such careless language, are internally resplendent with the wisdom of the mysteries. This is why, as the Apostle also says, we carry this treasure in earthen vessels.[42]

Isidore sets up an opposition between beauty and virtue. Since one can have one or the other but never the two together, the second must obviously be preferred—hence the condemnation of literature, defined as vain ornament: "In reading, it is not words which must be loved, but truth."[43] But do not be misled: the opposition is purely tactical. It only serves to justify the aesthetic guilty conscience of a Christian man of letters of the sixth and seventh centuries like Saint Isidore, who was torn between the formal sophistication of pagan literature and the (supposedly) raw quality of Holy Scripture.

A simple, direct solution to this internal tension would have been to repudiate the pagan texts, because they were pagan, and replace them with the Christian texts, because they were Christian. After all, if one believes in the Gospel, why continue to concern oneself with any manifestation of paganism? All that should matter is the truth expressed by the texts, and the rest would count for nothing.

Yet this is exactly the kind of alternative whose radicalness is inconceivable to Isidore of Seville, first out of social concern, because he does not want to throw out a culture that continues to make up a part of the world he lives in, but also, more importantly, because he has to legitimize the qualitative opposition he sees between the two categories of texts. It is precisely because the charm of the pagan texts is a nearly irresistible temptation to Isidore that it is indispensable for him to view the relationship between beauty and truth in a dialectical fashion. Had he been impervious to this beauty, he would not for a moment have considered denouncing its lies and inanity: the effort he puts into his lines of argumentation is an unwitting tribute to vice on the part of virtue and the paradoxical acknowledgment of literature as a force to be reckoned with.

Those who turn against literature are sometimes simply disillusioned with it for not living up to their expectations. Isidore seems to paint a picture of this disappointed bunch—including himself, perhaps—when he describes the "snobs" (*fastidiosis*) and "phrase-makers" (*loquacibus*) who dislike Holy Scripture "due to the simplicity of its language, because it seems disgraceful when they compare it to pagan eloquence, but immediately recognize the sublimity of what they had disdained about it if they ever pay humble attention to the mysteries it contains."[44]

A verse from the book of Psalms reinforces this anti-literary position: "For I have not known literature, I will enter into the power of the Lord."[45] This is anti-literature's biblical motto—but there is one qualification. The Vulgate reads, *quia non cognovi litteraturam*. In Latin, *litteratura* is not literature as such, but writing, the alphabet, grammar, or even knowledge. Modern editors of the Bible now reject this verse, regarding it as an interpolation by a scribe who, having failed to recognize the following word, noted in Hebrew on his copy that he "did not understand the letters."[46] Isidore, on the other hand, struggles to interpret these words in any way other than as a terrible divine warning issued to those unfortunates tempted to give in to literary seduction.

Two centuries earlier, Augustine had been less categorical: disconcerted by this biblical verse, he looked for variants and, having failed to find a satisfactory one, astutely suggested that the only writing or literature the psalmist could have been incriminating was that of "the Jews," which was the only one the psalmist knew, thereby exempting all other literature from condemnation.[47] And so the bishop of Hippo was able to continue reading the pagan and Christian authors with a clear conscience and to write a literary work that was, let us confess on his behalf, a guilty pleasure.

Isidore does not accept Augustine's cunning anti-Judaic hypothesis, choosing instead to take the verse at face value, while hastening to add to his commentary the formula for the antidote, namely that literature is not as dangerous as heresy:

> Grammarians are better than heretics: indeed, through persuasion, heretics invite men to drink a lethal juice, while the knowledge of grammarians can still be useful to life, as long as it is kept to better usages.[48]

The grammarians are saved by the gradation of errors and sins: literature will not be burned with the heretics—but neither will it escape the bonfire of the vanities.[49]

ISIDORE'S COMPLICATED, not to say tortured, relationship with literature and more generally with the art of language provides a fairly good illustration, even taking into account his scruples, of the prejudices of the fathers and doctors of the Latin church against an excessive concern with verbal beauty. In about the same period as the Sevillan, Pope Gregory the Great presented his *Morals on the Book of Job* not by apologizing for the fact that the work was poorly written, but by expressly priding himself on it:

> I have declined to follow even the art itself of eloquence, which the teachers of that external discipline (*disciplinae exterioris*) recommend. For just as the style of this letter also makes clear, I do not avoid the clashing of final "m," I do not shun the confusion of barbarism, I refuse to observe syntax and moods, and the cases governed by prepositions, as I am certain that it is unworthy that I should restrict the words of the Heavenly oracle beneath the rules of Donatus.[50]

Since Donatus, a great grammarian of the fourth century, was the teacher of Saint Jerome, Gregory's statement serves as a criticism of the patron saint of translators' concern for eloquence: over a period of two centuries, from Jerome to Gregory and from Augustine to Isidore, Christianity had taken a noticeably harder line on literature. Now, writers prided themselves on their grammatical errors as if they were the best safe-conducts to the heavenly kingdom: this is where zeal and piety now took up residence.

To tell the truth, this shameless indifference to language had originated much earlier, and from on high: its declared model is none other than God, or the Holy Spirit, or even Moses, to whom it is said that the Holy Spirit dictated the Pentateuch:

> For these [rules] have not been observed by any of the interpreters of the authority of Holy Scripture. Because our exposition arises from that, of course, it is certainly proper that a newborn child, as it were, should imitate the appearance of its mother.[51]

If the Word itself does not care about words, why claim to be more royalist than the king? God's sloppiness in Holy Scripture renders the

slightest linguistic affectation suspect and justifies any stylistic neg-
ligence on the part of God's commentators and followers. Elsewhere,
Gregory writes that eloquence is a property of lying and that a lack
of affectation is the touchstone of truth:

> The coeternal wisdom of God does not present itself with the dyed colors
> of India, for whoever truly understands it recognizes the distance that
> separates him from those men that the world honors with the name of
> wise men. The very terms of its precepts distinguish it from the wise
> men of this world, who, when they practice eloquence, speak words to all
> appearances stylish, thanks to the dye that decorates them, but which,
> because they remain foreign to the essence of things, falsely claim to
> be other than they are, thanks to verbal techniques (*verborum compo-
> sitionibus*) similar to a color dye.[52]

Bogged down by an inexpressible inferiority complex, and for
want of being able to instantly replace pagan culture with a Christian culture they considered of equal aesthetic value, the Christians
gradually constructed an ontological opposition between being and
appearance, truth and beauty, the Gospel and literature, in such a way
as to attribute the holiest virtues to their own shortcomings and to
present them as the best expression of faithfulness to the divine message. Indeed, God does not worry about the materiality of words: all
that matters to him is the intention from which they proceed. Such
is the rather ingenious argument put forward by Guibert of Nogent
at the turn of the twelfth century:

> [The] divine ear measures intentions rather than words. If you hiccup
> when you are praying, "Let the power of the Holy Spirit be present (*Adsit*)
> to us, Lord," and it comes out, "be absent (*Absit*) from us," it does not
> matter: God is not overly concerned with grammar (*non est Deus gram-
> maticae curiosus*). No voice pierces him, but a heart reaches toward
> him.[53]

During the same period, Pierre Damien provides the most striking and most radical expression of this disdain for form. He uses a
single word to excuse the coarseness of his writing and preemptively
reject the criticisms of men of letters as null and void: "my grammar
is Christ."[54] With a few variations, this is a motto that all extremists,
fanatics, and philistines of every religion, belief, and ideology can identify with. Pierre Damien wasn't expecting as much: he is satisfied to
demand the use of an unaffected, charmless, and even openly unpleasant style, since, as he reminds us by quoting the book of Ecclesiastes:
"The words of the servants of God should be like goads, their collected
sayings like nails firmly embedded in the sky."[55]

Ultimately, the anti-literary creed often aims merely to propose
another kind of literature, one that is simpler, less sophisticated, and
more essential: to walk on goads and nails, even if they are embedded
in the sky, is to propose a different kind of writing, one based on what
is bitter and sharp rather than soft and caressing. The crux of the
matter is that this opposition takes the form of an absolute rejection
of the art of writing, as if the conflict between Christ and literature
could be resolved not by literature's conversion, but by its negation
and destruction—the only acceptable outcome of a battle between
two fundamentally incompatible authorities.

In the Middle Ages, the word *poet* was long a synonym for a priest
or theologian of paganism: in this sense, Ovid and Virgil were "poets,"
since the *Metamorphoses* and the *Aeneid* were seen as the Old and
New Testaments of the Roman religion. In the twelfth century, in *Le
Roman de Troie*, Benoît de Sainte-Maure describes the funerals of
Patroclus and Achilles being performed not by priests but by many
"poets." The pagan "poets" and the biblical prophets are brought
face to face, as if they were two parallel, practically irreconcilable
worlds. One has to wait until Petrarch and Dante to find authors
claiming for themselves a title endowed with such suspect connota-
tions; these writers would do so precisely because they sought to
restore a lost continuity with classical Antiquity: their choice aimed

to be provocative, commensurate with the subversive charge of the word *poet*.[56]

WHAT IS STRIKING about Christian criticism of poetry in the Middle Ages is the moderation with which it is generally expressed: these clerics take infinite care to handle literature gently, in the same way that in Plato, Socrates recommended that the poet be accompanied to the gates of the city while being crowned with wool, as if the feeling prevailed that something of this dangerous practice needed to be preserved after all, if only to use it for one's own purposes. Sometimes criticism of poetry even turns into its most rousing defense. This is the case when Thomas Aquinas makes a list of arguments against the proposition that "Holy Scripture should use metaphors." The first argument is:

> That which is proper to the lowest science seems not to befit this science [theology], which holds the highest place of all. But to proceed by the aid of various similitudes and figures is proper to poetry, the least of all the sciences. Therefore it is not fitting that this science should make use of similitudes.[57]

But after the arguments against come those in favor, as is always the case in the *Summa Theologiae*. The first argument in favor of the use of metaphors is based on nature: since human beings acquire knowledge through the channel of the senses, it is legitimate for them to also acquire knowledge of spiritual truth through bodily comparisons.[58] Moreover, by hiding divine truth in figures of speech, scholars can exercise their abilities while avoiding the mockery of the impious—an argument that is practical, in discriminating among reading publics, but also evangelical, for Jesus advises not to give that which is holy to dogs.[59] Finally—and this is probably both the most sophisticated and the most paradoxical argument—Aquinas develops a philosophical poetics of metaphor as the coincidence of a concealment and a revelation:

[The use of metaphor] is more befitting the knowledge that we have of God in this life. For what He is not is clearer to us than what he is. Therefore similitudes drawn from things farthest away from God form within us a truer estimate that God is above whatsoever we may say or think of Him.[60]

Thus, according to a paradox consistent with negative theology, the more vulgar the comparison, the more accurate the idea it will provide of divine truths, which are infinitely superior to our own: by exposing their inability to directly name them, comparisons express the distance that separates us from these truths. Later, the *Summa* suggests a dizzying correspondence between the inferiority of poetry and the superiority of God:

Just as human reason fails to grasp poetical expressions on account of their being lacking in truth, so does it fail to grasp Divine things perfectly, on account of the sublimity of the truth they contain: and therefore in both cases there is need of signs by means of sensible figures.[61]

Here God and poetry are put on the same level, if it is true that both elude human reason, even though for opposite reasons—the former because He is beyond reason, and the latter because it cannot reach reason's heights. With this idea, Thomas Aquinas manages to turn several centuries of discourse against poetry into an argument ultimately in its favor: its lack of rationality is precisely what makes it valuable. Situated in relation to us in the same way that we are situated in relation to divinity, poetry is the very image of our condition. Far more than that, it speaks the very language of God, which is that of figures, a language given to humankind to explore the two infinities between which we are torn: the below-rational and the above-rational.

What higher praise could one give poetry? It is not by chance that it was possible to express this in the thirteenth century, when poetry was no longer automatically assimilated to paganism: the troubadours had sung, the *chansons de geste* had spread, Chrétien de Troyes had written his *Story of the Grail*, and Aquinas himself produced theological hymns. A few decades later, the greatest and most beautiful poem in the history of Christianity would be written by Dante Alighieri. If literature was no longer a threat, but a tool in the service of faith, it would be utterly absurd to prosecute it for abuse of authority. After all, didn't the Bible itself contain poetry, at least in Psalms and the Song of Songs? And in retrospect one understands the theologians' scruples about condemning poetry: they were not targeting poetry itself, but rather the pagan religion for which it appeared to be an indissociable vehicle. Fundamentally, anti-literature was anti-paganism. Why pursue an indictment that was now without content? Though Christian resistance continued to be expressed at least until the seventeenth century, Aquinas cleared the way for the advent of Dante and Petrarch—later to be joined by Charles Péguy and Georges Bernanos.[62]

THE SAME IS TRUE of every period and culture in which literature is stripped of its authority, or when this authority no longer poses a problem: when the principal charge disappears, almost all the others vanish, as if by magic.

It is revealing that after Plato's attacks on literature, no one in Ancient Greece bothered to target what no longer represented a threat. It is possible that we have lost any evidence of these attacks, but it is even more probable that with the political transformation of the Greek cities after the Macedonian conquest and the modification of tragic ritual in the fourth century, when participation in choruses lost its traditional role in the civic education of Athenian youth, it was no longer relevant to start proceedings against poets. Societies without anti-literature are either societies in which literature is considered pure entertainment, a game with no stakes, or those in which literature entirely subordinates itself to authority and does not claim an authority of its own. In fact, playfulness and submission often go hand in hand.

So it was in Ancient, pagan Rome, where it would have been impossible to find any trace of anti-literary discourse. Why would anyone have gone to the trouble of composing such a thing? The *litterae*—poetry, history, philosophy, treatises on agriculture and natural history, plays—served at most as a reservoir of examples for orators. They allowed Romans to prove how cultured they were at banquets, showing off in the vainest, most prodigal manner, as in the *Deipnosophistae* of Athenaeus and the *Table-Talk* of Plutarch. Distinct from the public affairs that the Roman citizen had a duty to be engrossed in, the *litterae* fall under the category of play and *otium:* neither serious nor farcical, just entertaining. In Rome, there was no reason to question an activity that, without claiming the slightest authority, was entirely subjected to a complex social system of envois, dedications, gifts, and favors.[63] If anti-literature is the symptom of a struggle for power, then in the absence of struggle it is superfluous.

THERE IS NO TRIAL for abuse of authority, then, when literature does not claim to have any; neither is there one when the very principle of authority is ridiculed, when there is no recognized authority or every authority is contested—which is more or less the situation in societies that are at the forefront of democratic progress.

But no need to worry: in these cases, anti-literary discourse shifts to other arguments.

Second Trial

Truth

5 P.M. at Cambridge University. A brief appearance by John F. Kennedy. A false symmetry. Homophobia suits anti-literature. Literature leads straight to Auschwitz. Benda, an unwitting moderate. Writers are cowards. Adorno. Nobel hopes for Baron Snow. And then there was Leavis. Third culture and third realm. Arnold and Huxley. The Homeric laughter of Monsieur Renan. Children sucking their thumbs. Does Mister Spock like literature? The geometer and the poets. God, poetry is so boring! Translations without an original. I embrace poetry, only to suffocate it. Return to Plato. When poets attacked philosophy. The classical ideal of the man without letters. Cup of coffee versus cup of tea. Behaviorism in Homer, Shakespeare, and others. The myth of the crazy writer and the Nazi lover of literature. Fighting for the territory.

In a vast neoclassical room whose only fanciful touch was a tile floor with a dizzying repetition of diamonds embedded within each other in a black-and-white jacquard pattern, two superposed rows of nine tall windows faced eighteen similar windows (to simplify the count, I am proceeding as if one of these windows had not been replaced by a dull, opaque wood door, the architect having eventually had to accept that even at Cambridge University, humans are not pure spirit and that the symmetry so carefully laid out consequently had to be broken to provide at some selected spot what is commonly known as an *entrance*). In this vast room, then, one found some thirty-four twinned windows (to which one must add the five windows of the short east side, the west side having none, for a total of thirty-nine). In short, quite a large number of more or less symmetrically arranged windows allowed the warm light of a late spring afternoon typical of the English countryside to illuminate a gathering of about four hundred people. Unless, of course, clouds were obstructing the sky that day and rain was pouring down, a detail history has refrained from recording, though it would not have been unlikely in this verdant part of leafy England, even in May—on May 7, 1959, to be specific. The clock had just struck five: it was not time to drink tea, but rather for a man of respectable height and girth, who would probably not have turned down a few extra scones, to head for the lectern standing at one end of the room in front of a recess paneled in dark wood and topped by a large pediment resting on four pilasters. The lecture was about to begin.

All this solemn symmetry in such an imposing setting was perfectly suited to the topic of the day: "the two cultures," according to the invitation card, just as one might say *The Two Towers* or *The Two Gentlemen of Verona*. In fact, the full title announced was longer: "The Two Cultures and the Scientific Revolution." Yet history would only remember the first part, and it is under this abridged title that the much-reissued text was read around the world and made a big impression, sometimes even generating outrage: another triumph for symmetry, whose power to illustrate overshadows the complexity of the real.

According to the orator, the two cultures are the literary culture and the scientific culture, which quietly stare each other down from opposite sides of a room without ever meeting in the middle. The literary types know nothing about the second law of thermodynamics, that old chestnut of modern physics, and the snobbish ignoramuses even dare to be proud of it. As for the scientists, they don't ever read literature, preferring to devote themselves to the simple pleasures of gardening or, in the unlikely event that they should pick up a book, to use it merely as a tool (hard to say whether a hammer or a shovel).[1] Is modern civilization forever fated to be torn between these two poles, without any possible communication between the two? Not at all, says the man at the lectern. On the contrary, we must fill the cultural gap by reforming the educational system, providing elites with the scientific abilities they sorely lack, and allowing the world to develop harmoniously through moral and technological progress that promises to unite all its peoples. In broad terms, this was the human-ist, generous credo, so obvious it was incontestable, proclaimed in Cambridge that day in May 1959 in the context of the prestigious Rede Lecture series founded three or four centuries earlier by an equally generous donor.

The lecturer had all the necessary qualities to measure the conse-quences of the scandalous gulf between the two cultures: a chemist by training, Sir Charles Percy Snow had begun his career as a researcher at Cambridge and then worked as a consultant to the government during the Second World War, recruiting the scientific community to help reach military objectives. At the same time, he had begun early on to publish novels describing the scientific life, and these had been relatively successful. Wearing the two hats of an administrator for scientific research and a fashionable author regularly participating in public discourse, Snow could claim to speak authoritatively on the lecture's double subject, the division between literature and science— a division to which he prided himself on being a happy exception.

Snow was indeed able to make the most of this double legiti-macy, which created a halo around his slightest comment on this dual subject. In just a few months, the transcript of the lecture was printed, translated, and commented upon all around the world (except in France, oddly enough).[2] Its author was hailed as an intellectual of the first rank and triumphantly welcomed wherever he set foot, starting with the United States. As early as 1960, Columbia University had started assigning *The Two Cultures* as required reading for every student, and future president John F. Kennedy promised himself to use it in his speeches.[3]

Readers today would find it difficult to explain the extraordinary impact of Snow's discourse when faced with this text, which is not only unconcerned with stylistic elegance—despite the fact that its author delighted in being called a writer—but written in ordinary prose redeemed neither by its succession of good-natured platitudes and pretentious personal reminiscences along the lines of "I myself knew such and such a great physicist, who personally told me . . . ," nor especially by its failure to provide a precise meaning for the principal terms employed, least of all the term "culture," which is curiously endowed with the ability to change meaning from one page to the next. Unless *The Two Cultures*'s very banality is responsible for its international success—as if in a certain way the future Baron Snow (for this was the title later bestowed on him by the queen for achievements that one can only hope, without much conviction, did not include *The Two Cultures*), as if this baron in the making had paradoxically been the first and principal beneficiary of the degeneration of culture that he so clumsily sought to denounce.

A book about anti-literature would have nothing to say about this lecture whose undeserved reputation is still strongly felt in the Anglophone world—though it is now less often considered in its own terms than as a historical moment best left in the past[4]—were it not for the fact that alongside its explicit condemnation of the division of society into two cultures, Snow's lecture at the same time spread the insidious voice of a discourse aiming to depreciate actual literary culture. It is one thing to use a generous philanthropic vision to promote a more inclusive, unified culture that puts the humanities and the sciences on equal footing and provides everyone with the means to participate in both intellectual spheres for the purpose of facing the challenges of the present. The objective is laudable—utopian perhaps, poorly stated no doubt, but certainly laudable, like any effort to raise humankind's general level of knowledge. But it is something else entirely to take advantage of this denunciation of the lack of communication between cultures to hide a unilateral criticism of the shortcomings and harmful effects of literary culture, and only literary culture. For, contrary to what the apparently equitable title of the lecture would suggest, the two cultures were not treated equally: the stated symmetry was as false as the symmetry of the windows in the Cambridge University hall where the famous lecture was delivered.

Two cultures? Without a doubt, but one of them is systematically credited with every virtue: sincerity, truth, simplicity, usefulness, effectiveness, altruism. That would be science—or scientists. It's hard to know exactly because Snow doesn't think twice about combining several distinct realities under the name of science: a method for constructing knowledge, the social and professional practice to which it corresponds, the environment in which this practice is carried out, the individuals that participate in it as well as their ways of life outside their professional context—Snow undoubtedly believes he can allow himself this rampant confusion because of his use of the word *culture*. As for the other culture, it is exactly the opposite: hypocritical, lying, snobbish, stuck in the past, artificial, egocentric, downright harmful—enough already! Believe it or not, this is Snow's description of scholars, writers, artists, intellectuals, and the like. Obviously deriving pleasure from reinforcing this contrast, Snow could not be harsher in his criticism of literary culture, which he constantly and without explanation refers to as "the traditional culture," as if this term made any sense. (Is it the culture based on tradition? The dominant culture? That of the people, the elites, etc.?)[5] Contrary to what its title seems to promise, the lecture appears to be less a lament about the lack of understanding between the two cultures than a lampoon of the misdeeds of literary culture, the alleged cause of every ill besetting the modern world.

Some will say I'm exaggerating. Hardly: in fact, in 1959 Snow was toning down what he had said in a first version of the lecture published a few years earlier in the left-wing weekly the *New Statesman,* under the same title of "The Two Cultures." Let the reader be the judge:

Its tone [that of scientific culture] is, for example, steadily *heterosexual.* The difference in social manners between Harwell and Hampstead, or *as far as that goes* between Los Alamos and Greenwich Village, would make an anthropologist blink. About the whole scientific culture, there is an absence—surprising to outsiders—of the feline and oblique. Sometimes it seems that scientists relish speaking the truth, especially when it is unpleasant. The climate of personal relations is singularly bracing, not to say harsh.[6]

Ah, the warm and harsh virility of relations among scientists! A welcome change from the effeminacy and feline slyness of literary types. Who wouldn't prefer to live in the New Mexico desert, with the rugged real men of Los Alamos, rather than with the sissies of Greenwich Village and Hampstead?

Here we get the full measure of the talent that earned Sir Charles so many honors: rejection of unfair generalizations, attention to local and social specificities, subtle and objective analysis of personal experience, respect for others, and abolition of all prejudice.

One wonders what detailed sociological research allowed this intellectual to achieve such a finely shaded perception of reality. Two years earlier, in 1954, the brilliant British mathematician Alan Turing had committed suicide after being convicted of homosexuality. A hero of the Second World War, which the Allies might not have won without his contribution to decrypting the Enigma machine, Turing had gone on to do nothing less than develop the fundamental principle of computers and artificial intelligence. So yes, with one less homosexual in its ranks, the British scientific establishment could perhaps pride itself on having preserved a proper, "steadily heterosexual" atmosphere. But had science benefited? Snow clearly did not ask himself that question: one hopes, with no real conviction, that he would have answered in the negative.

Curiously, the contentious passage from the 1956 article was removed from the 1959 Cambridge lecture, as was the one in which Snow remarks that a scientist asked about his reading habits might answer: "As a married man, I prefer the garden."[7] Not simply, "I prefer the garden," but "as a married man," which was undoubtedly important in Snow's eyes. The argument is clear enough: literary culture only interests homosexuals and is sterile, perverse, and dangerous.[8]

In 1959, then, the more or less direct homophobic allusions in which Snow displayed the same "feline and oblique" character he denounced in the literary world were deleted. On the other hand, the danger of literature is still present, looming larger than ever. It is—and this is the key word—*political*:

> I remember being cross-examined by a scientist of distinction. "Why do most writers take on social opinions which would have been thought distinctly uncivilized and démodé at the time of the Plantagenets? Wasn't that true of most of the famous twentieth-century writers? Yeats, Pound, Wyndham Lewis, nine out of ten of those who have dominated literary sensibility in our time—weren't they not only politically silly, but politically wicked?"

Then comes the fundamental question in all its terrible ridiculousness: "Didn't the influence of all they represent bring Auschwitz that much nearer?"[9]

But of course! The invention of the extermination camps had nothing to do with Hitler, Nazism, the crash of 1929, the invasion of Poland, the outbreak of the Second World War, the development of nationalism and racial theories in the nineteenth century, two millennia of constant anti-Semitism in the West. A handful of British and American poets of the interwar period were most certainly to blame. What took everyone so long to realize that?

Joking aside, if Snow had not specified that the speaker was a well-known scientist, one might have thought he was repeating ill-conceived drawing room chatter from one of those dinner parties where after the meal and in a cloud of cigarette smoke, alcohol leads the conversation off the rails. But this is "a scientist of distinction": anyone other than Snow would have drawn the reasonable conclusion regarding the value of this much-vaunted scientific culture and the intelligence it is supposed to confer—but anyone other than Snow would probably not have chosen to repeat such a statement, unless it was to laugh at it.

After such a pronouncement, one expects Snow to take the reins of the conversation and rectify the scientist's judgment. After all, there were plenty of potential responses. For example, that Yeats, Pound, and Lewis did not have a wide audience in Great Britain, much less in Germany, or that James Joyce, Thomas Mann, and Marcel Proust, among many other writers, could hardly be suspected of being in league with the forces of fascism and anti-Semitism. Or that many scientists participated in making Auschwitz possible: the anthropologists Francis Galton and Georges Vacher de Lapouge, engineers like Wernher von Braun and Hermann Pohlmann, who invented the V-2 rocket and the Stuka, doctors like Josef Mengele, and of course the chemists of IG Farben. Or that literature has no more and no less responsibility for all this than the society that it was simply an expression of. In other words, there was no shortage of arguments.

Instead of which, the future Baron Snow continued:

> I thought at the time, and I still think, that the correct answer was not to defend the indefensible. It was no use saying that Yeats, according to friends whose judgment I trust, was a man of singular magnanimity of character, as well as a great poet. It was no use denying the facts, which are broadly true. The honest answer was that there is, in fact, a connection, which literary persons were culpably slow to see, between some kinds of early twentieth-century art and the most imbecile expressions of anti-social feeling. That was one reason, among many, why some of us turned our backs on the art and tried to hack out a new or different way for ourselves.[10]

One can only be stunned by so many outrageous statements: not defend the indefensible, half-forgive Yeats because at the end of the day he was a good guy. With friends like Snow, literature doesn't need enemies.

The most unbearable is the orator's clear conscience in spouting such foolishness: he was convinced that he represented the good and the moral, that the future was on his side, and that he would be heard as an oracle. But a clear conscience devoid of intelligence is worthless.

As I have mentioned, Snow was a repeat offender. In the version published three years earlier, he had written:

[Scientists] have nothing but contempt for those representatives of the traditional culture who use a deep insight into man's fate to obscure the social truth—or to do something prettier than obscure the truth, just to hang on to a few perks. Dostoevski sucking up to the Chancellor Pobedonotsev, who thought the only thing wrong with slavery was that there was not enough of it; the political decadence of the *Avant garde* of 1914, with Ezra Pound finishing up broadcasting for the Fascists; Claudel agreeing sanctimoniously with the Marshal about the virtue in others' suffering; Faulkner giving sentimental reasons for treating Negroes as a different species. They are all symptoms of the deepest temptations of the clerks—which is to say: "Because man's condition is tragic every-one ought to stay in their place, with mine as it happens somewhere near the top."[11]

When dealing with such bad faith, what purpose would it serve to counter all those names with those of Tolstoy, Zola, Orwell, Gide, Breton, or Steinbeck? No doubt the Anglo-Saxon modernists had a frequent though not exclusive propensity for the right and even the extreme right of the political spectrum: is that a reason to stamp all of literature without exception with the seal of infamy?

It was possible to think otherwise. Thirty years earlier, in France, Julien Benda had also painted a bleak picture of the "betrayal of the clerks."[12] Immediately after the Second World War, long before Snow dreamed of criticizing contemporary literature's "Alexandrianism" and its disconnect from the people and from reality, Benda made the case against the "Byzantinism" of the writers of his era, which could be summed up as the "triumph of pure literature."[13] Yet despite his aggressive tone, the French critic never dreamed of lumping all of literature together and arguing for its eradication: only a few writers were targeted.

Snow is not as scrupulous. He continues the scathing description in the 1956 version as follows:

> From that particular temptation, made up of defeat, self-indulgence, and moral vanity, the scientific culture is almost totally immune. It is that kind of moral health of the scientists, which, in the last few years, the rest of us have needed most; and of which, because the two cultures scarcely touch, we have been most deprived.[14]

End of article, case closed: *sic transit Gloria litteraturae.* Immunity, "moral health": Snow's references are to biology and medicine, in keeping with an intellectual framework that, paradoxically, is identical to that of his enemies on the extreme right: the opposition between scientific and literary people is of an organic nature, which is why it is impossible to eliminate.

A few years earlier, a German philosopher of a different caliber had also taken literature to task, particularly poetry: "To write poetry after Auschwitz is barbaric."[15] Or: "All post-Auschwitz culture, including its urgent critique, is garbage."[16] These statements were motivated by the feeling that art, as defined in traditional bourgeois terms, was absolutely powerless in the face of Nazi barbarity, but their unexpected violence also expresses the necessary rejection of nostalgia as well as the will to radically transform the usual practices.

In Adorno—for it is him we are speaking of—the energy of this call to critical revolution was proportional to the disappointment and distress experienced. Solutions had to be invented from scratch; and if there was one place where it would be unwise to try to find them, it was in the so-called scientific and technological culture whose triumph the philosopher considered one of the fundamental reasons for the catastrophe known as Auschwitz. Science would not help us escape from the historical logic that had led to absolute barbarity: it was nothing other than the most successful expression of the primacy given to practical efficiency, with the results we know. In contrast to the technological and scientific pragmatism celebrated by Snow, Adorno argued that a general critique needed to come first, with the full force of its negativity.

Nothing could be further removed from the good baron's thinking, both in content and in form. If Snow had read Adorno, it is likely that he would have used his ideas as additional evidence of the incorrigible "Luddite" temptation specific to literary culture, which according to him was traditionally opposed to industrialization and technological progress.[17] Snow has simple ideas: unlike Adorno, he is hardly inclined to destroy or change everything and start over from scratch. That would be far too much work. He finds his solution in what already exists: it is called science. Simple as that.

Naturally, Snow also wants another literature. He believes it is possible, and he personally works to bring it into existence with his own novels: a generous literature, attuned to psychological and social realities, and not afraid to champion ideas.[18] A literature that incorporates the virtues of science and subordinates itself to it. Yet that is still not good enough, for to Snow the literary endeavor appears to be rotten to the core, and the world will not find its salvation there.

According to Snow, literature—even good literature—is no longer necessary. Never does he make an attempt to balance his argument by pointing out science's shortcomings in dealing with contemporary problems; never does he advise science to glean the slightest thing from the qualities of literary culture. The symmetry on display is false: there are two cultures, but only one culture matters. All the rest is . . . literature.

The most interesting thing about this episode is the global success with which Snow's proposition was met in the few months following the lecture, despite all its approximations, oversimplifications, absurdities, and untruths. It is as if the world had been waiting for exactly that: a discourse radically opposing literary principles and scientific principles and elevating the value of the latter at the expense of the former. A discourse confirming the idea, which was being insisted on everywhere with imperturbable force, that in the second half of the twentieth century, literature had been definitively supplanted by science and now belonged to a bygone era. That it no longer had a place in the modern world. If so many people were blind to the flagrant naïveté of the lecture delivered on May 7, 1959—so many intellectuals, critics, journalists, and politicians—it is because it was merely using the dazzling power of pseudo-obviousness to repeat a theory everyone was already absolutely convinced of, sometimes without even daring to admit it: literature and progress had proven to be incompatible, and since the postwar world was now on the irresistible path to humanity's material and moral improvement, since everyone was genuinely delighted about it, since the fast-approaching year 2000 seemed to promise the fulfillment of the wildest utopias, anti-literature could now become the official discourse of the elites. Endowed with a truth and an effectiveness that literature was lacking, science had won, once and for all. This creed was the most widely shared thing in the world, and Snow was its prophet.

Snow's and Adorno's theories were radically opposed to each other. This did not prevent either of them from being swiftly disseminated. In the German-speaking world and beyond, the phrase "to write poetry after Auschwitz is barbaric" became a slogan nearly as well-worn as "the two cultures" was in the Anglophone world. The coincidence of these two successes is surprising, given how contradictory the positions were. It is as if the cause of their success was to be found in their only common denominator, their anti-literary content. Public opinion was ready for such a message: the era of media-driven anti-literature could finally begin.

RESISTANCE TO SNOW'S lecture long remained in the shadows. Everyone had applauded the orator, or pretended to. No one seemed

to notice that behind the writer's apparently generous, humanist system for reconciliation of the two cultures, a purely anti-literary war
machine was being launched. For three years, everything was just fine,
so to speak. In 1962, Sir Charles, the future Baron Snow of Leicester,
was peacefully enjoying his international fame. Nothing seemed out
of reach to him now, and he dared to hope that a Nobel Prize for
Literature might eventually honor his body of work and crown his
achievement as a great thinker and a great writer.

Then an annoying interloper stepped in. Not just any interloper
either, but Frank Raymond Leavis, the most famous and influential
critic at Cambridge, if not in the entire United Kingdom, a merciless
foe of literary mediocrity whose keen opinions altered the canon to
his liking, making and unmaking reputations. His journal, *Scrutiny,*
had long championed the position of literature as one of the highest
achievements of the human spirit and the central element of any rigorous intellectual education. While it goes without saying that Snow's
lecture and ensuing success had upset the critic, who was perfectly
aware that Snow's apparently irresistible influence was on the verge
of dashing his own efforts to establish the study of English literature
as the basis of the university curriculum, Leavis nevertheless bided
his time: he did not publicly express himself on the subject until February 28, 1962, the date on which he had been invited by students
to deliver the Richmond Lecture. The context was far different from
that of the Rede Lecture that Snow had given three years earlier: the
Richmond Lecture was limited to a single college, Downing, where
Leavis taught, and was not open to the general public. Journalists
were deliberately excluded. Not for want of trying, either: the press
had been attracted by the smell of blood and a title that could not be
mistaken for irenicism: "Two Cultures? The Significance of C. P. Snow."
An air of scandal surrounded the event.

The lecture lived up to expectations—or fears. Several members
of the audience noisily left the room after a few minutes, and the very
next day all of Cambridge was abuzz with speculation about what had

transpired inside the walls of Downing College.[19] Rumors about the lecture reached London, and, to put an end to the false allegations that were beginning to circulate in the major newspapers, Leavis quickly decided to entrust his text to *The Spectator.* The conservative weekly published the piece on March 9, 1962, with its cover entirely devoted to what was becoming a major controversy. This controversy continued for a month, in every issue of the magazine: reactions to Leavis's article, counter-reactions, counter-counter-reactions, etc. Political and intellectual notables as well as ordinary readers had a field day, with those favoring Snow taking precedence over his detractors, since his cause was championed by the vast majority of establishment thinkers. A prime example was the poet Edith Sitwell—Dame Edith Sitwell, to call her by her full title—whose concision was as brutal as it was scornful:

> I read with an entire lack of interest, but some surprise, Dr. F. R. Leavis's non-stop and malevolent attack on Sir Charles Snow in your last issue.
>
> I read to the end of this attack solely because I could not make out what it was all about, or why Dr. Leavis wrote it.
>
> Is it possible that Sir Charles may have offended Dr. Leavis by the fact of his great fame, or by the fact that he—Sir Charles—can write English? Only this can explain such a silly exhibition.[20]

Most of the other reactions were of the same type: the publication of the opinion piece turned markedly to Doctor Leavis's disadvantage at least in *The Spectator*'s letters section, to the point that the paper had to explicitly come to the critic's defense.[21]

It has to be said that Leavis had not pulled any punches during his lecture at Downing College. Let the reader be the judge:

> The peculiar quality of Snow's assurance expresses itself in a pervasive tone; a tone of which one can say that, while only genius could justify it, one cannot readily think of genius adopting it.[22]

And:

> The judgement I have to come out with is that not only is he not a genius; he is intellectually as undistinguished as it is possible to be.[23]

As well as:

> Snow is, of course, a—no, I can't say that; he isn't; Snow thinks of himself as a novelist. I don't want to discuss that aspect of him, but I can't avoid saying something. The widespread belief that he is a distinguished novelist (and that it should be widespread is significant of the conditions that produced him) has certainly its part in the success with which he has got himself accepted as a mind. The seriousness with which he takes himself as a novelist is complete—if seriousness can be so ineffably blank, unaware.[24]

Leavis continued to demonstrate the literary pretensions of this novelist who was incapable of breathing life into his characters or producing anything other than a dry, utterly external approximation of what a real novel should be. Incapable, even, of allowing the reader to perceive what really drives the scientists who are his characters, to the point that Snow's own reputation as a scientist is called into question: "That [Snow] has really *been* a scientist, that science as such has ever, in any important inward way, existed for him, there is no evidence in his fiction."[25]

Is this a case of literary incompetence or scientific incompetence? Leavis slyly fails to shed light on the question, omitting any mention of the affair that drove Snow to give up his career as a researcher in the 1930s. The much-publicized announcement that he had found a way to artificially synthesize vitamin A had been followed by the no-less-talked-about revelation that the discovery was false—a disappointment that Snow would use as the subject of one of his first novels, *The Search* (1934).[26] At best, the critic continues, Snow is merely a technocrat, familiar with what he calls "the Corridors of Power," which are actually far more fascinating to him than the humble routine of lab benches and microscopes. His view of the world is no less technocratic: according to him, science should serve only to produce economic growth for the entire planet, the purely material satisfactions to which he boils down the aspirations of the human race, or the "jam" to be spread on one's toast, according to an expression Snow uses several times and whose deplorable triviality Leavis is quick to point out.[27]

No one would deny that science can make human action more effective. But, the critic asks, what is the purpose of this action? Scientists in their labs are no more qualified than anyone else to decide. This is exactly what literature considers: ultimate purpose. Leavis cites the writings of Joseph Conrad and D. H. Lawrence, whose reflections on the role of technical progress in advancing social well-being and individual existence seem more finely shaded than Snow's: there is a reflective dimension specific to literature that neither the academy nor humanity in general can do without and that can certainly not be replaced by the third-rate journalism practiced by Snow and his friends. This is Leavis's response to accusations of the alleged immorality and dangerousness of literature.

But there is more, Leavis continues: it is the very principle of a comparison between science and literature that is fundamentally flawed. It would be absurd to deny Sir Charles's claim that science is a marvelous human creation. However, "there is a prior human achievement of collaborative creation, a more basic work of the mind of man (and more than the mind), one without which the triumphant erection of the scientific edifice would not have been possible: that is, the creation of the human world, including language. It is one we cannot rest on as something done in the past. It lives in the living creative response to change in the present."

Yet, the critic continues,

It is in the study of literature, the literature of one's own language in the first place, that one comes to recognize the nature and priority of the third realm (as, unphilosophically, no doubt, I call it, talking with my pupils), the realm of that which is neither merely private and personal nor public in the sense that it can be brought into the laboratory or pointed to. You cannot point to the poem; it is "there" only in the re-creative response of individual minds to the black marks on the page. But—a necessary faith—it is something in which minds can meet.[28]

This admirable and nearly desperate profession of faith in literature attempts to save the field in the face of science by drawing attention to an order of realities that is specific to it: that of this intermediate "third realm," inserted between a person's innermost being and the external world, between pure subjectivity and hard objectivity. This is the shared world of intersubjectivity: aesthetic values and judgments on which the possibility of public life is based. How could we refuse literature the eminent, leading role it can play in exploring this vast domain? Leavis's argument is a powerful one.

Yet, at the same time, it would be hard to deny that the academy also includes an entire body of disciplines that can make an equally legitimate claim to the study of this shared world: those generally known as the social sciences. Snow sensed that this was a card he could play against Leavis. In the reply he published a year after the Richmond Lecture, he emphasized a "third culture" that could bridge the gap between the first two: "social history, sociology, demography, political science, economics, government (in the American academic sense), psychology, medicine, and social arts such as architecture."[29] In short, just about every discipline possible outside of the exact sciences—except literature. Surprise, surprise! In his lecture, Snow had already stressed that the historians and sociologists of his acquaintance vigorously refused to be "corralled in a cultural box" with literary people.[30] In other words, there was no chance that

Snow would recognize literature's claim to exploring any world, including that of intersubjectivity: it was time to make way for the new human and social sciences, which, strangely, he now employed as reinforcements in the battle of the two cultures.[31] This is not the only time they would be enlisted on anti-literature's side, whether they liked it or not.[32]

However, it is far from certain that the counterattack of the social sciences succeeded in completely dispossessing literature. For that to take place, the "third culture" heralded by Snow would have had to perfectly match the "third realm" discussed by Leavis. As it happens, the two fields are as poorly assorted as literature and sociology: while literary works include noteworthy sociological and anthropological reflection, as seen in Conrad, Lawrence, and Dickens, the literary experience goes far beyond simple description of a shared world.

According to Leavis, this experience has three parts: a linguistic experience, contributing to the foundation of a common language; an aesthetic experience, allowing the establishment of a canon and a tradition of reference; and a moral experience, aiming to produce a "criticism of life," to quote Matthew Arnold's famous expression.[33] Involved at the origin of any community of thought, literature participates in the functioning of society as effectively as science. Truth falls to science, good and beauty to literature. How could science ever render literature obsolete, if we recognize that the moral question and the aesthetic experience must remain at the heart of all education and civic existence? Science is the instructor of truth, literature the teacher of good—and, secondarily, of beauty: this is the position defended by Leavis, for better or for worse.

How long could this partition of the empire and the ensuing gentleman's agreement persist? No matter how secure literature's position might have appeared, it was the result of a retreat to its basic principles, after it was forced to relinquish truth to the power of science. Additionally, this fallback position did not appear to be ironclad. If

Snow could conflate literary culture and evil in such an absurd way without raising an outcry, it had to be expected that literature would eventually be evicted from the moral camp. While Flaubert had made such an attempt a century earlier in France (not without difficulty), the literary systems on either side of the Channel were too different for his example to bear fruit on British soil.[34]

In the meantime, and despite his attempted retort, Lord Snow of Leicester never completely recovered from the furious attack launched against him by F. R. Leavis. The publication of Leavis's denunciation in *The Spectator* was followed by numerous indignant responses, as we have seen, but perhaps in the eyes of the victim the most important thing was missing: genuine praise of his work as a novelist, which would have offset the pernicious discrediting of his literary reputation by the Cambridge critic. Snow's friends ventured only half-hearted attempts. The American critic Lionel Trilling found fault with Leavis's form but did not express any significant disagreement with the substance of his argument.[35] Snow asked George Steiner, whom he had hired at Churchill College, to take his defense from a purely literary point of view, but the brilliant young Cambridge Fellow found a paradoxical way to offload his responsibility with a magnificent tribute to Leavis, supplemented for good measure with a few sincere paragraphs on the "ignoble performance" of the Richmond Lecture and the critic's lack of humanity.[36] And so Baron Snow saw the Nobel Prize inexorably slip out of his grasp; in any case, he was convinced that Leavis had been the cause of this failure—or what he experienced as such.[37]

Yet could Snow decently claim to have it both ways and win on the literary *and* the anti-literary front? All in all, perhaps a more appropriate prize for Snow would have been a Nobel Prize in Anti-Literature, had there been such a thing. Even that is not a given: Snow was a popularizer of anti-literature, not an inventor. Leavis had said as much with the full weight of his contempt: "in himself negligible," Snow was primarily relevant as a "portent" or a symptom.[38] He was the ideal pseudo-thinker for an age in which lack of culture prevailed: his success singlehandedly spelled the intellectual degradation of a society that demeaned itself by taking him so seriously.

LET'S PUSH ON EVEN FURTHER: Snow was only a stage, neither the first nor the last, in the long history of the fight of science against literature, one that was repeated several times in nearly identical terms, with education as the primary focus. The Leavis-Snow controversy was simply a reprise in more violent form of the genteel conflict that had opposed Matthew Arnold and T. H. Huxley a century earlier, also in England. On the occasion of the inauguration of the new Mason Science College in Birmingham in 1880, Huxley had defended the principle of an education based exclusively on the sciences, in keeping with the wishes of the college's founder.[39] Arnold responded in 1882 with a lecture at Cambridge, in the series instituted by Sir Robert Rede, which would provide the prestigious setting for Sir Charles Snow's famous remarks almost eighty years later. The lecture was entitled "Literature and Science," and Arnold repeated it no less than twenty-nine times during the course of a subsequent major tour of the United States and Canada.[40] His position was deeply conciliatory. In essence, Arnold's argument went as follows: "Literature conflicts with science? But literature as I conceive it calls on everything that makes us human beings; it includes science, it presupposes it! While the reverse is not true. So that, all in all, if I had to choose between the two, I would choose the first and not the second. But God forbid that I should have to choose!" All of this expressed in the politest, friendliest of terms.

However dissimilar the tone of the lecture, neither the issues nor the arguments presented were particularly different from those characterizing the polemics that would one day erupt in the same location—with unprecedented fierceness. Lionel Trilling was not wrong to complain that Snow and Leavis were merely repeating a well-known controversy and that Sir Charles had failed to display any knowledge of his distant predecessor's lecture.[41] Those who do not know history are doomed to repeat it—often in a farcical mode.[42]

That both events took place at Cambridge in the context of the Rede Lectures is an entirely superficial coincidence. Their real similarity is elsewhere, in the fact that the antagonism between science and literature appears in both as the commonplace of anti-literature. The argument is that since science has dispossessed literature of truth, literature no longer has a rightful place in education or society in general. It would be difficult to be more straightforward—or dismissive. But why stop while you're ahead? Science can itself be recognized as having ethical and critical content that makes literature superfluous: eighty years apart, Huxley and Snow were saying the same thing. In the meantime, the prodigious development of modern science had only exacerbated the antagonism.

Yet this repetition should not obscure the difference between the two controversies: the first saw the clear-cut success of the pro-literary argument, via the good word that Matthew Arnold triumphantly preached all across North America, from Massachusetts to Virginia and from Ohio to Wisconsin and Quebec, while the second saw the official victory of the anti-literary position championed by Snow—at least until Leavis entered the fray. Many things had changed between these two moments: science and technology had experienced tremendous development; technocracy, as most perfectly embodied by Sir Charles, had prevailed; literature, now under formalism's sway, had largely reduced its social ambition since the romantic age of which Arnold was a late representative; finally, postwar Western societies had undergone sweeping democratization and no longer had the same relationship to a culture and a tradition perceived as elitist.[43] A long and rich career lay ahead for anti-literary discourse, which was now in a position to dominate. It had become a less shocking discourse, which made the threat it represented all the more painfully apparent to the last partisans of literature. This was all it took to bring things to a head—or at least to send the newspapers into a tizzy. The personalities of the opponents did the rest. The impassioned response to the dispute matched this level of tension.

Nonetheless, there was something irresistibly déjà vu about the polemic. Snow and Leavis were merely unwilling links in an infinitely longer story, the reluctant actors of a scene played out a thousand times in many countries—notably in the context of debates about education. There was a distinct lack of subtlety in this case, but one could hardly complain about the passion or character of the episode: anti-literature is more like a gladiator fight than an academic dispute.

WE NOW MOVE TO AN ENTIRELY different scene, one far more courteous and high-society, though perhaps no less disturbing, owing to its incongruity. It takes place in Paris, in the late 1880s, shortly after Matthew Arnold's much-talked-about Cambridge lecture on "literature and science." We are at the literary salon of Madame Arman de Caillavet, the inspiration for Proust's Madame Verdurin. This evening, the guest of honor is none other than Ernest Renan. He holds court by the fireplace, his massive body supported by a flimsy gilt chair on the verge of collapsing. Guests are introduced to him one by one. A thin young man approaches. Awkward and shy, this recent arrival from his native Provence can think of nothing better to do than to tell the writer how much he admires his "Prayer on the Acropolis," which many writers at the time thought contained the most perfect page of prose ever written in French.[44] The hostess joins in, adding her own compliments and those of all her guests for this magnificent prayer, and then . . . But let's give the floor to Charles Maurras, who described the events almost half a century later with full knowledge of the facts, for he had once been that shy young man:

> Then, then, what a surprise! First M. Renan began to go very red in the face, then he suddenly burst out laughing, but with a god's laugh, as mysterious as it was uncontrollable, a laugh whose object we tried in

vain to discover. The more we tried to explain to him all the reasons we admired this great page—the most beautiful in French literature, we kept repeating—the more he laughed wholeheartedly, to the point of making the gilt chair shake and groan.

If he had been reminded of a bad little book of juvenilia, riddled with indecent trivialities, would he have reacted any differently?

We didn't give up. We tried to make him recite that beautiful text, but he laughed even harder. There was nothing left to do but be quiet. And I have no memory of that laugh coming to an end, for I hear it to this day.[15]

Sometimes anti-literature is just a laugh. This is how the divinity mocks those who bring her offerings in thanks for what they regard as a godsend: the recovery from ill-health of a family member, a much-needed rain, an abundant harvest. "These are trifles," she replies, "that are not worth the trouble. Celebrate me for what is really important: the creation of the world, the movement of the planets, the birth of life, what have you . . . I can see that these things have merit. For the rest, leave me alone; I have serious work to do."

For Renan, literature was merely an amusing pastime to undertake in between archeological digs or epigraphic studies, pursuits that were helping to advance science. His disdain for the literary veneration he was universally granted was unprecedented. He did not even try to use this reverence to add to his fame. His rejection of hypocrisy here, as in his other activities, was absolute, and his moral attitude irreproachable—but anti-literary.

In 1891, Jules Huret came to see Renan in the context of research for his *Enquête sur l'évolution littéraire* (Study of literary development). Ceremoniously entering the vast office Renan used as an administrator of the Collège de France, the journalist finds him hard at work, wholly absorbed in several quartos lying open around him. Huret struggles to get Renan to take an interest in the question that has brought him, the development of contemporary literature:

As I was making incredible efforts of dialectic to link literary trends to the developments of the philosophic spirit, M. Renan said to me, with both his hands lying flat on his knees:

—Literary trends . . . are puerile, childish. That's not interesting, no, really it's not. In two years, no one will talk about it.

And he added:

—You see, literature is itself a mediocre concern.[46]

Renan suddenly appears to change his mind and begins to speak highly of Racine, Voltaire, Leconte de Lisle, and Sully Prudhomme, but it is clear that his praise is pro forma. Huret asks him about Zola. By a stroke of luck, Renan has just read *La Faute de l'Abbé Mouret* (The sin of Father Mouret) and remarks that there are too many overlong passages. He continues:

And also, there are a great number of repetitions; it is not written, it is not crafted, oh no! . . . It was done too quickly, that is clear. It would have taken another year of work to finalize it, and he should have pruned, pruned a lot. . . . But after all, [Zola] is undoubtedly a worthy man.[47]

A master would not have proceeded any differently had he wanted to destroy his student's work—for Renan is a master, though he has nothing but contempt for the art form in which he is a past master.

The interview is coming to an end. It has lasted only a short time: Professor Renan has other things to do. With a final push, the journalist tries to bring him back to the subject of the day:

After all, I had to utter one last time the fundamental words of this study, and with a final effort, I managed to say: symbolists, psychologists, naturalists.

To which M. Renan replied:

—They are children sucking their thumbs.[48]

That was the end of the interview and the end of the study. Things couldn't have been much loftier on Mount Olympus. Huret's experience is every bit as bad as the laughter at Madame de Caillavet's.

Renan does not live on Mount Olympus, but he might as well: he looks at literature in the context of an overall conception of the history of humanity. His contempt is anything but a tantrum or the resentment that follows a failed love affair. It is a very strong feeling that goes back to his formative years. Matthew Arnold alluded to it in his 1882 lecture at Cambridge, rightfully reproaching the illustrious thinker, whom he greatly admired, for having come away from his literature courses at school with the memory of a "superficial humanism," admittedly "elegant," but "slight and ineffectual," having nothing to do with "positive science, or the critical search after truth," and even appearing to him to be "the opposite of science or true knowledge."[49]

Indeed, Renan has only a single credo: humanity is fated to science, and the scientific contemplation of truth will soon replace the meager pleasures provided by literary lies:

> Let us then say without fear that if the wonder of fiction has thus far seemed necessary to poetry, the wonder of nature, once revealed in its full splendor, will constitute a poetry one thousand times more sublime, a poetry that will be reality itself, that will be both science and philosophy.[50]

Renan was twenty-five when he put this profession of faith into words in *L'Avenir de la science* (The future of science). Though he would not publish this early work until the very end of his life, in 1890, the idea that science will render art and literature obsolete is an underlying theme throughout his work. It seems that revolutions encouraged Renan to speculate. Just as the reflections collected in *L'Avenir de la science* were inspired by the events of 1848, the turmoil of 1871 yielded the following:

Even great art will disappear. The time will come when art will be a thing of the past, a creation made once and for all, a creation of the nonreflective ages, which man will adore but recognize no further need for. This is already the case with Greek sculpture, architecture, and poetry.[51]

All the arts are fated to eventual extinction, including literature, which the infinite expansion of truth and good will one day cause to be stored away with the other antiquities:

> Each art, with the exception of music, is thus tied to a state of the past; music itself, which can be considered the art of the nineteenth century, will one day be done and complete. And the poet? . . . And the good man? . . . The poet is a comforter and the good man is a nurse, which are useful but temporary duties, for they presuppose evil, the evil that science aspires to greatly diminish.[52]

Beauty will itself no longer be necessary. Humans will have turned into beings of pure reason, not unlike *Star Trek*'s Mister Spock (though the comparison, it goes without saying, is not Renan's):

> Perhaps there will come a time (we see this day dawning) when the great artist and the virtuous man will be outdated, nearly useless things; the scholar, on the contrary, will always be increasingly valuable. Beauty will nearly disappear with the advent of science; but the extension of science and man's power are also beautiful things.[53]

Literature is just a crutch: useful during the childhood of humanity, but ready for the scrap heap when it reaches adulthood. This philosophy of history is more radical than the succession of the arts proposed by Hegel because it is tinged with a cruel nostalgia—the same cruelty one cannot help but hear in Renan's uncontrollable laughter, as it continues to ring out in Madame de Caillavet's salon, or in his haughty replies to the journalist Huret.[54] Renan uses the same insensitive cruelty to close "Prière sur l'Acropole," which is in fact a eulogy for literature and religion, considered on an equal footing: "The faith one has had must never be a chain. One is done with it once it has been carefully rolled into the crimson shroud in which dead gods sleep."[55]

On a lovely Paris evening, Monsieur Renan's laughter painfully revealed the irony of this nostalgic farewell to literature—and his own conversion to anti-literature.

LET'S GO BACK another century. Third scene: after Snow's lecture at Cambridge and Renan's laughter at Madame de Caillavet's, we now find ourselves at the Académie Française, in 1760, on the feast day of Saint Louis. It is August 25, and the mathematician Jean Le Rond d'Alembert is sharing his "Reflections on Poetry, Written on the Occasion of the Texts," submitted to the Académie's annual competition. One might well be surprised to learn that the Académie had entrusted a geometer with the task of writing a speech on poetry. And indeed, some people were surprised. Although the spirit of the time revolved around science and philosophy, which were considered able to govern everything, including poetry, d'Alembert knew that his speech would be received as that of a scientist and that the conservatives would hold it against him; nonetheless, he dove right in.

Why, d'Alembert asked, do old men have less taste for poetry? It is because poetic fictions get worn out; with time, the same endlessly repeated topics become boring; poetry does not take enough interest in great ideas. In fact, the boredom of old men is that of the entire century, which is no spring chicken:

> Most types of poetry seem to have successively gone out of fashion. The sonnet is nowhere to be seen, the elegy is expiring, the eclogue is on the decline, even the ode, the proud ode is starting to wane; satire, finally, even though it has every right to be welcomed—satire in verse is boring when it is long; we made it more comfortable by allowing it to move into prose.[56]

As for the "little verses" that appear in the periodicals, is it even worth mentioning them? They are completely out of favor. Even the epic poem, which d'Alembert initially seems to preserve from the disaster, no longer interests people: Homer and Virgil have themselves become unreadable. Only Torquato Tasso is spared, along with Voltaire—but in his case, friendship is at play.[57] Generally speaking, long poems have become impossible; it is difficult to maintain a uniform quality throughout, and even if it can be done, monotony threatens: "verse stops being pleasant as soon as it is careless, and on the other hand pleasure becomes dulled by continuity itself."[58] Even the "continuous exactitude and elegance" of Racine are eventually tiresome.

Yet if brevity disappoints and length is boring, what are poets left with? When there are so many problems whichever way one turns, it's best to give up: "The versifying population sadly recognizes the appreciable growth of the discredit into which it has fallen."[59]

The century has become too philosophical to enjoy this kind of balderdash. The Académie itself has complained of the low standard of the poetic pieces it receives: the quality is going down.[60] (Clearly, this argument is nothing new; d'Alembert would repeat it each time he was responsible for the poetry competition and in 1772 even chose not to award a prize because of a lack of sufficiently worthy contestants.)[61]

The solution? D'Alembert announces that it exists and will come from philosophy itself. It is time to put an end to the preconception that verse alone can make poetry interesting: ideas—real ideas, great ideas—have to be put into poems.

These were the many provocations scattered throughout d'Alembert's speech, cleverly hidden behind remarks apparently commending good poems. Yet one did not have to dig deep to find a fundamental challenge to the very idea of poetry—of *any* poetry. It was one thing to say that long poems had become as unbearable as the short ones: after all, one could try to come up with an unlikely happy medium. But there was worse—a proposal that d'Alembert pretended not to dwell on, if only to try to attenuate its brutality: "In a word, it seems to me that our century imposes on poets the following rigorous but just law: it now only recognizes as good in verse what it would consider excellent in prose."[62]

In essence, d'Alembert is simply stating that poetry is absolutely reducible to prose; that the harmony of language that it imposes on itself as an additional constraint is only useless embellishment; and that, all in all, if one can do without the embellishment, one can do without the rest, which is to say poetry itself. Then d'Alembert goes to an even greater extreme, couched in the language of philosophical experimentation:

> We believe that rhyme is as indispensable to our verse as versification to our tragedies: whether this is reason or prejudice, there is only one way to liberate our poets from this form of slavery, if indeed it is one: it is to write tragedies in prose, and verse without rhyme, which would in fact be worthy enough to justify this license. Until then any reasoning on either side will be in vain, with some believing they have reason on their side, and the others claiming usage and habit, before which reason must be silent.[63]

Verse without rhyme, tragedies in prose: d'Alembert was putting the spotlight back on a debate over the usefulness of verse and rhyme, which had been stirring in France since the late seventeenth century and was crashing head-on with the literary system of the period.[64] In a later speech, the scholar made the no less paradoxical proposal to use translation as a touchstone of poetic beauty: "Any poem, it will be agreed, loses in translation, but perhaps the most beautiful one is the one that loses the least."[65]

The proposal was not absolutely new: it can be found earlier in Isocrates, and Charles Perrault had borrowed it during the quarrel between the ancients and the moderns as a practical tool for comparing the two sides' poems.[66] In this case, however, it serves as a direct attack on versification.

The poet Évariste de Parny would remember it: in 1787, he presented his *Chansons madécasses* as a translation of an unknown (and most likely nonexistent) source text of poems by natives of Madagascar. And so the prose poem entered French literature by proving that the most beautiful poetry can do without verse: d'Alembert's posthumous triumph.

The very year that the mathematician delivered his provocative remarks to an audience at the Académie, James Macpherson published his first *Fragments of Ancient Poetry Collected in the Highlands of Scotland, and Translated from the Gaelic or Erse Language,* which was soon followed by many others; the original, attributed to a bard named Ossian, was as imaginary as that of the *Chansons madécasses.* In a way, the unprecedented success of these translations without an original, which were in turn immediately translated throughout Europe, proved d'Alembert's theory right; at the very least, it proved its historical pertinence.

Walter Benjamin concisely expressed this argument in describing the aesthetic theory of German romanticism, notably that of Friedrich Schlegel: "The idea of poetry is prose."[67] At the beginning of the nineteenth century, the philosopher Carl Gustav Jochmann prophesied "the regression of poetry," which would be reduced to nothing by humanity's progress.[68] D'Alembert was clearly a pioneer in this history or this philosophy of history, the same thread that would later include the reflections of Renan.

If his 1760 speech is more directly akin to anti-literature than Schlegel's and Jochmann's romantic writings, it is because it was received by his contemporaries as a deliberate act of aggression against poetry on the part of science and philosophy. *L'Année littéraire,* the literary periodical founded by Élie Fréron, no friend to the *philosophes,* published an anonymous letter (possibly written by Fréron himself) "on the remarks d'Alembert made against poetry and poets at the Académie Française on the feast of Saint Louis." It read:

Here, Sir, are the lapses we are subjected to by this geometric spirit, much vaunted today as the only one worthy of enlightening the arts, but in actuality more terrible for poetry and music than the iconoclasts were for painting and sculpture.[69]

A few years later, a poem "on the fate of poetry in this philosophic century" related the fateful reversal of fortune that poetry had been subjected to since Urania, the muse of philosophy, had taken its place in human hearts and the most austere works had prevailed over games and laughter:

> Thus came about this sudden change
> From a poetic century to a philosophic one.[70]

The author had the good idea to advocate for the reconciliation of the two muses: he walked away with an honorable mention from the Académie Française.

By 1760, d'Alembert was well aware of the risk he was running: that of uniting against him the anti-philosophic camp, which was already hostile to him, and the defenders of poetry, who would certainly be irritated by his radical critique. Since such a coalition would be good neither for his own affairs nor for those of the *philosophes,* he had to do everything in his power to break up the common front and distinguish between what was at stake for the different parties:

> [The versifying population] attacks that pernicious *philosophic spirit,* already accused of far more serious iniquities; for the philosophic spirit must also be charged with that particular wrong.
>
> Perhaps our century does not truly deserve the honor or injury we claim to do it by calling it, as a compliment or an insult, the *philosophic century;* but whether or not they are philosophers, the poets have no grounds for complaining of our century, and it will be easy to justify it to them.[71]

He returned to the charge in 1771: "There have been complaints that poetry is discredited among us, and it is this *philosophic* century, thus named *in praise* by some, and *in denigration* by the rest, that is indiscriminately held responsible."[72]

To defuse the situation, it took nothing less than the publication of a "Dialogue between Poetry and Philosophy, to Serve as a Preliminary to and Basis for a Treaty of Peace and Perpetual Friendship between the Two"—a freewheeling dialogue in which d'Alembert, speaking behind the mask of philosophy, attempted to put the pieces back together by giving the poets the floor and proclaiming his good intentions toward them:

PHILOSOPHY

I protest that I want much good for you.

POETRY

Your protestations might well resemble the line from *Britannicus*: I embrace my rival, but it is to suffocate him.

If you want so much good for me, why then do you constantly decry me? Why do you constantly repeat that verse is no longer wanted?

PHILOSOPHY

Me, decry poetry! Me, say that verse is no longer wanted! . . .

POETRY

Yet won't you admit that you do not read much verse?

PHILOSOPHY

I admit it, and it is not without reason. I read a great deal of it in the past, but I got so caught up in it, that I hardly ever expose myself to it anymore. . . .

POETRY

All of that is marvelous; but by feigning to attack only bad artists, it
is against art itself that you bear a grudge.[73]

Luckily, the conversation ends well, and poetry and philosophy
go their separate ways as friends forever—especially after the latter has touted its project to "introduce tragedies in prose and verses
without rhymes," exactly as d'Alembert had suggested in 1760.[74] The
most important thing was thus intact, except that this final retraction
can cast legitimate doubt on the sincerity of the entire dialogue. The
retraction itself seems to have been prompted by tactical considerations aimed at restoring peace within the Académie and the Republic
of Letters. In any case, d'Alembert had seen the error of his ways—
or made a show of seeing it. Did he succeed in convincing poetry's
defenders? They would have been mistaken to settle for his gestures
of good will: through his voice, science had made the first assault on
poetry. As we have seen, it would not stop there.

IN FACT, the indictment of poetry in the name of truth had not begun
with d'Alembert. As is always the case with anti-literature, we have
to go back to Plato to find the first example of such a conflict—with
one difference, however, and a significant one at that: in Plato, the
truth in question is not exactly that of science, in the modern sense
of the term, but that of a discourse. The opposition between poetry
and truth did not play out as a clash between two incommensurable
worlds or two totally disproportionate practices, as would be the case
with Renan and Huxley. Snow took perverse pleasure in describing
these two parallel universes that never meet, even at the high table
in Cambridge's colleges: scientific and literary types rubbed shoul-
ders while ignoring and being invisible to each other the whole time.
Modern science made the divide between the two fields infinitely
more unbridgeable.

There is almost none of that in Plato, for whom truth is a discourse, like poetry, but *other:* a discourse *of truth,* strictly speaking, or a philosophical discourse. The opposition of poetry and truth pits two types of utterances against each other. These most often contradict each other, but they can sometimes be in agreement. Thus Socrates accuses the poets of spewing one lie after another about the gods: if one were to believe the poets, the gods do harm, metamorphose, and do not hesitate to deceive both humans and other gods. But this is all nonsense, says Socrates: the philosopher knows that the divinity can only do good, that it is immutable and only produces acts and words of truth; otherwise, it would not be a divinity. Poets must therefore be forbidden to spread so many lies about the gods. Nothing could be more simple: take away the choruses the poets request and they will be reduced to silence.[75]

In this case, the opposition between poetry and truth does not reflect a difference in nature or essence: poetry can sometimes express the truth, and in the good republic imagined by Plato, it must even be required to tell the truth—except, possibly, when this truth is dangerous, in which case it is important to keep it quiet.[76]

As one might suspect, this argument does not go far enough for those who want to make philosophy the only legitimate discourse. *The Republic* therefore proposes a second argument with the ability to wholly invalidate poetic discourse. It appears in *The Republic*'s last book, like a coup de grâce delivered to literature. The thesis is that poetry is only imitation—and not just any kind of imitation, but the lowest level or worst possible kind of imitation. There are three levels in the production of objects. Take a bed, for instance. The first level corresponds to the idea or essence of the bed: only the divinity is capable of this idea, just as it produces all the objects that make up the universe. Then comes the next level of production: the carpenter who makes the bed by focusing his mind on the idea of the bed. Seen in this light, the actual bed is already an imitation. Finally, at the lowest level, the painter comes in, reproducing the image of the bed in his painting. This is the third degree of production, the least worthy of interest because the furthest from the original idea. The painter is unable to build the real bed: he has no skills as a carpenter; he produces the imitation of an imitation, nothing else—an imitation of a bed devoid of any of the qualities one expects from a real bed.

Well, the poet is on the same level as the painter: while Homer gives the impression of knowing something about leadership in war and government in *The Iliad,* we do not know whether he ever commanded an army on the battlefield or governed a city. He knows absolutely nothing about these types of things and provides only an illusion of competence. Furthermore, if the poets had been useful in any way, if they had been able to improve humankind, they would not have led the itinerant life they are known to live, and cities would have competed to be associated with them. Yet not only are poets not useful, they are truly dangerous: their art excites only the worst parts of the soul, those furthest removed from reason: love, anger, and the pleasant and painful passions that are aroused at the mere sight of an imitation, without regard for the truth.[77] Socrates therefore concludes that we must turn away from poetry:

> Just like the men who have once fallen in love with someone, and don't believe the love is beneficial, keep away from it even if they have to do violence to themselves; so we too—due to the inborn love of such poetry we owe to our rearing in these fine regimes—we'll be glad if it turns out that it is best and truest. But as long as it's not able to make its apology, when we listen to it, we'll chant this argument we are making to ourselves as a countercharm, taking care against falling back again into this love, which is childish and belongs to the many. We are, at all events, aware that such poetry mustn't be taken seriously as a serious thing laying hold of truth, but that the man who hears it must be careful, fearing for the regime in himself, and must hold what we have said about poetry.[78]

What proper language for such a severe condemnation! Especially proper given how radical it is: one regretfully lets go of poetry in the same way one lets go of a childhood love (d'Alembert would make the same argument: there is an age for poetry and an age for philosophy), but one nevertheless resolves to let go because poetry is an art that cannot reach the truth.

Of course, most of Socrates's anti-poetic arguments can be challenged. The poet describing a bed may be referring less to the object than to the idea of the bed, which exists in his mind as it does in the carpenter's: the imitation is therefore not so far removed from the original idea, even less so if the idea is a human invention rather than a divine one, as could legitimately be argued. Even Homer's alleged ignorance is debatable: Homer could not lead an army or pilot a ship, but could a general write *The Iliad* or a sailor *The Odyssey*? Writing poetry is a specific skill, one that is too easily reduced to divine inspiration or delirium, as Socrates does elsewhere.

We will not venture further into contesting Plato's arguments against poetry on rational grounds. Ultimately, it doesn't make much difference, for Plato was not the first to attack poetry; Socrates mentions that even in his era the quarrel between philosophy and poetry was already ancient.[79] The poets' invective against the philosophers attests to it:

> That "yelping bitch shrieking at her master" and "great in the empty eloquence of fools," "the mob of overwise men holding sway," and "the refined thinkers who are really poor" and countless others are signs of this old opposition.[80]

Socrates is particularly smug in reporting these pleasantries in stark contrast with the measured strictness he imposes on himself: in doing so, he implicitly emphasizes the excesses of poets, who are unable to curb their language. Philosophers, of course, are made of different stuff.

If there is one thing to take away from Socrates's line of argument, it is that poetry is, as a matter of principle, in the realm of imitation. It has nothing to do with truth; in fact it even dismisses the truth. In contrast, the task of "true philosophy" is "the turning of a soul around from a day that is like night to the true day; it is that ascent to what *is*."[81] Several sciences lead to it: arithmetic, plane geometry, the geometry of solids, astronomy, harmony, and finally, the crowning achievement, dialectics.[82] Ultimately, poetry and philosophy are different in nature. That difference is the basis for condemning the former in favor of the latter.

Once the sentence was handed down and the poets were exiled, philosophical discourse could occupy the space left by poetry. It is not by chance that immediately after the trial of poetry in the name of truth, *The Republic*'s dialogue ends with a myth, that of Er the Pamphylian.[83] The reader might object that she thought we were done with myths once and for all after the last poet had been evicted. Yes, but it is a *philosophical* myth, which changes everything, since, unlike the Homeric poems, it expresses a truth reached by philosophy—in this case a theory of justice and its consequences in the hereafter.

Truth be told, in formal terms a philosophical myth is just like an old wives' tale, and the tale of Er the Pamphylian is no exception, with its description of the underworld, the three Fates, and the souls of heroes popping up like celebrities encountered by the narrator at every turn: he is no luckier than a tourist visiting Los Angeles who comes upon one of the movie stars whom everyone knows can be spotted on every street corner in the city.

Nothing could be more like bad fiction—except that Socrates was careful to distinguish between the two discourses beforehand. It's true that the tale of Er could have fooled us. Did it completely pass the test? Nothing is less certain: no one is forced to take Plato's philosophy as an article of faith—outside of *his* republic. Witness d'Alembert:

> I know that Plato banned poets from his republic, but between us, and I only dare whisper this to you, Plato was an ingrate, far more worthy still of being included among the poets than among the philosophers.[84]

Let's take it a step further: there may be more human truth in book 11 of *The Odyssey*, in which Odysseus encounters the dead, than in the heavy-handed, allegedly scholarly myth of Er the Pamphylian. Sometimes anti-literature is just a way to get rid of an irritating competitor.

THE DEVELOPMENT OF MODERN science did not systematically result in an opposition to literary culture. Leonardo da Vinci was criticized for being a "man without letters" (*omo sanza lettere*),[85] but in fact he prided himself on this, knowing that he was endowed with the "good disposition" and genius that are far better than a simple veneer of literary culture and as likely to produce writers and artists as engineers and scholars: "Good letters are born of a good disposition; and since the cause is more to be praised than the effect, I will rather praise a good disposition without letters, than good letters without the disposition."[86]

Good letters and good science were supposed to be products of the same cause. This is a long way from the dichotomy of cultures proclaimed by Snow—but then again Snow had none of Leonardo's genius, neither in letters nor in science, which may explain a lot.

Even Descartes, who "completely abandoned the study of letters" and resolved "to search for no knowledge other than what could be found within [him]self, or else in the great book of the world," "held oratory in high regard and was enamored with poetry." "But," the French philosopher adds, "I thought both were gifts of the mind, rather than fruits of study"[87]—in other words, the same "good disposition" proclaimed by Leonardo. Near the end of his life, Descartes wrote verses for a ballet to celebrate the end of the Thirty Years' War, which he dedicated to Queen Christina of Sweden: the separation between letters and sciences was not yet experienced as an insurmountable tension.

Scientific knowledge on one side, poetic pleasure on the other: this modus vivendi finally settled in on a permanent basis among the poets themselves in the late sixteenth century. Responding to the rediscovery of Aristotle's *Poetics,* which attributed the plea-sure of poetry to the mere pleasure of imitation, poets and the erudite now strove to make their own distinction between poetry and knowledge. A notable example is Lodovico Castelvetro's famous commentary on the *Poetics,* which was studied through-out Europe:

> The material of the sciences and the arts cannot serve as a subject for poetry for another reason that is even more obvious to common sense, namely that poetry was invented solely for delectation and recreation—I mean to say, for the delectation and recreation of the mind of the rabble and the common people, who do not understand the reasons, distinctions, or subtle arguments, far removed from regular custom, used by philosophers in their search for the truth of things and artists in their organization of the arts, and since they do not understand them, they can only be bored and unhappy when discourse turns to that.[88]

This argument was a last resort for turning the separation of poetry and truth—which in Plato was merely one count of the indictment—into a distinctive feature and almost a title of nobility: anything can be turned to good use. The natural side of art was increasingly valued, at the expense of sophistication and pedantry; after all, art was just a matter of entertaining honest folk. Poetry thus came to define itself against *literature* understood as *knowledge* (the French expression "avoir de la littérature"—"to have literature"—was then equivalent to saying one was cultured): one could be—in fact one *should* be—a poet without having letters.[89]

Thus was classicism born. "A good poet is no more useful to the State than a good skittles player," as Malherbe put it.[90] Plato couldn't have said it better: had he experienced classical poetry, he would probably have approved of the poets' ironclad modesty—and then he would have gotten rid of these useless mouths to feed.

The theory of classicism is a direct product of the distinction between literature and truth: sometimes anti-literature can lead to the birth of a new kind of literature.

THE TRIAL OF LITERATURE in the name of truth has been repeated in every era: repetition is one of the great pleasures of anti-literature. Literature may change, but the arguments remain surprisingly stable.

In 2011, the *Times Literary Supplement* published an article by the English philosopher Gregory Currie claiming that the psychology in novels has nothing to do with real psychology as it is brought to light in laboratories.[91] According to Currie, science shows that conscious will plays a very limited role in our daily activities. Rather, the decisive influence comes from our environment: mere contact with a cup of hot coffee is enough to provoke an altruistic feeling; hearing the names of friends produces the same effect; repeating a customer's order word for word automatically increases the customer's generosity and, consequently, the server's tip; imagining a professor for five minutes increases one's intellectual capacity far more than imagining a hooligan; and so on and so forth. Well, the philosopher continues, if we read the great so-called psychological novelists Henry James and Marcel Proust, we will find none of these psychological truths based on experience, but instead, a mythification of character and will that has very little to do with the empirical reality of human behavior. This is proof enough, Currie concludes, that novelists know nothing about psychology; literature can therefore not be defended on the grounds that it provides readers with psychological insight, contrary to what Lionel Trilling, F. R. Leavis, and, more recently, Martha Nussbaum have stated. This is the substance of Currie's argument.

There are, in fact, a lot of things one does not find in novels: the recipe for veal Marengo, how to replace a washer to fix a faucet, the proper way to pick up a heavy object without throwing out your back. And, yes, it is likely that one does not find much in James or Proust about the influence of hot coffee on altruistic feelings, nor for that matter on the latest developments in molecular genetics and digital miniaturization. It is true that Proust discusses the influence on human bliss of a madeleine dipped in tea; sadly, he failed to do the same about coffee. Surely this oversight was worth an article in the *TLS*.

But seriously: can one reasonably criticize two early-twentieth-century novelists for not having taken into account the latest psychological discoveries of the following century? Let's imagine that James and Proust had done so, through some unprecedented miracle: wouldn't the usefulness of contemporary psychologists and the need to fund their research programs with huge grants be called into question if a relatively observant novelist had obtained the same results a century earlier by sitting alone at his desk?

As it happens, anyone willing to consider things with a modicum of good faith will see that this is exactly what took place. Gregory Currie presents as the last word in contemporary psychology the thesis that "our conscious decisions are not what bring about our actions, but are a product of the underlying and unconscious causes of the actions themselves."[92] You don't say! This very thesis has been constantly illustrated in literature since time immemorial. One would have to be totally blind—or else thoroughly lacking in good faith—to fail to see that this alleged last word in contemporary psychology is simply the old chestnut from *In Search of Lost Time:* when Swann says, "I wasted years of my life," "wanted to die," and "felt my deepest love, for a woman who didn't appeal to me, who was not my type," isn't that precisely the revelation that love is produced by a set of circumstances in which volition and conscious inclinations do not play any part?[93]

But let's not go on and on about Proust, who is clearly not Gregory Currie's cup of tea. Would Valéry earn his approval? All of *La Jeune Parque* proceeds from an attempt to provide a never entirely conclusive, after-the-fact explanation for a sob and a hand "absently submissive to some deep-hidden end."[94] And what about Colette, whose entire body of work deals with the hold that circumstances have on her characters' moods: the coat of the cats they pet, the cups of hot chocolate they drink in the late afternoon, the lark they hear in the distance amid the dew and the scents of morning. Or Baudelaire, whose *Spleens* returns again and again to the influence of time, light, and setting on the poet's melancholy. Surely Molière's *Misanthrope* is the most behaviorist play in the repertoire, with its characters driven by the whim of circumstance to go against the person they most sincerely believe themselves to be: Célimène badmouthing her lover in the heat of discussion, Alceste dismissing the woman he loves on a sudden impulse.

But maybe the most behaviorist drama is simply *Hamlet,* whose theme appears to be the very impossibility of expressing one's will or remaining aware of it when circumstances oppose it. Has Gregory Currie read Shakespeare—or Homer? For Homer speaks of nothing else: the fact that the heroes' deeds are incommensurable with what is said to be their nature. Facing Odysseus, Ajax, and Phoenix, who have come to negotiate with him, Achilles struggles to find a reasonable justification for his stubborn refusal to fight after his fit of anger at Agamemnon. Later, he gives Priam the body of the man he hates the most in the world for the simple reason that the old king of Troy reminds him of his father. Odysseus remains on the island of Calypso for seven years, kept there by the charms of the nymph and against his conscious desire to return to his beloved Penelope.

Not that behaviorism must be considered the final word in psychology *sub specie aeternitatis:* Currie's obvious bias toward this fashionable theory should in itself lead one to proceed with caution. Just as the behaviorist framework I suggest for interpreting these masterpieces should not exclude all other interpretations. But at least it is applicable, if one is willing to go to the trouble.

The problem is that Gregory Currie is not willing to go to the trouble: his entire inquiry aims to incriminate literature using the most specious arguments. For instance, the philosopher quotes a 1990s study of "creative groups," according to which "only one in fifty writers was free of psychopathology (Maupassant)"; worse, writers were the group that "contained the highest proportion of individuals with severe pathology (nearly fifty percent), compared with scientists, statesmen, artists and composers."[95] (Such a shame the study has nothing to say about plumbers, highwaymen, and raccoons, but no doubt they would not supplant writers, whose case clearly appears to be hopeless.)

Currie goes on to conclude, in the most serious manner, that given the propensity of people with schizophrenia and bipolar disorder to overinterpret the slightest detail, writers cannot be trusted to provide accurate psychological insights. (It goes without saying that one could mount just as reasonable a defense of the opposite position, namely that attention to detail makes writers far more sensitive to the environmental conditions that determine action—in the same way that certain forms of autism boost mathematical aptitude or the ability to learn.)

In case the reader has failed to understand him, Currie drives home his point by quoting a pseudo "expert on creativity" who suggests that "people in the arts are more prone to such disorders than those in the sciences, and especially prone if they are operating at high levels of originality." Suddenly, the old opposition between the sciences and the arts is back on the table, this time in the form of an ad hominem attack: it is no longer worth examining literary works in detail to see if they deserve their despicable reputation; one need only discredit the authors themselves, and the game is over.

One would like to know what method, undoubtedly very scientific, made it possible to retrospectively evaluate the level of psychopathologic suffering of fifty writers who died long ago and lived in societies and cultures other than our own. One would like to know how such a method, should it exist, could be compatible with the behaviorist theory with which the article's author aligns himself. One would especially like to know how credible a method could be that singles out Guy de Maupassant, of all people, as the only writer "free of psychopathology"—unless the author of the study considered that the paranoiac madness that overcame Maupassant before he turned forty and destroyed him in short order is a sign of perfect mental health?

It is flabbergasting to find so many prejudices, outrageous remarks, and simply naïve statements concentrated in only two pages, particularly coming from a philosopher who holds a senior position in an institution of higher learning. Nothing like this has been seen since Baron Snow, to whom Currie refers extensively, and who at least had the excuse of being an *amateur* philosopher.

Despite all that, Currie claims that he is not attacking literature in and of itself, but simply those who represent it poorly. Yet he does not attempt to mount a better defense: his blows are squarely aimed at writers and literary works.

Two years later, Currie published an article of the same vintage in the *New York Times,* entitled "Does Great Literature Make Us Better?" in which he repeats the old anti-literary cliché of the Nazi who loves literature. While Currie pretends to hold it at arm's length, he ultimately does not clearly distance himself from it.[96] How blinded does one have to be by the hatred of literature to fail to see the weakness of such arguments? There may certainly have been well-read Nazis, but there were far more who were utterly uncultivated, of whom not a word is spoken. And what about Nazi scientists, Nazi musicians, Nazi artists? What about Nazi philosophers, the Carl Schmitts and Heideggers, Mister Philosopher? What about Nietzsche's Nazi readers?

"Does Great Literature Make Us Better?" Currie asks. Maybe not, but it doesn't need to do that to be great literature. It is far more worrisome that philosophy does not make us think better.

FUNDAMENTALLY, Gregory Currie is not saying anything different from what Charles Percy Snow had proclaimed in the beautiful senate chambers at Cambridge University half a century earlier. He has simply adapted it to a new behaviorist and psychological flavor.

By a curious coincidence or concerted irony, the same issue of the *TLS* contained a review of a book by a learned psychologist who included a short piece of fiction that he had written to illustrate his main points. According to the reviewer, the fictional piece was so weak as to spoil the entire book.[97] In other words, it takes more than solid knowledge of psychology to write a good novel.

But would this be sufficient reason to attack psychologists, declaring them to be poor writers and then accusing them of being neurotic? Such an attack would certainly be deemed absurd—and justifiably so.

Yet this is the treatment writers receive when someone claims to discover that a novel's quality does not necessarily rest on psychological accuracy. The double standard is glaring: out of principle, it is always literature's territory that is contested. The question of truth is only an excuse, but one that is highly significant in the scientific world and the academy, where every department wants to expand and add a few positions, to the detriment of its neighbors. From this perspective, the future looks rosy for anti-literature, and the Snows and Curries will proliferate for years to come.

Third Trial
Morality

Madame Bovary in the seventeenth century. Family business. Proof that one can simultaneously be a Hellenist, a Protestant, a liberal, and a gallant. Socrates, the Calvinist. The child prodigy, and the associated method. The best Hellenist in France. The prodigal and parricidal son. Unnatural poets. The school of vice. Were David and Moses poets? Immorality of form and futility of poetry. A bourgeois condemnation of literature. Enter a young and likable champion of the literary cause. On the cremation of heretical books. A patron saint and martyr of anti-literature. Acting the fool with the fool. Against the castration of writers. The censor censored. The duel of the sons. The versatility of Virgil. The ideal of a serious and sincere poetry. Racine, father and son. Psychoanalysis of anti-literature. An extended phase of teenage angst. Huck Finn in the rye. Trigger warning on Ovid. An American anti-literature? A very smelly cheese. Instability of the moral lesson. Every reader is immature. An anti-literature competition. How poetry toppled two empires. The hypothesis of the clog maker-poet. Rousseau, the burner of libraries. Weakened by literature. The beginnings of art for art's sake. Mardi Gras in Florence. The bonfire of the vanities. Orpheus, the first sodomite. Truths that should not be spoken. A citizen is always a minor. Irrationality of poetry. In praise of Soviet and Sulpician literature. The disciple's reply to his master. There is nothing virtuous about virtuous plots. Of the usefulness of bad passions. Plato caught in the act of writing poetry. Reading novels and Alzheimer's disease. When the poison is also the remedy.

THE CONNECTION BETWEEN the trial over truth and the trial over morality is easily drawn. In 1668, the Oratorian father Bernard Lamy published his *Nouvelles Réflexions sur l'art poétique* (New reflections on the art of poetry). Hidden behind this innocuous title was a scathing indictment of poetry. The author, a Cartesian and a mathematician, criticized poetry for containing fanciful images and for turning readers' attention to created beings while at the same time hiding their imperfections, thus causing readers to forget the Creator. This was the classic, Platonic argument against the false world created by fiction.

Father Lamy then claimed that this lie had a moral consequence: not only does poetry inspire bad passions, but, even if these passions were good, poetry would render them pointless and even "criminal" because they would be focused on nonexistent objects. He takes the example of a woman who reads novels: "If such a woman is accustomed to the marriages that are described in novels, and fails to find all the false and imaginary qualities of a hero in her husband, she is not well disposed to love him."[1] Two centuries later, this would be the gist of *Madame Bovary.*

IN THE MODERN ERA, women are seen as the principal victims of literature, along with children, and the anti-literary diatribe is unleashed in the name of conjugal and family values. The instrumentalization of these values to champion questionable causes is not a new phenomenon.

In fact, families are often the source of the first literary trauma, just as they are of so many other problems. One such example is the strange story of a father, his daughter, and his sons, in which a poorly handled Oedipus complex finally manifests itself as an acute and memorable case of anti-literature.

TO BEGIN WITH, the father. Tanneguy Le Fèvre, a professor at the Protestant Academy of Saumur, was one of the most famous French Hellenists of the seventeenth century. He published editions of Anacreon, Sappho, Aristophanes, Plato, and Lucian, not to mention the Romans Terence, Horace, and Lucretius—free-spirited, even libertine writers who were in principle not compatible with the Calvinism to which Le Fèvre had converted shortly before turning thirty.

A conversion of convenience? More likely an indication of a spirit of reform resulting from the study of humanist and liberal texts, which is consistent with Tanneguy Le Fèvre's reputation as a gallant man, fond of the fair sex. In fact, Le Fèvre hesitated to accept offers of professorships at universities in Germany and the Netherlands for fear of shutting himself into a Protestant austerity for which he had little affinity. Perhaps it is no coincidence that he died unexpectedly before finally leaving to take a position in Heidelberg.

His preface to his French translation of the *First Alcibiades* suggests an inner torment, a kind of Augustinian, or even pre-Baudelairian, dual aspiration:

> There is no man under the sun who is master of his thoughts, who can remain firm in the most holy resolution in the world and does not grow tired of the highest contemplation to which he sometimes lifts his soul.[2]

This is true of virtue:

> We feel certain powerful and magnanimous emotions that lead us to this great idea [of virtue]; we give it our applause and our esteem, I still confess; but after having given it our esteem and our applause, we refuse it our love. It is as beautiful as can be, this idea that is so loudly praised; but we do not love this beauty; we will adore it, if you like, we will present it with incense in front of a large public, and we will be very pleased that history speaks of it; but despite this appearance of worship, it does not, however, claim our heart.[3]

What a beautifully lyrical way to express human weakness and the inability to live according to one's ideals. One can feel that these words are the product of personal experience: that of a man who, seeing good, does the evil he does not want, as Saint Paul wrote, himself repeating a commonplace of Greek thought found in Euripides.[4] Le Fèvre and Saint Paul come to the same conclusion: one can only love virtue and get better at it with "the assistance of divine grace." This is exactly what Socrates says at the end of the dialogue, when he warns Alcibiades that he will only be able to become virtuous if "he pleases God": in this regard, Plato is in agreement with—and even heralds—the Apostle. Le Fèvre adds:

> Would to God that this monstrous morality that today dishonors the face of Christianity had taken some lessons from Socrates and taken advantage of some of the reasoning in this dialogue![5]

Here, Le Fèvre is taking aim at Catholicism and its blind trust, according to the Reformed church, in the ability to achieve salvation through good works and rites, in other words through effort alone. This is how one reconciles the philosophy of the pagans and the most orthodox Calvinism.

For Le Fèvre's second—if not first—religion was the literature and thought of the Ancients, which he tirelessly shared with young people. He had a reputation as an extraordinary educator, and for the next two centuries, his *Méthode pour commencer les humanités grecques et latines* (Method for starting on Greek and Latin humanities) was steadily republished, commented upon, and discussed.

Le Fèvre did not put this method into practice only at his school; he also tried it out at home, on his own children, and with considerable success. In fact, he probably would not have considered publishing the method and sharing it with the world at large if the opportunity had not presented itself through a family tragedy: the death of his eldest son, Daniel, in whom he had placed the most brilliant hopes. The famous *Méthode* was a funerary monument to this son lost too early, whose premature death cruelly emphasized the effectiveness of the education he had received:

"I went about it in such a way," wrote the father,

that by the time he died (which happened at the end of his fourteenth year), he had twice read *The Iliad* from start to finish and did justice to its parts as readily as a reasonably good teacher would (for he was never undecided and never hesitated). He also knew Virgil's *Aeneid*, Terence, Phaedra, Ovid's *Metamorphoses*, Sallust, Plautus's first comedy, the first and second by Aristophanes, and the first three books by Titus Livius, aside from the other minor authors one must know in order to understand those works I have just mentioned and which are probably the most beautiful ones in the two languages.

The supplementary books I used to achieve an understanding of the others were Eutropius, Aurelius Victor, Justin, Aesop's *Fables*, and the five historical books of the New Testament. I forgot to say that around the time he was thirteen, I had him learn the Hebrew verbs orally from one of my friends, for I thought that this language could be very useful for finding an endless number of word origins in Greek.

Now, I ask everyone with common sense: what kind of man would such a child one day have been, had he but reached his twentieth year? Imagine what we could have raised on such good foundations.[6]

The *Méthode* therefore presents itself as the narrative of the intimate relationship between a father and his son and concludes, as it had begun, with a "small outburst of pain and tenderness": two poems in Latin mark the end of this short work, like two stelae erected in memory of the dead child.[7]

Yet the book is not without contradictions: on the one hand, it celebrates the exceptional nature of a lost son, while on the other, it affirms that "to do as much, and perhaps even more, only one thing is needed: a good teacher"—that is to say, a good method.[8] As if, in some way, pedagogy had the power to bring back the miracle of a family joy that had been shattered.

And why not? To be a good teacher, Le Fèvre specifies, it is not enough to have a good grasp on what one is supposed to teach: one must also have "a father's affection for his disciple," which amounts to making this disciple into a new son.[9]

LE FÈVRE'S RELATIONSHIP to literature was inseparable from an ethics, an affect, of the most intimate personal experience. His own family experienced it—and it is here that we duly enter into the conflict.

Le Fèvre had five children. The unfortunate prodigy was the second child. Before him, there was a daughter, Anne. The *Méthode* says nothing about Anne: at the time, a daughter mattered little, and her education even less. Yet unbeknownst to her father, Anne took advantage of his lessons, learned Greek and Latin by imitating her brothers' work, and was eventually recognized as a marvelously gifted student, so much so that after a few years she had become the most famous Hellenist in France and "the most scholarly woman in the world."[10] She is not known to us by her maiden name but by that of her husband, André Dacier, a student whom Le Fèvre had agreed to board. Anne was none other than the famous Madame Dacier, whose translation of *The Iliad* and *The Odyssey* caused such a commotion at the beginning of the eighteenth century that it sparked a literary and poetic revolution—a revolution that we will have occasion to return to.[11]

EVERY FAMILY EXUDES its antinomies: Anne, the good little girl, tried hard to take the place of the lost son—and succeeded brilliantly. It fell to the youngest of the siblings to play the part of the rebel. His name was Tanneguy, like his father. The burdens of a shared first name and the memory of a dead older brother were probably too heavy: if Anne was the child prodigy, Tanneguy was the prodigal son. Or rather the opposite, for it is not in debauchery that Tanneguy would lose himself. Far from the liberal humanism professed by his father, he shut himself into an austere Calvinism, chose to study mathematics, moved to Neuchâtel to serve as a minister, and then settled in Amsterdam and later in England before returning to his sister's home in Paris and recanting his Protestant faith in order to receive a pension from the king—one cannot be a prodigal son without returning to the fold.[12]

Just as one cannot be a prodigal son without wanting to kill one's father. Tanneguy made a methodical attempt to do so with *De futilitate poetices*, an opuscule in Latin published in Amsterdam in 1697, the full title of which translates as "Futility of Poetry, by Tanneguy Le Fèvre, son of Tanneguy, Minister of the Divine Word." The shared first name painfully emphasized the generational difference between, on the one hand, the vain poetry enthusiast and famous editor of Anacreon, Sappho, and Horace, and on the other, his dignified minister of a son—if Tanneguy the elder had not already been fifteen years in the grave, this new text would certainly have sent him there. A tombstone is a poor shield against family quarrels.

There was no more effective way of killing the father than by settling the score against the invariant goal of his existence, the occupation by which he hoped to survive in human memory: reading and commenting on the Ancient writers and poets. Throughout the history of anti-literature, there have been few attacks as systematic and premeditated as the one launched against poetry in the late seventeenth century from the fine city of Amsterdam by a minister not yet thirty and deep in the grips of an Oedipal crisis. Woe betide him whose enemy has not resolved his childhood problems.

In nineteen chapters, Tanneguy the younger literally sends literature *ad patres*. One has only to read the chapter titles, which are repeated like a refrain: "That the love of poetry has engendered the contempt of truth," "That the ancient poets were impious," "That the poets of our time are even further from piety than the Ancients," "That the crimes of poets are the most certain effect and proof of their impiety," "That by their own admission the most famous poets were the vilest of men."[13]

And so on and so forth, nineteen times over, to be sure to drive home the point—or rather to drive the knife into the paternal remains nineteen times over. There is nothing ambiguous about the son's project:

> If, through invincible arguments, I show that the art of poetry is one of the most harmful sources of ignorance, impiety, and every crime, it will be readily apparent that its charm and the other qualities which are attributed to it should not make it any less worthy of contempt.[14]

This young minister has the spirit of a Savonarola. Might the target seem too elevated for such a greenhorn? Tanneguy anticipates the objection:

> No matter if I am illustrious or obscure, famous or unknown, for that has no impact on this matter, and certainly nothing is more unjust than to judge based on hatred, love, or the affection one has for the parties present! The poets in all their writings constantly correct each other, they declaim out loud and we listen to them; how can it then be forbidden to attack in prose those whom they themselves attack in their satirical poems, and to do out of concern for the truth what they do simply out of carelessness?[15]

He goes on to quote with irony a passage from Juvenal that contains the famous line *Semper ego auditor tantum*: "Shall I always be stuck in the audience? Never retaliate for being tortured so often by hoarse Cordus' *Song of Theseus?* Let them get away with it then—this one reciting me his Roman comedies, and that one his love elegies?"[16] This quotation from the Latin satirist is anything but innocent: its message of vengeance reflects Tanneguy's own resentment toward a father obsessed with poetry and literature, who subjected his children to a classical education made particularly effective by the fact that it was totalitarian. In the long run, all these lessons produced the opposite of the intended effect, and the best teacher wound up training the most hateful disciple—who happened to be his son.

Any method will do when it comes to fulfilling this desire for revenge. Tanneguy is not above malicious gossip:

If we examine the lives of the poets whose works are presented as the canons of art, we discover that some were drunkards, others debauched, others adulterers, and others yet were infected with execrable vices that are in our parts rightly punishable by death: Aeschylus wrote his tragedies under the influence of alcohol; Homer and Hesiod suffer the torments of Hell, one hanging from a column, the other being bitten by snakes for eternity, and this fiction regarding Homer and Hesiod gives a clear indication of how they were perceived; Horace and Sophocles, immersed in the pleasures of the body, were guilty of abominable passions; suffering from the same disorder, Virgil sang his own desire through the figure of Corydon in the second *Eclogue;* similarly, Pindar breathed his last on the lap of the boy he cherished; Aristophanes ruined his reputation through the most shameful traffic in calumny and the death of Socrates; Terence won the favor he enjoys through the help of those to whom he prostituted his modesty; due to obscene verses and other crimes, Ovid was sent into exile by Augustus, the wisest of emperors, despite Augustus's well-known benevolence toward men of letters and his universal clemency; finally, Euripides hated women and was among those whom Apocalypse calls *dogs,* which is exactly why God wanted to have him torn apart by dogs, soiled as he was by crimes to which nature is loath to give a name.[17]

What frenzied, intoxicated pleasure Tanneguy the younger finds in recalling in a single sentence, nearly a single breath, every last crime of the poets! How could one defend poetry after hearing such a list? Who would dare? And who would entrust their children to such tutors? Who would have them read Homer, Aristophanes, Ovid, Terence, or Virgil? Yet this was exactly the education that Tanneguy Le Fèvre the elder had given his family. He had even bragged about it: what an unworthy or at the very least unthinking father!

In fact, there is basically only a single crime that constantly appears in the honorable minister's work: sexual debauchery and, more specifically, what was then called sodomy and is now better known as homosexuality. The prudish Tanneguy does not even risk naming it: to paraphrase Oscar Wilde, it is the crime that dare not speak its name. Guilty only of writing under the influence and of spreading malicious gossip, Aeschylus and Aristophanes are no match for Virgil and Pindar in the race to ignominy: the real crime of the poets is first and foremost the crime against nature. Two hundred and fifty years later, the British physicist Charles Percy Snow said exactly the same thing, though he said it in a more roundabout way and under a more liberal facade.[18] Homophobia and anti-literature fight the same fight: that against an activity considered useless, asocial, counterproductive, and anti-family. Unlike Snow, Tanneguy the younger at least had the excuse of religious fanaticism and a traumatic childhood.

Reading the poets is no more, no less than a school for vice:

> Yet here are these famous prophets whose oracles so many men meditate with incredible zeal, that they translate into various languages, learn by heart, invoke every day in order to uphold or refute the opinions that are being debated. Here are these divine masters of morality whose writings inflame young people for the best that there is, namely vengeance, debauchery, arrogance, and all the vices, in such a way that daily association and seduction finally make them in every way similar to their tutors.[19]

Studying, translating, learning by heart, quoting: once again, the education described by Tanneguy in his tract is the very one he received from his father. By demolishing the famous *Méthode pour commencer les humanités grecques et latines* point by point, *De futilitate poetices* strikes back at the paternal education.

Tanneguy must nonetheless respond to the classic objection from those partisans—if there are any left—who want to defend poetry at all costs: What about Christian poetry? What about the poetry in the Bible itself? Wasn't poetry "consecrated by God and cultivated by the wisest men, those most respectful of justice?"[20] No need to get flustered over details, replies Tanneguy:

> It is easy to refute this misleading quibble and destroy the entire soph-ism. Indeed, those who make this argument manifestly rely too heavily on the ambiguity of the name *poet*. By this appellation, one refers to a writer whose verse contains a certain number of feet (as was once the case in Greece and Rome) or consists of two, three, or more syllables, the last of which, if the lines are seen in pairs, have the same pronunciation (as is today the case in France, where it is not even rare to give three or four lines the same ending).
>
> Yet far from being contained, constrained, and forced into strict boundaries, as in Greece, Rome, and France, Hebraic poetry was freer, nearly like prose, so that sometimes one counted the feet, sometimes the syllables, sometimes one was satisfied with the similarity of the endings, and sometimes it was enough to stray from the habitual and common way of speaking (*communi loquendi consuetudine*).[21]

In other words, one could say that David and Moses were poets, but their writings lacked the formal dimension that is generally considered part of the poet's work. They were poets in the sense that Cicero is thinking of when he writes that Plato, who wrote in prose, was more of a poet than the "authors of comedies, whose works, other than the fact that they are written in verse, are in no way different from everyday language."[22]

Nearly twenty years in advance, these are the very terms of the dispute over Homer that would cause deep divisions among French lit-térateurs of the early eighteenth century: the translation of *The Iliad* by Tanneguy's own sister, Madame Dacier, was attacked as unpoetic for being in prose, and its critics proposed to write a version in verse without out even knowing Greek. One sees that the minister from Amsterdam was preemptively taking his sister's side in this dispute, which would lead to a new definition of poetry, unrelated to verse, and open the way to a new—romantic—conception of literature by preparing for the coming of the prose poem. Anti-literature is often no more than a type of anti-formalism, which can sometimes be a prelude to the appearance of new literary forms.

David and Moses were also not poets in the etymological sense of the term, in other words in the sense of:

he who *does*, that is to say who *invents* many things, and consequently who often lies and exaggerates the inventions of others through new lies, by alleging, for example, that it is glorious to take revenge for an injustice received or to deflower a multitude of young girls in a single night, as it is said of Heracles.[23]

On the contrary, the biblical prophets aim only for saintliness, piety, and truth; David and Moses have nothing in common with Homer and Virgil.

Though he expresses himself under a mask of irony and condemnation, one cannot avoid noticing that Tanneguy the younger takes perverse pleasure in relating the details of Heracles's sexual exploits—it is said he deflowered forty-nine virgins in a single night[24]—and that, in contrast, the prudish minister gives short shrift to the horrors described in the Bible, the monstrosities presented there as models of virtue, and the misconduct of David and Solomon. He even overlooks the fact that an erotic poem entitled the *Song of Songs* is at the very heart of the Old Testament. Fanaticism is rarely in good faith.

Interestingly, Tanneguy establishes an inverse relationship between poetic form and the morality of the content: the more refined, constrained, and complicated the form is, the less moral the content will be—so much so that the very nature of poetry is eventually revealed to be depraved. Formal refinement induces a moral lapse because it comprises an amoral dimension in and of itself: it is not morally correct to devote so much time to an activity as futile and needlessly sophisticated as poetry. The inversion of the scale of aims and priorities involved in the work of poetry, placing what should remain at the bottom at the very top, can only go hand in hand with an inversion of the scale of values in general behavior. There can be no aesthetic order without ethical confusion.

TANNEGUY'S BOOK takes its title from the key word *futility,* from which fragility, frivolousness, absence of authority, and, finally, lack of truth directly follow. To all appearances lightweight and often ridiculous, this attack by Tanneguy Le Fèvre the younger nonetheless aims for the most vulnerable spot. It is easy to caricature poetry and accuse it of deception, lying, and artificial seduction, of being a teacher of vice and error: Tanneguy does not hold back on these criticisms from the anti-literary vulgate, which were heard long before him and would continue to be heard long after. Yet by leveling these charges, the critic continues to grant poetry power and authority, however deviant.

Infinitely more insidious and cruel is the accusation of insignificance implied by the term *futility.* If Homer and Virgil are futile, there is no need to consider them, even for the purpose of refuting them: it is enough not to mention them. If poetry is speech, there is no more effective way to kill it than to silence it: silence is the acid that leaves no trace, and Tanneguy is a master at using it. Never does he openly and explicitly oppose his father, never does he even mention his name— aside from the title page, in order to distinguish himself from his progenitor. This silence is as powerful as any poison or dagger. One can only learn such perfidy through family life.

Here is the moral of the story—at least the one Tanneguy draws in the conclusion to his lampoon:

One must devote as little effort to reading the poets as possible, that is, only as much as they are necessary for gaining a better understanding of languages (*ad linguas melius intelligendas*)—they whose life and works are, for the most part, full of acts of infamy and impiousness, and whose daily use weakens the spirits and crushes all the nerves of masculine virtue. Poetry can only be much loved by those who overindulge in their free time, since the enormous energy it demands is used in an obviously criminal way if one produces texts contrary to good moral standards and the fear of God, and in an absurd and nearly profitless manner if the intention is instead to work usefully and in the interest of the state. If, however, one must write in verse, one should follow the example of Moses and David, and it is always much better to pay attention to the meaning rather than the rhythm and the sound structure (*vocum structuram*). Finally, the time that many spend on vain and harmful cogitation would be better spent on the study of the superior arts, since expending vain efforts only to produce futile or immoral tales and ramblings at the cost of much fatigue is pure madness.[25]

After the many extreme arguments expressed throughout the tract, this conclusion seems surprisingly moderate: Tanneguy recognizes that poetry can be somewhat useful for learning languages, puts forward a model of writing drawn from the Bible, and admits that poetry sometimes aims to do good, though with meager results. But in fact the principal argument here is of a different stripe. Avoiding the usual rhetoric of anti-literary discourse, which revels in grandiloquence and excess, this argument centers on a pragmatic and, one might venture to say, *bourgeois* calculation of the advantages and disadvantages of the study of poetry: the bookkeeping of profit and loss.

It is not insignificant that the book was written and published in Amsterdam, an industrious trading city—and by a minister at that. As Max Weber showed, Protestantism played a crucial role in the birth of modern capitalism. Tanneguy the younger's emigration from France to the Netherlands corresponds to the transition from an aristocratic regime based on lavish spending, of which poetry is the linguistic analogue, to a bourgeois, merchant society attentive to the profitability of industry and exchanges. The only relevant moral code here is that of work: Is it useful? Can one see the results? Is the intended goal worth the effort expended?

Up to this point, the moral condemnation of poetry had been absolute and was based on a dogmatic opposition between good and evil, defined *ex cathedra*. Now good and evil came to be defined and measured in relative terms: good was assessed according to the amount of evil required to attain it, evil according to the good it could lead to. Categorical denunciations were a thing of the past; now it was enough to compare and calculate. This double-entry bookkeeping is the only language understood by the shopkeeper, the only one heard by a society founded on the pursuit of the greatest profit and the optimization of spending—such as our own, perhaps.

In such a society, it would be counterproductive to threaten novice poets with the suffering of hell in the hereafter: hell always attracts people, if only out of a desire to provoke. One only has to show hell or boredom here on earth, in a literary activity spinning its wheels and having no goal or usefulness: in poetry, the torture of Sisyphus is in the here and now.

And so the underlying principle of this book by Tanneguy Le Fèvre the younger consists of one of the most powerful anti-literary diatribes possible, which is also one of those most often heard today. I certainly have qualms about saving it from the oblivion into which it had fallen for more than three centuries, just as a biologist might hesitate before exhuming the plague virus from the ice where it has remained buried for millennia. I can only hope that it does not seize this opportunity to recover its strength.

SUCH AN ATTACK could not go unanswered. A year after publication of Tanneguy Le Fèvre the younger's *De futilitate poetices*, on Sunday June 29, 1698, the young academic Friedrich Wilhelm Schütz presented a public refutation of it in Leipzig.

How had he become aware of the tract? Although quick dissemination of such a text from Amsterdam to Leipzig would not have been impossible, it may have been aided by a particular set of circumstances. It appears that sometime around 1655, Friedrich Wilhelm's father, Christoph Georg, a town councilor of the city of Leipzig, had spent some time in Saumur, the very city where Tanneguy Le Fèvre the elder was teaching Greek.[26] Since both men were Protestant, it is possible that the Schütz and Le Fèvre families established a friendship at this time, which would have allowed Friedrich Wilhelm to quickly get a copy of Tanneguy the younger's book and to prepare a response to it only a few months after it was published.

Friedrich Wilhelm Schütz belonged to an honorable Leipzig dynasty, whose members included the illustrious Heinrich Schütz, the most famous musician in Germany and the young man's great-uncle. In 1696, shortly after turning nineteen, Friedrich Wilhelm had presented a disputation—one dare not say a *fiery* disputation, given the subject matter—entitled *The Cremation of Heretical Books,* which suggests that he was already keenly sensitive to the question of freedom of expression and attacks against literature. The disputation had been presented in two parts: the first was of a historical nature and was delivered on January 28, 1696; the second, from the moral perspective, was delivered on December 30 of the same year, in collaboration with Johann Christoph Schwedler, Friedrich Wilhelm's fellow student at the University of Leipzig.[27] The two disputations explicitly displayed the anti-Catholic and anti-papist leanings of the authors, both of whom were students in reformed theology: Schütz would eventually become a minister at the St. Nicholas Church in Leipzig, while Schwedler would become a minister in Niederwiese, in Silesia, and would gain fame for his liturgical hymns.

The line of argument deployed to protest against the burning of heretical books was based on the distinction between a work and its author. How absurd, wrote the two students, to condemn a book because its author has a bad reputation, even if the book itself does not touch on religion. Hadn't Melanchthon's *Grammar* stupidly been burned for the sole reason that its author was a follower of the Reformed religion?

How could one believe that a good book should be destroyed because its author is evil? Who would look away from roses in disgust on account of the fact that they are born of a mother covered in so many thorns? Does Seneca not say, in favor of impartiality, that "one should not be ashamed of a bad writer when he speaks well"?[28]

The cause defended in 1698 was considerably vaster. In facing Tanneguy the younger, it was no longer only heretical books that had to be defended and saved from the flames, but all of poetry. It is all the more surprising to find that Schütz's refutation of *De futilitate poetices* opens with a call for severe punishment:

> If the wisest of kings judged that Zoilus deserved to be tortured simply for having slandered Homer, whose statue he attempted to flog with a whip, as reported by Claudius Galenus, what tortures would be worthy of those whose insults and slander tear to shreds every poet, and even poetry itself?[29]

Could it be that the very flames from which Schütz had tried to save the heretical books were now being stoked for the author of *De futilitate*? Such intemperate zeal is unexpected on the part of a self-declared opponent of literary cremations. But actually, this threat of torture was not written by Schütz himself: it was an epigraph taken from the Italian humanist Giglio Gregorio Giraldi, whose complete works had just been published in Leiden two years earlier—clearly, the young student and enthusiastic reader was keeping up with the latest in literature.

Zoilus was a grammarian in the fourth century BCE, famous for having publicly criticized the flaws and contradictions in *The Iliad* and *The Odyssey;* he was nicknamed the "Homer whipper" (*homeromastix*) and apparently died a violent death—crucified, burned alive, or thrown off a cliff, depending on the account (however much one dislikes denigrators of poetry, one likes to think he was not subjected to all three methods of execution, either at once or in succession). Were anti-literature to require a patron saint—and a martyr to boot—Zoilus would perfectly fill the bill: as early as Antiquity, his name was used to refer to any excessive and malicious critic.

One should not underestimate the ironic quality of this epigraph being used by a declared champion of the freedom of expression of heretics. Nonetheless, it is not insignificant that the young man is less severe toward enemies of religion than enemies of poetry, as though tampering with poetry were the more fundamental taboo. It is also true that the two previous disputations were primarily aimed at Catholicism and that the heretical books were Protestant books: a good theology student from Leipzig had no choice but to defend them. In the case of poetry, he was speaking from the heart.

Le Fèvre's tract initially sent Schütz deep into shock, the stages of which he carefully describes at the beginning of his refutation:

> Last year, a book was published in Amsterdam entitled *On the Futility of Poetry,* by *Tanneguy Le Fèvre, minister of the word of God.* One might well be surprised that the son of the illustrious *Tanneguy Le Fèvre* and brother of the highly learned *Anne Dacier,* born into a family so fond of literature and poetry, should choose a radically different path. I admit that as soon as I came upon these pages, I, who have loved verse and poets since childhood, expected nothing more than a joke, a game, or the pranks of an unrestrained intelligence, for I did not think that there existed people who would seriously endeavor to disparage poets or work to undermine the study of verse. I knew, of course, that in some people malice is like a stain and a blot, even when dealing with what is best, but to think that there were men capable of hounding poetry with a hatred strong enough to accuse it of futility was impossible. Yet when I picked up this opuscule again, I soon recognized the author's hostile intent toward poets and their art. Indeed, I saw that he set out to show that *poetry, because it is difficult, because it is based on assiduous reading of pernicious books and proves nearly incapable of producing the slightest*

fruit, must be avoided by men of letters. Immediately, in response to this outrageous remark, my mind caught fire; I could not bear to see the honor of such a holy and venerable art attacked, and right away, driven by I know not what impulse, I took the opposite side, and, increasingly excited, I finally decided not to leave poetry defenseless and to publicly stand up for it against such an audacious opponent. I put this in writing in the present exercise, in which I tried to show, insofar as I could, all the frivolousness and fickleness of the arrows fired by Le Fèvre, and their complete inability to reach poetry, which emerges safe and sound.[30]

Here we have the autobiography of an opponent of anti-literature: at first he does not believe what he is reading and thinks he is dealing with a hoax; then he finally has to recognize the attacker's sincerity, however outrageous, absurd, and monstrous his arguments. His irritation then grows to match the attack's fundamental inanity and aggressiveness—in general, the more inane an attack, the more aggressive it is. What should he do next? Close the book and do something else, at the risk of letting people believe this nonsense? (One never knows, after all, how gullible readers will be: can one rely on their intelligence and their love of literature?) Or counterattack, at the risk of giving credence to the enemy and granting him more importance than he deserves? Friedrich Wilhelm Schütz hesitates, wrestling with these very questions:

> Obviously, I do not doubt that most will consider this work vain and unnecessary, that they will be convinced that no one would applaud the inanities of this Le Fèvre and that there is no need to fear that a single man's audacity could be enough to remove poetry from the pinnacle of glory to which it has been raised unanimously by the most eminent men in every field. To seek to refute balderdash is to produce more balderdash. Contempt avenges the art of fiction well enough that it does not appear necessary to devote great effort and care to its defense. That is what people will think. And certainly, I could not deny that there will

be no one, or very few people, who agree with Le Fèvre's opinion, and these will only be the enemies of any kind of beauty; I also admit that Le Fèvre's enterprise is marred by much foolishness; but it is precisely for that reason that it is acceptable to subject the opponent's arguments to evaluation, so that their futility is brought to light and so that people do not believe—who knows?—that among all these arguments there is a single one likely to weaken a divine science. And if, when *Lactantius* turns to refuting Epicurus's balderdash in his treatise on *The Works of God*, he says he wants to play the fool with the fool, for fear that the latter will otherwise feel too intelligent, what prevents me from being able to balderdash a little myself?[31]

So many precautions before launching on a point-by-point refutation of Le Fèvre the younger's foolishness! The audience for this lecture might indeed have considered that it was hardly worth it: the august members of the municipality of Leipzig, the consuls, proconsuls, town councilors, and magistrates for whom the young student's exercise was primarily intended may have had other concerns than to sit through a long and tiresome defense of poetry; there is more important business to attend to when managing a city.

Yet Friedrich Wilhelm did not consider sparing their patience. The lampoon *On the Futility of Poetry* had nineteen chapters; its refutation has the same number, to take apart each of the Amsterdam minister's propositions, without leaving out a single one. To clarify his argument, Schütz notes the title of the corresponding chapter of Le Fèvre's book in the margin of each of his chapters, in such a manner that the refutation also serves as an objective summary of his opponent's positions. In other words, a true academic exercise, superbly printed, with its marginal notes, its duly referenced citations, and even—the cherry on top—its concluding corollaries, including:

> Without reading the poets, eloquence remains incomplete.
> Poets' fictions are not lies.

Poetry is not older than prose.

It is permissible to stage tragedies and comedies.

To castrate Ancient authors [i.e., to expurgate them] is to put one's zeal to bad use.

The poet must concern himself with words no less than with meaning.[32]

There are nine corollaries in this style, as many as there are Muses. The student obviously enjoyed scattering some taunts throughout his text, such as when he criticizes Le Fèvre for the suspect way that he dwells on the poets' obscenities:

If it is so vile to read indecent verses of this kind, why, I ask, did you, Le Fèvre, read them? Worse, why did you include them in your text? Since you said earlier that no one would be able to convince you to study the *Priapus Poems* or, similarly, many poems by Martial, who finally succeeded in doing so? For above, on pages 21, 34, and 36, you quote verses that clearly deal with obscene subjects and also make your own book unfit to be read (*propter quae nec tuus ipse legi debet liber*).[33]

It's the old joke of the biter bit—or the censor censored.

Elsewhere, Friedrich Wilhelm defends poetry in an entirely personal, lyrical spirit, such as when he upbraids Le Fèvre for his accusations against poetic beauty, judged to be nothing less than "puerile," "ridiculous, impious, and criminal":

You are blind, Le Fèvre, yes, you are blind to all the power of poetry and all its beauty (*elegantia*)! Indeed, when pleasure (*delectatio*) is born equally of the meaning and the structure of words (*verborum structura*), something indescribably extraordinary appears. I do not refer to those privileged joys that only poets experience, when they believe they are rising above the human condition (*supra rerum humanarum fastigium*) and touching the stars with their sublime foreheads each time they create something that produces within them, through the seductive power of the subject (*argumenti suavitate*) on the one hand and the softness of the words and the rhythm on the other, an incomparable pleasure; I am referring only to that charm (*jucunditatem*) that others, whether readers or listeners, experience from these same objects, an absolutely infinite charm that sweeps them away despite themselves.[34]

One would think one was listening to Valéry speaking about poetic creation and the "pendulum" that endlessly swings between sound and sense to leave the reader in an inexpressible state of perpetually renewed hypnosis and ecstasy.[35] Two pages later, Schütz makes a reference to Montaigne's taste for the Roman poets and for Ovid's *Metamorphoses,* which the wise man of Bordeaux recommended for children.[36]

We find in Friedrich Wilhelm Schütz an enthusiasm for all things poetic and a tone of sincerity that betray the author's youth and make him eminently likeable. I have little in common with this student of Protestant theology and scion of a wealthy family who used his paternal fortune and connections to publish elegant academic booklets and to court the town councilors of Leipzig, yet I cannot help but feel a nearly fraternal communion, across the centuries, with this young and passionate academic who out of pure love of poetry undertook to tilt at the windmills of foolishness, arrogance, and narrowmindedness.[37] There was no point in this undertaking: the attacks would die out on their own. But nasty and stupid anti-literature sometimes has the effect of producing a valorous champion of the literary cause—a cause that remains impervious, since it can take care of itself: all that is required is to read the books.

TANNEGUY THE YOUNGER's lampoon made waves, more so than we might think it would.[38] But one does not write an anti-literary diatribe with impunity when one is either the son of a great humanist and translator of poetry or the brother of Madame Dacier. Tanneguy was both at once: all the more reason for his book not to go unnoticed. Which was exactly what he wanted.

There followed what could be called the duel of the sons. In 1747, fifty years after publication of the lampoon, another writer's son published a riposte. In his *Réflexions sur la poésie* (Reflections on Poetry), Louis Racine, the youngest child of the playwright Jean Racine, responded to two classic accusations leveled at poetry: "it corrupts hearts with dangerous images," and "it feeds the mind frivolous fables and fictions."[39] He mentions the most recent attacks, including that of Bossuet, who had accused poets of exclusively seeking to please without any concern for whether what they say is true. Racine notes that Bossuet gave as an example Virgil, who

> at times describes in magnificent verse Plato's system on the system of the world, and at others reels off in beautiful verse Epicurus's system on the fortuitous concourse of atoms. "It is indifferent to him," adds M. Bossuet, "whether he is a Platonist or an Epicurean: he has satisfied the ear, he has showed off the beautiful turn of his mind, the beautiful sound of his verse, and the vividness of his expression: that is more than enough for poetry."[40]

Then comes the turn of an unidentified Englishman who "has had printed in London, in the last few years, a book whose purpose is to prove that poets are the enemies of reason and morals."

Finally, Louis Racine addresses "the brother of Madame Dacier" and his *De futilitate poetices*. *De futilitate* was still drawing attention: in the century that saw the rise of the bourgeoisie, when progress in industry and the arts was acclaimed everywhere, it was not good to be accused of frivolousness.

In this context, it is symptomatic that Bossuet's accusation that poetry does not tell the truth no longer took the form, as it had in Plato, of a full indictment of the lies and errors of the poets—they are no longer even worth the trouble. To a certain extent, the question of whether poetry tells the truth seems to have been settled: it is now agreed that one cannot ask poets to do something that they are not capable of, in any case. They are instead reproached for something that is both less serious, because it has a smaller impact, and more discouraging, because it is the ultimate proof that one should not have faith in poets even when it comes to little things: Shouldn't poets at the very least be expected to take their own work seriously and ensure that it is logical? Yet Virgil, in being now a Platonist, now an Epicurean, according to the circumstances and the poetic effect desired, displays a deplorable inconstancy.

The issue here is no longer the absence of a correspondence between poetry and reality, but poetry's lack of internal coherence: fundamentally, what is being questioned is not so much the onto-logical value of poetry (which had already been relinquished) as its ethics. Or: after having lost in the realm of ontology, poetry was now also being defeated in the realm of morality—not the morality of a universal ethics, but that of poetry itself, with which the writer should in principle comply. "A poet is a light being," as Plato had written long ago: how true![41] And the poet must pay the price for this lightness.

It would take a few more decades for a new conception of poetry to take root, one far removed from the light and frivolous society games criticized by Bossuet and Le Fèvre the younger, a poetry proclaiming absolute seriousness and, above all, sincerity: what would come to be known as romanticism.

While awaiting this aesthetic revolution, Louis Racine devotes a few dozen well-chosen pages to a defense against the accusations of futility and frivolousness, thereby providing a moving record of the poetic and lyrical crisis at the heart of the French eighteenth century—an apologia haunted here and there by the ghost of a playwright father as admired as he is unnamed, whose image stands like a com-mander at the beginning of the book, as if *Réflexions sur la poésie* were somehow giving itself the task of paying an impossible debt. The preface concludes with a poignant confession:

When such a modest father was taken away from us by death, I was still at that age when, though one is free with one's tears, one does not have enough reason to shed them in the case of genuine misfortune.[42]

He who cried without a reason refused to cry when a reason was given to him: an unforgivable mistake. *Réflexions sur la poésie* ideally makes up for this deficit of tears, belated amends offered by Louis Racine at the age of fifty-five for the wrong he had done when he was only six.

THE BATTLE BETWEEN Louis Racine and Tanneguy Le Fèvre is the battle of filial appreciation against filial ingratitude. Think, too, of the defense of poetry by Friedrich Wilhelm Schütz: it coincides with his appreciation of a beloved and respected father, as shown by the dedications of his books. Or of Sartre's *The Words,* in which keeping literature at a distance is identified with challenging a paternal figure—in this case, the character of the grandfather.

Over and above these four authors' individual cases, a kind of psychoanalysis of literature takes shape: to attack poets is to want to murder the ancient teachers of humanity; to defend them is to maintain the link with the original language and with tradition and to perpetuate the thread that unites each generation both to the one that preceded it and the one that will follow. How could one avoid seeing the fantasy of killing the father in this primal scene of anti-literature, as experienced by those who received a strong literary education at an early age and eventually turned against it?

MORE GENERALLY, if the accusation of immorality leveled at literature is among those that continue to elicit a response and still today serve to justify the banning of various books, it is because this accusation primarily concerns childhood and education and raises the image of readers who are defenseless before the representation of evil, incapable of opposing it by using their intelligence and their own moral conscience. Anti-literary discourse often supposes that literature initially had an implicitly recognized moral authority that was later rejected, as if literature had not been equal to the task with which it had first been entrusted. The ethical judgment an individual is supposed to be able to exercise in a real situation, faced with flesh-and-blood people, is considered to be lacking when that same person is confronted with a literary text: literature apparently deprives the reader of moral autonomy, which is why readers should be emancipated from literary custody.

If literature really enjoyed such powerful authority, there might be reason to worry; luckily, the very existence of anti-literature proves that the moral emancipation of the reader, which it refuses on principle to acknowledge, is in fact possible.

This is simply how family quarrels work: as long as paternal authority is recognized, teenage angst can always resurface; it is only once that authority is left behind that adulthood begins. There can be no authority without the agreement of those who submit to it, if only to challenge it; anti-literature is often no more than a prolonged fit of teenage angst on the part of certain thinkers. Some say the analyst's couch might do them good.

YET ONE should not think that these trials of literature on moral grounds were restricted to ancient times or totalitarian regimes. Democracies are not immune to the phenomenon. Even in the most powerful liberal democracy in the world, the United States, one finds books removed from school curriculums, banned from libraries, or, in the best case, simply purged of those expressions or passages considered offensive. And naturally all of this is done to protect children and young people.

This would be a relatively inconsequential matter if the volumes in question were only marginal works or books that were explicitly and intentionally subversive from a moral perspective. It is regrettable that Henry Miller's *Tropic of Cancer* was not legally published in the United

States until 1961—a full twenty-seven years after the first edition was issued in France—and still with considerable trouble. Yet it must be admitted that the book was directly at odds with a certain number of American moral codes governing literary and artistic representation: under such circumstances, the conflict, though unfortunate, was utterly predictable.

Attacks are more unexpected and significantly more damaging when the works targeted are generally considered classics, have long been taught in schools, and have for decades been considered peaks of global literature, but then suddenly spark controversy and are deemed unacceptable: every Homer, every Virgil will eventually give rise to his Tanneguy Le Fèvre.

Works dear to young people often bear the brunt of this multifaceted censorship: look no further than *The Adventures of Huckleberry Finn* and *The Catcher in the Rye*. Upon publication, both of these seminal works of American literature were reproached for providing young people with bad examples: vulgar, familiar language, explicit references to sexuality, the undermining of so-called family values and conventional social mores.[43] Nonetheless, beginning in the 1960s, both works became classics of young people's literature; they were read and discussed in middle schools and high schools precisely because they allow students to deal with subjects directly relevant to them. This is the way to put literature to good use: not as a compendium of moral and religious precepts that are immediately applicable and transposable to reality, but as a place of reference, exchange, discussion, and debate.

Mark Twain's and J. D. Salinger's masterpieces have experienced the paradoxical fate of being included both in school curriculums and on lists of banned books, of being both the most widely read and the most often challenged books—perhaps the most often challenged precisely because they are the most widely read: the more children read the adventures of Huck Finn and Holden Caulfield at school or in the library, the more likely it is that some parent will be offended and initiate legal proceedings. Luckily, these attempts at censorship have not always been successful.

Literature's moral and ideological compliance is a difficult thing to assess, not only because literary works are fundamentally ambiguous, their interpretation constantly shifting and being subject to discussion, but also because dominant ideologies are themselves no less changeable than moral references. For instance, the nineteenth century was scandalized by the rudeness and vulgarity of Twain's novel: shortly after the novel was published in 1885, the library in Concord, Massachusetts, declared the book unworthy of its oh-so-respectable bourgeois readers and banned it from its shelves.[44] This could be termed right-wing, conservative censorship.

A century later, the pendulum had swung the other way and censorship came from the left. If *Huckleberry Finn* sparks controversy today, it is no longer because of its use of popular vernacular, but because of its treatment of the question of race. The problem is as follows: Does the book denounce the racial prejudices it describes, or does it make them its own? Scholars are still arguing the question.[45]

Particularly at issue is the repeated use of the term "nigger," a word that was common in Twain's time and could then be relatively neutral in value, but which became exclusively pejorative and insulting in the twentieth century. How can we give such a book to today's children, who could be shocked or disturbed by the word because they were not aware of its history? One of the solutions reached was to bowdlerize the novel and publish a new version, among other expurgated editions, in which the word "slave" was substituted for every occurrence of "nigger."[46] The paradox is that to make the novel more readable and socially acceptable, the editors chose to replace a period term that was more or less neutral, but had racial significance, with a term that has no racial significance, but explicitly refers to an inferior and dominated social condition whose mere existence is today considered intolerable. "Slave" is certainly more offensive than "nigger," but since there are happily no more slaves in the United States today, no one would feel targeted or offended by the term. The idea is not to improve the book from a moral perspective, but to avoid any misunderstanding on the part of the reader, irrespective of the integrity of the actual novel.

The right solution would instead be to educate children and teach them about the variability of language and judgment. The right solution would be to teach young people to maintain a certain distance from works of literature, to understand that they come from another world, which demands to be studied for what it is, and that these works are not always about us. The right solution would be to allow the texts the freedom to speak for themselves.

Even more recently, the Latin poet Ovid, who was himself exiled by the emperor Augustus because of the licentiousness of his writings, continued to cause a scandal in the United States. In 2015, a student at Columbia University complained that reading passages in *The Metamorphoses* describing the abductions of Persephone and Daphne had triggered a memory of her own traumatic rape: she now felt unsafe in the classroom.[47] There followed a university-wide, then national, discussion over whether the study of classics like *The Metamorphoses* should receive trigger warnings in curriculums. In this case, what is the happy medium? Where do we draw the line? There are rape scenes in *The Metamorphoses,* but also scenes of zoophilia, torture, and massacre; in terms of religion, polytheism prevails. In France, I encountered a Muslim student who refused to read *Faust* because the devil appears in the play.

It is probably too easy to make fun of this trigger warning policy, which aims to spare adult readers from encountering anything they might find shocking, upsetting, or simply vaguely disturbing. After all, this is not a case of actual censorship, but of a pedagogical procedure intended to prevent uncomfortable situations in the classroom and to preserve an atmosphere of trust within the university community. Texts are neither suppressed nor altered, only made optional for those who may not feel strong enough to face them. But such a policy does not have any theoretical limit: if the measurement scale is readers' varying sensitivity, even the most innocuous text could require a warning, for there will always be someone who might be traumatized by some more or less manifest aspect of a text.

These are cases of something other than individual censorship. If it were only that, these examples would not have a place in a volume whose principle is to avoid anything dealing with censorship of specific works in order to focus on *general* and *absolute* condemnations of literature as a whole.

As it happens, the specific condemnations leveled at the works mentioned above entail something other than these works merely being inappropriate in the context of contemporary American society. They are the result of a reductive and castrating vision of literature. They promote an art of language that would no longer be literature such as we know it, as an autonomous and independent art, but a system in which works would ideally limit themselves to providing a pure and, if possible, improved reflection of the society in which they are read. To refuse literature the right to shock, provoke, and make people uncomfortable is to impose upon it the constantly redefined duty of offering readers only what they expect—what they can accept, understand, and absorb. It is to refuse the power of reading to confront us with alterity. It is to demand that literature propose only sameness, that is to say something with which readers can wholly, blindly identify, without calling on their critical and hermeneutic faculties. It is to turn every reader into an eternal minor.

What is rejected here is alterity itself: the alterity of the past, the distant, the ancestors, the neighbors. And the strangest thing is that this rejection of alterity is expressed in the name of respecting the other: Should I force literature into silence and deprive my contemporaries of it just because it does not correspond with my expectations and values and personally disturbs or upsets me?

Ultimately, literary texts are considered the equivalents of sacred texts: they contain every truth and only truth. Literature is seen as the place where beauty, good, and truth come together. In Anglophone countries, a long tradition, notably represented (though to different degrees) by Ralph Waldo Emerson and Matthew Arnold, has established the study of literature as the secular equivalent of reading the Bible: continuing debates about the composition of the canon, particularly in the United States, echo this way of regarding reading as a sacred instrument of intellectual and moral education.

The literary canon has therefore developed on the model of the biblical "canon"—but a canon that is subject to the principle of the freedom of inquiry, in keeping with the tradition of culturally Protestant countries. As Emerson pointed out in "The American Scholar," every work must be placed on the Procrustean bed of individual inquiry: its value resides in us, in its compatibility with "the Divine Soul which also inspires all men."[48]

The problem is that literary texts, including those that are apparently the most virtuous, do not always offer examples of good morals. What are we to do with those texts in which crime mixes with virtue, beautiful language with the colloquial, and horror with the sublime? What are we to do with those that precisely do not want to be taken literally or read as gospel, but land before us because tradition has passed them down, because they provide pleasure, hope, or joy, or because of the very fact that they take apart every norm and rebel against everything and everyone? What are we to do with texts that disturb us or make us ill at ease? The truth is that every text does this: if you look at it closely enough, every text carries a force of destabilization.

Literary texts are precisely *not* the law: Plato was certainly clear that he held that against them. They state neither the truth nor moral goodness. They are also neither the Bible nor the Koran, which require believers to wholly subscribe to their content. Literature, on the contrary, demands distance, a critical gaze, and hermeneutical perspective. Literary texts cannot be assimilated to any others. They come from another world, and that is exactly why we read them: because they avoid every known interpretative framework, and because they enrich us with something other than ourselves.

To stigmatize *The Metamorphoses* for describing rape scenes or *Huckleberry Finn* for using the word "nigger" is to attempt to demand from literature something that does not apply to it. It is to ask it for a perfect, irreproachable, unchallengeable sacred text, that is to say, precisely what it is not. Literature exists to fill us with wonder or enthusiasm, to transport us, but also to be discussed, commented upon, and critiqued. It fully participates in the entire system of language exchanges that makes us full-fledged human beings.

From this perspective, the typically American movement to subject the canon to the demands of political correctness or democratic representativeness, while motivated by good intentions, is often the result of a total ignorance of literature's specificity, which is precisely that it avoids being pinned down. It is a resistant and illegitimate discourse.

To refuse a book the possibility of shocking those who read it is to impose on literature constraints that should not be its responsibility and to deprive it of its ability to bring us the new, the strange, and the unknown, if it is true that the new, the strange, and the unknown, by which I mean the truly new, the really strange, and the genuinely unknown, are necessarily shocking or provocative. In this refusal to grant literature the power to destabilize every value and every certainty, in this requirement imposed on all works of literature to rub their readers the right way and arouse empathy, and in the correlative obligation implicitly foisted on every reader, and particularly on students, to agree with works as if they were sacred texts, one can perceive a negation of literature in terms of what has specifically made it literature since Plato, namely as a weapon of subversion and seduction (in the sense of its etymological root, that is of secession or separation: literature *divides*). Behind these individual acts of censorship, a more general and timeless force is at work: the very force of anti-literature, which refuses literature the right to exist as literature.

IN A GENERAL WAY, to refuse literature a moral value is to deny the reader the possibility of making an autonomous judgment. This is the case with Jean-Jacques Rousseau and his condemnation of the use of La Fontaine's fables for the moral education of children. To argue his point, he chooses the fable that is the best known and apparently the simplest, *The Fox and the Crow*, and asks naïve questions about the text. Sometimes the questions are silly and are just used to play to the gallery:

> *Held in his beak a cheese.*
> What cheese? Was it a Swiss cheese, a Brie, or a Dutch?[49]

More often, the issue is realism:

> *Tempted by the odor of a cheese!*
> This cheese held by a crow perched on a tree must have quite an odor to be smelled by the fox in a copse or in his hole! Is this the way you give your pupil practice in that spirit of judicious criticism which does not allow itself to be impressed except by real likelihoods and knows how to discern truth from lie in others' narration?[50]

One could have said something entirely different, however, and come to the conclusion that, for instance, the cheese in question was a smelly aged Muenster (Camembert did not yet exist). But either because his knowledge of cheese was deficient or because his anti-literary leanings won out, Rousseau chose to accuse the text rather than the cheese. (The latter hypothesis is most likely the right one.)

Elsewhere, it is the poem itself that is deemed to be weak, clumsy, or difficult for a child to interpret:

> *How charming you are! How handsome you seem to me!*
> Padding, useless redundancy. The child, seeing the same thing repeated in other terms, learns slovenly speech. If you say that the redundancy is part of the author's art and belongs to the plan of the fox, who

wants to appear to multiply the praises with the words, this excuse will be good for me but not for my pupil.[51]

Even those parts of the poem that Rousseau recognizes as being well executed are shown to be failures:

He opens his big beak, lets fall his prey.
This verse is admirable. The harmony alone produces an image. I see a big ugly beak opened; I hear the cheese falling through the branches. But this sort of beauty is lost on children.[52]

Finally, the moral does not escape criticism:

This lesson is doubtless worth a cheese.
This is understandable, and the thought is very good. However, there will still be very few children who know how to compare a lesson with a cheese and who would not prefer the cheese to the lesson. One must, therefore, make them understand that this remark is only mockery. What finesse for children![53]

The lesson is clear: in every scenario, whether clumsy or successful, the fable is beyond the understanding of children or, worse, corrupts it. The moral: there is no morality there—at least not in fables, even the simplest ones, and pupils should be kept away from any kind of poetry, which is more likely to lead them to stray from the straight and narrow than to teach them how to behave themselves.

Rousseau's argument does not lack for finesse or humor in the way it shows the traps awaiting the teacher in every line of the fable. But it is flawed in its manner of exaggerating certain difficulties, of considering them all on the same level, and of proceeding as if they cannot be overcome. Education is aimed precisely at providing the child with the means to resolve problems: if the text had no pitfalls, what could be gained from studying it? Learning demands obstacles—or there is nothing more to be learned.

However, one argument is fundamental: the ambiguity of the moral lesson. Children identify less with the crow than with the fox, who takes advantage of another's credulity (hence the choice of the cheese rather than the lesson); they see themselves less as grasshoppers than as ants, which greedily attend to their own well-being; they see more advantages in the majesty of the lion, even if it is mixed with injustice, than in the innocence and placidity of the ass: thus the lesson of the fable is lost.[54]

This reasoning is not without merit, and it is not enough to object that the teacher's task is precisely to guide the pupil's reading in the right direction, to correct errors in interpretation, and to help students understand the proper meaning. Even though there is one meaning that is more probable than others, or at least preferable in certain conditions and according to certain parameters, the possibility exists for each reader—Rousseau is not wrong to insist on this—to interpret the tale in a unique way and to see themselves in it differently depending on their mood and the circumstances.

Thus, the most edifying apologue can become a lesson in immorality if the emphasis is put on one character rather than another. Sade appears to have made use of this lesson when he shifted from Justine to Juliette and from the description of the "misfortunes of virtue" to the symmetrical one of the "prosperity of vice"—practically the same fable, but arousing admiration rather than pity. There is a certain instability in fictional projection that is made use of by the best novelists as well as the cleverest fabulists.

Childhood is clearly the major issue here, and enemies of literature are not wrong to focus most of their criticism on the question of its educational value. We all know that it is such a sensitive age, so impressionable and at the same time so wicked, capable of turning the most decent fable into a handbook of deceit. It is more prudent to keep the fable out of children's hands, or better yet to take away the entire book, or, to be absolutely safe, to lock up the whole library.

"I hate books," Rousseau finally confesses. "They only teach one to talk about what one does not know."[55] It would have been more accurate to say, "They teach one what one *did* not know," which is the definition of what it actually means to learn; but for the author of *Émile,* there is no knowledge that does not come from experience.

One should acknowledge that for those who want to condemn literature, it is easy to use the example of an immature and ill-intentioned reader. It is hard to imagine what could stand up to such treatment: science, ethics, religion, philosophy—what could avoid becoming bad if it were placed in the wrong hands? Does reality itself escape this criticism? Is it any less ambiguous than fiction, or less easily co-opted?

Rousseau finds the solution in practical education—putting the child in direct contact with the world. He recommends taking a child to see the sun rise. "There is here a half-hour of enchantment," he writes, "which no man can resist. So great, so fair, so delicious a spectacle leaves no one cold."[56] A melancholy, suicidal, or insomniac person might disagree. Extreme cases? Perhaps, but no less than the malicious and unhinged reader postulated by *Émile.*

Some will say I'm biased. But no more than Rousseau himself. In this case, literature is like the ass in the fable: innocent and peaceful, it is bound to be the guiltiest—because it is the least able to defend itself, having been stripped of its attributes over so many centuries. An ideal victim, and an ideal culprit too.

CHILDHOOD MUST BE PROTECTED—the childhood of the individual. But it was regarding another childhood—the childhood of humankind, lost for good—that Rousseau launched his first assault against literature; the pedagogical argument would not come until later.

In 1749, the Academy of Dijon selected the following question for its competition: "Has the restoration of the arts and sciences contributed to the purification of morals?" The philosopher set about crafting a response in the negative; he sent his text to the academy, which awarded him the prize. This was the genesis of Rousseau's *Discourse on the Arts and Sciences.* It was also the real beginning of his career: the discourse made waves, responses were written, the author replied. In a few months, his reputation had been established.

Diderot spread the rumor that he himself had directed Rousseau, who was hesitating over which position to take in his entry to the competition: "There is no need to waver, I told him, you will take the position that no one will take. —You're right, he answered me, and he worked accordingly."[57] It was to be a discourse *against* literature. Still open to doubt are the truthfulness of the anecdote and the decisive nature of Diderot's intervention; less puzzling, however, is the paradoxical nature of the discourse. Was it really as paradoxical as Rousseau and Diderot claimed? If that had actually been the case, the Academy's question would not have been the topic of the competition, and Rousseau would not have won the prize.

In fact, mistrust of the moral value of letters was in the air—a real cliché of anti-literature. One need only think of Tanneguy Le Fèvre the younger or Bossuet, and to the objections to their arguments that Louis Racine still felt it necessary to make in 1747.[58] One also need only think of Plato—but we'll come back to this later.

It is true that Rousseau did not pull any punches: according to him, far from contributing to the purification of morals, the sciences and the arts had had the opposite effect. The progress brought about by the restoration of letters in the Renaissance had only been superficial, exclusively affecting appearances; in reality, letters provoke the degeneration of morals, today just as in Antiquity.

This was the case in Rome, which began to decay with the first appearance of Latin poetry:

It was not till the days of Ennius and Terence that Rome, founded by a shepherd, and made illustrious by peasants, began to degenerate. But after the appearance of an Ovid, a Catullus, a Martial, and the rest of those numerous obscene authors, whose very names are enough to put modesty to the blush, Rome, once the shrine of virtue, became the theater of vice, a scorn among the nations, and an object of derision even to the barbarians.[59]

The same was true of China and its learned Mandarins:

There is in Asia a vast empire, where letters are held in honor, and lead to the highest dignities in the state. If the sciences improved our morals, if they inspired us with courage and taught us to lay down our lives for the good of our country, the Chinese should be wise, free and invincible. But, if there be no vice they do not practice, no crime with which they are not familiar; if the sagacity of their ministers, the supposed wisdom of their laws, and the multitude of inhabitants who people that vast empire, have alike failed to preserve them from the yoke of the rude and ignorant Tartars, of what use were their men of science and literature? What advantage has that country reaped from the honors bestowed on its learned men? Can it be that of being peopled by a race of scoundrels and slaves?[60]

Sparta won because, alone in Greece, it did not engage in the delicacies of the arts. Letters only teach laxness, hypocrisy, and deference to the powerful. Rousseau claims that they are (to use Le Fèvre's term) purely futile: "Your children will be ignorant of their own language, when they can talk others which are not spoken anywhere. They will be able to compose verse which they can hardly understand."[61]

In this century of industry, poetry distracts from real work and actual enterprises: "A man who will be all his life a bad versifier, or a third-rate geometrician, might have made nevertheless an excellent clothier."[62] A convincing argument—at least among bourgeois, industrious families. But is it admissible from the future apologist for the state of nature, for whom "the odds are a hundred to one that he who first wore clogs was worthy of punishment, unless his feet hurt"?[63]

In this case, if Rousseau had been consistent, he would at least have given poetry credit for the fact that if the inventor of clogs had been a poet, he would never have become a clog maker.

The philosopher went so far in his violent attack on letters as to praise the burning of books. First, to note that the barbarians only abstained from the practice in order to weaken their enemies:

> When the Goths ravaged Greece, the libraries only escaped the flames owing to an opinion that was set on foot among them, that it was best to leave the enemy with a possession so calculated to divert their attention from military exercises, and keep them engaged in indolent and sedentary occupations.[64]

Next, to regret that the pope had not personally burned the library of Alexandria rather than leaving this honor to the caliph:

> It is related that the Caliph Omar, being asked what should be done with the library at Alexandria, answered in these words. "If the books in the library contain anything contrary to the Alcoran, they are evil and ought to be burnt; if they contain only what the Alcoran teaches, they are superfluous." This reasoning has been cited by our men of letters as the height of absurdity; but if Gregory the Great had been in the place of Omar, and the Gospel in the place of the Alcoran, the library would still have been burnt, and it would have been perhaps the finest action of his life.[65]

It is hard to know which to admire more: Rousseau's irony or his cynicism. He later claimed that he had not suggested "overthrowing existing society, burning libraries and all books," or "destroying colleges and academies." He justified himself: "I have seen the evil and tried to discover its causes: others, more daring or more foolish, may seek to find the cure."[66] A poor justification, tantamount to admitting that the only solutions could come from recklessness or madness, and to regretting that it was impossible to hold the book-burnings that he was accused of wanting to organize.

What inconsistency, what fragile suppositions, what unlikely historical simplifications Rousseau deploys! But also what vigor, what animosity, what resentment. The *Discourse* is both a masterpiece of rhetoric and the tomb of history and logic; for in truth, it must be said, without the arts and sciences, what evidence of virtue would have been preserved? Would we even know what it was? The same goes for vice: the periods and civilizations we believe to be free of any depravity are highly likely to be those whose archives have not been preserved or which never even kept archives and were idealized after the fact. It is too easy to imagine that they were better than those that succeeded them; in all likelihood, they were only more ignorant and less self-aware, less able to make moral distinctions and less concerned with leaving a written trace of their existence. Rousseau's entire reasoning is based on the fundamental inconsistency that involves concluding that the absence of documents means the absence of vice, as though virtue lay strictly in ignorance—which is essentially the philosopher's central thesis, but is a circular argument in terms of the question asked.

This can be recognized as a final development of the Pauline ethics partially inherited by the philosopher from Geneva: it is written law that creates sin, and spontaneity is always good in the state of grace (which in Rousseau becomes the state of nature, before the expulsion from Eden). As a matter of principle—or dogma—letters are the foundation of sin.

It is more than a little paradoxical that the virtue so highly praised in the *Discourse* ultimately comes down to fervor in combat and is measured by the number of battles won. The least peaceful of virtues, then, and the least compatible with the state of nature, the least Rousseauist, though undoubtedly the most virile: pure *virtus* in the etymological sense. (It should be mentioned that the question asked by the Academy of Dijon focused on morals, which is not exactly the same thing as virtue.) In contrast, letters belong in the realm of laxness, weakness, and femininity—a caricature that reflects the characteristic gendering of anti-literary discourse. As we have seen in the Second Trial, one still found traces of this in the twentieth century in C. P. Snow.

This is far from the only contradiction displayed by the *Discourse*'s author, the principal one being that in order to condemn letters he deploys every resource of eloquence, at which he excels. His replies to his opponents provide abundant examples, always to his advantage. There is no better weapon against letters than letters themselves: this duplicity may be the worst criticism that can be leveled at them.

Since he was unable to physically do away with all the literature that preceded him, Rousseau would later write *The New Heloise* and his *Confessions* in a bid to create a new kind of literature that was free of hypocrisy and closer to the truth of feelings: here, anti-literature is no more than a prelude to a revolution in discourse—a revolution that would be called romanticism and was destined for a great future. The declared disconnect between letters and morals and, in parallel, the detachment of literature from life, prefigure, in an inverse manner, the future developments of art for art's sake and the independence of literature: one can see the entire future of literary art in the nineteenth century implicitly take shape in the anti-literary discourse of Rousseau, as well as in Bossuet and Le Fèvre the younger.[67]

Despite his hatred of books, Rousseau would continue to write, more than ever, in fact, and would justify this activity throughout his career, simultaneously finding in it his punishment and the only consolation for his existence. His condemnation of letters applies only to the common people, he explains, and the problem is that all of society wants to learn literature, when only an intellectual and moral elite should have access to it: sometimes anti-literature is a form of aristocratism, even on the part of the thinker behind *The Social Contract*.[68]

ROUSSEAU WAS SORRY that there were no book-burnings but denied having suggested any should be organized—an unexpected example of casuistry on the part of the scourge of hypocrisy. Others did not have his scruples.

On Tuesday, February 7, 1497, the eve of Ash Wednesday, the usual Mardi Gras celebrations did not take place in Florence. The previous Sunday, Fra Domenico da Pescia, a companion of Savonarola's, had inveighed from the pulpit against books in Latin and in the vernacular, as well as artistic representations of any kind: the anathema had been pronounced.

On Tuesday, February 7, then, thousands of children (who had long been recruited by the Franciscans, as they are today by terrorists of every stripe) streamed through the city, knocking on the doors of private homes and demanding that their inhabitants hand over any object likely to be used sinfully: statues, paintings, jewels, wigs, veils, perfumes, mirrors, dice, playing cards, masks, and musical instruments, as well as, of course, books of Latin and Italian poetry, including those by Dante, Petrarch, and Boccaccio, to mention only the most illustrious. It is said that Botticelli contributed a few of his paintings.

On the Piazza della Signoria, a huge pyramid of books and other contraband was erected with eight faces, rising fifteen levels, twenty meters (sixty-five feet) tall and equally wide, with a monstrous image of Satan looming over it. It was set on fire and burned merrily into the night, to the sound of the children singing canticles. That very morning, thousands of Florentines had received communion at the cathedral, abjured every pleasure, and sworn perpetual chastity, even though some were already married. "It was as if," said an eyewitness, "the angels had come to live with men, and that was indeed the case."[69] Having gotten rid of all this immorality, Florence was able to observe Lent with dignity, in the holy austerity of the ignorant, the brutish, and the illiterate. Oh the wonders of virtue!

This "bonfire of the vanities" (*rogo della vanità*) is the most famous book-burning in history, but neither the only one nor the first—nor, sadly, the last. It is also the most emblematic, for the role that children played in the proceedings: by finding the noblest of its pretexts in the protection of children, the accusation of immorality leveled at literature keeps readers of all ages ipso facto in the grips of an eternal infancy. Many crimes against the mind have been committed in the name of pedagogy and purity. And many continue to be committed, by the best-intentioned souls. Real or imagined threats justify every prohibition, and the supposed victims are all too often the first executioners.

A little over a year later, on May 23, 1498, Savonarola and his acolytes were also burned, on the same Piazza della Signoria, though it was no doubt a less charming sight. It should be noted that their executions were not carried out in the name of literature: popes burn people for more serious reasons, and while literature may be immoral, it does not hold a grudge.

SAVONAROLA WAS NOT AN ISOLATED accuser: since Mussato, Petrarch, and Boccaccio had advocated the reading of the Ancients, the new humanism was a constant subject of controversy among clerics. Should one encourage the reading of the pagan authors, at the risk of endangering the teachings of the church?[70] In 1455, the bishop of Verona, despite his reputation for encouraging the development of letters, thought it wise to oppose certain overly zealous partisans of the Ancients by coming up with two long speeches, "Against the Poets." For it was poets who were directly targeted, rather than orators and philosophers, whose works, on the contrary, were recommended by the prelate.

As for the poets, the condemnation was absolute:

There has never been a time when poets were not scorned, disdained, or rejected; at no time, in no country have they ever been able to obtain the slightest dignity, a dignity that all the other arts, on the other hand—this is an established fact—obtained or could obtain.[71]

The bishop was certain of his stance, and it's a good thing for him and for the church that there is no doctrine of infallibility to protect such nonsense, for all this was obviously wrong, completely wrong: there are countless examples throughout history of cities honoring poets, from Pindar to Sophocles, and from Mussato to Petrarch. But the good prelate did not care: what was important to him was to remind people of the profound immorality of all poets, starting with Orpheus, the very first poet, but also the inventor of pederastic (*paedicaria*) and sodomitic infamy (*turpitudo sodomitica*), which he had the misfortune of introducing to Greece and, consequently, to Italy and throughout the world:

> Who could still believe that he was born of the gods, he who instituted for his own gods a cult so abominable, he who introduced debauchery so horrifying and even so contrary to natural dignity and the propagation of mankind?[72]

As I have earlier had occasion to note, anti-literature has always been highly compatible with homophobia, all the way through the twentieth century.

The most paradoxical thing is that these lectures against poetry exclude two, and only two, authors from general disgrace—Horace and Virgil, neither of whom is particularly known for the purity of his morals, and whose works display many examples of activities *against nature,* to use the excellent bishop's words. It was necessary to compromise with the humanist movement, and Virgil had already long been considered a precursor of Christianity. The defense of morals does not make the partisans of anti-literature any better readers or any more consistent.

THE CONDEMNATION of literature in the name of morality goes back at least as far as Xenophanes of Colophon and Heraclitus of Ephesus.[73] Yet it was Plato who would establish himself as the grand inquisitor and *The Republic* as the bible of anti-literature through the centuries. Bossuet, Tanneguy Le Fèvre the younger, Rousseau, and even Savonarola were no more than epigones—Savonarola's only advantage was that he exercised power and was able to get a lot done in a short time.[74]

We have seen that Plato criticizes poets for not telling the truth. If at times they do tell truths, those truths are ones that should not be made public, which is even worse. For not everything about the gods should be told. An example is Cronus's rebellion against his father Uranus, which is told by Hesiod with plenty of scabrous details—most notably, an emasculation by scythe followed by disposal of the genitals in the sea. Regardless of its veracity, the story is not universally comprehensible; its interpretation can lead to confusion, and it offers a poor example of filial piety.[75] Those most likely not to understand the tale of Cronus are children, who, according to the philosopher, are incapable of judging "what is allegory (*huponoia*) and what is not":

> What they take into their opinions at that age has a tendency to become hard to eradicate and unchangeable. Perhaps it's for this reason that we must do everything to ensure that what they hear first, with respect to virtue, be the finest told tales for them to hear.[76]

This is the first time in the history of anti-literature that childhood is invoked; going forward, it will rarely be left out. For in anti-literary argumentation the child is the ideal figure of the reader: an unemancipated reader, lacking judgment and unable to think independently. This view recognizes that literature is an invincible but poorly utilized authority, which should be replaced by a different one.

However old they are, citizens of Socrates's republic are moral and intellectual minors, under the guardianship of the city. This guardianship extends to poetry itself, which is censored because of the danger it poses to general morals. Poets are wrong to show heroes and, even more so, gods, who laugh and cry or are intemperate or greedy. They must be represented as impassive, like sages; this is the only example that should be given.[77] Poets are also wrong to describe Hades as a frightening place, thus weakening the courage of the citizens, who should always be ready to die for the state and for their freedom.[78] This is why it is important for the republic to exercise moral censorship of artists and poets, including by forbidding them to practice their profession; the well-being of the city demands it.[79]

It is no accident that poetry is dangerous; it is dangerous by nature: "the more poetic [the poets] are, the less should they be heard by boys and men" because they are all the more persuasive.[80] Socrates also condemns imitative poetry in general, which tends to give more importance to the representation of disorderly acts than to acts that are rational, prudent, and peaceful; the latter are "neither easily imitated, nor, when imitated, easily understood, especially by a festive assembly where all sorts of human beings are gathered in a theater," in a state of mind not inclined to moderation.[81] The wise man would make an unsatisfactory hero for the members of the audience, who on the contrary want violence, passion, pain, fury—something to move them to the depths of their being, without restraint.

For a poet, nothing is easier to portray than madness. Here he is, encouraging the part of each audience member's soul that is most irrational instead of dealing with the reasonable part, producing "a bad regime in the soul of each private man," "just as in a city when someone, by making wicked men mighty, turns the city over to them and corrupts the superior ones."[82] All those who provoke sadness, laughter, or erotic pleasure through imitation disrupt the audience member's morality, "fostering and watering [these afflictions] when they ought to be dried up, and setting them up as rulers in us when they ought to be ruled so that we may become better and happier instead of worse and more wretched."[83]

It is unacceptable for poets to create in each citizen so many poorly run little republics, each of which is headed for ruin. Like states within the state, they dissolve the latter's power. The Platonic homology between the citizen and the city, both formed according to

the same model, matches moral condemnation and political indictment, and the verdict is incontrovertible: the imitative poet who writes
epics, tragedies, and comedies must be banished, and "only so much
of poetry as is hymn to gods or celebrations of good men should be
admitted."[84] In other words, only those poems that are the least dangerous morally and the best suited to help those in power maintain
control.

If this were a question of restoring the sumptuous lyricism of Pindar or Alcaeus, why not? But one has to be realistic: over the course of
history, the Platonic program would far more often produce an official
literature—Soviet or Sulpician, it's all the same—that is, monotonous,
without passion or sincerity. This literature is not necessarily more
truthful than the other, but it uses lies for the benefit of the state.
When it is given the means of coercion—God forbid!—the moral condemnation of literature inevitably turns to ideological and political
subjugation.[85]

PLATO'S WARNING against the moral danger of poetry (or the warning
he put in Socrates's mouth) did not remain unanswered for long. The
response that was the most beautiful and most intelligent, as well as
the most ironic, came from his favorite disciple, Aristotle. On at least
three occasions, the philosopher of the Lyceum set forth a theory that
directly countered his master's propositions. From this perspective,
the *Poetics* can be described as an anti-*Republic*.

In the third book of *The Republic*, Socrates reproaches poets and
prose writers for showing that "many happy men are unjust, and many
wretched ones just, and that doing injustice is profitable if one gets
away with it, but justice is someone else's good and one's own loss."
He adds: "We'll forbid them to say such things and order them to sing
and to tell tales about the opposites of these things"—a simple, quick
way of dealing with the problem.[86]

But is there actually a problem, and is the suggested solution really
so effective? According to Aristotle, in the *Poetics*, the issue is far more

complex than Plato is willing to admit: tragedy's function is not to portray heroes in a certain state—happy, unhappy, or whatever it may be. Tragedy does not describe a fixed state; it describes a *change* of state, from happiness to misfortune or vice versa. If this change should purely and simply reproduce the moral norm, tragedy would be completely lacking in interest.

Showing a villain falling from happiness into adversity, as *The Republic* recommends, would not cause spectators to feel any emotions specific to tragedy: neither pity, for pity is extended only to victims of an undeserved misfortune, nor fear, which is aroused by the misfortunes of someone similar to one's self, and spectators generally do not consider themselves similar to villains. The virtuous plot dictated by Socrates would not have any moral use, because no one would be interested in it.

In contrast, Aristotle stresses the importance of choosing a hero who is ethically compatible with the members of the audience—neither perfectly good, nor perfectly bad—in such a way as to allow for identification. This hero must become a victim of misfortune as a result of some mistake he makes, but a mistake whose effect is disproportionate to the character's responsibility, in order, once again, to preserve the feelings of fear and pity.[87] This is Aristotle's first reply to Plato.

The second reply contradicts Socrates's entire indictment of the devastating effects of imitative poetry, which is alleged to engage the irrational part of the soul to the detriment of its rational part.[88] Aristotle's retort has a name as famous as it is misunderstood: catharsis. "Tragedy," writes Aristotle, "is an imitation accomplishing through pity and terror the catharsis of such emotions."[89] In other words, the pity and terror provoked by poetry are not its final products—if this were the case, it would indeed be regrettable, for they are bad passions. Instead, these are inevitable but intermediate stages of the tragic process, at the end of which the audience member is emotionally and physiologically improved. For Aristotle, the simultaneously cognitive and humoral mechanism by which catharsis is carried out in concrete terms rests on the necessary complementarity of fear and pity: what Socrates considers the tragedy's most unforgivable flaws are nothing less than the actual remedy.[90]

Ultimately, perhaps the best response to Plato is to go on the offensive and show that he is guilty of the same failings that he accuses poets of. This is exactly what Aristotle does in his *Rhetoric:* he lists the different types of comparisons that can be used in making a speech and points out that prose must generally avoid them, or else it risks becoming poetry. Several examples are cited, four of which happen to be drawn from *The Republic.*[91] And the last comparison is the very one Plato used to disparage poetry itself, accusing it of owing its charm to superficial embellishments, like a face that is without real beauty but is enhanced by the fleeting, fragile allure of youth:

> For when the things of the poet are stripped of the colors of the music and are said alone, by themselves, . . . they . . . resemble the faces of the boys who are youthful but not fair in what happens to their looks when the bloom has forsaken them.[92]

With this description of faces, Plato's disciple catches his master in the act of poetry just as the master is accusing poetry of adorning itself in deceptive colors. The irony is rich. Aristotle uses the opportunity to remark that the Platonic indictment of poetry is the work of a poet in disguise, who is using authoritarian means to substitute his own discourse for that of his colleagues, rather than acting like a true philosopher and impartially thinking about the positive and negative aspects of the art form he is attacking.

To justify his disagreements with his own master, the author of the *Poetics* calls himself a friend to Plato, but even more so to truth.[93] He is no less a friend to poetry.

ARISTOTLE DEFENDED the art of poetry by putting forward not only psychological arguments, but physiological ones. This is an entire vein of discourse on literature that today seems to have dried up: the ideas of doctors, or those claiming to be doctors, regarding the organic effects of written works. Looking back, it is difficult to imagine the influence of this line of thinking, for literature and the body now seem like completely separate worlds. But this was not always the case: in the eighteenth century, the medical profession did not hesitate to address the question of literature, regularly blaming the reading of maudlin novels for causing bodies to become weak and feminized.[94]

At the tail end of the century, Kant criticized novels for making female readers—women were those most affected—perpetually distracted, and for exacerbating memory loss:

> This practice in the art of killing time and making oneself useless to the world, while later complaining about the brevity of life, is one of the most hostile attacks on memory, to say nothing of the mental disposition to fantasy that it produces.[95]

Could the novel be the cause of Alzheimer's disease? Here's a hypothesis that contemporary researchers have probably not considered exploring.

Kant's argument is the following: unlike the representations made by a sequence of real events, characterized by their logical and cohesive (*conjunctim*) character, fictional objects appear scattered (*sparsim*) and disrupt the unity of understanding (*Verstandeseinheit*) in such a way that the mind of the reader—most often, that of the female reader—gets accustomed to a state of perpetual distraction, which is harmful.[96]

One could use the same points to make the opposite argument, namely that the scattering due to fiction forces the mind into a state of tension, creating a capacity to generate coherence that is not exercised by more cohesive discourses that lead the reader by the hand and describe reality as it is. From a single argument, one can draw two equally probable, but opposite consequences.

Which one should you choose? It couldn't be simpler: all it takes is an inclination for the anti-fiction side, as a matter of principle. Anti-literature is often merely the product of a certain intellectual laziness and adherence to general opinion, even on the part of philosophers in Königsberg.

Kant's attack was neither the first nor the last to accuse novels of disconnecting readers from reality: there had been *Don Quixote,* there would be *Madame Bovary,* and criticism of fiction was commonplace from the sixteenth through the eighteenth century. However, one aspect of Kant's criticism is specific to him: it is the well-organized world of the critic of pure reason, arranged in its carefully labeled boxes, just like the critic himself, an obsessive man with excessively hygienic daily habits, from sunup to sundown, taking meals and walks at fixed times.[97] This world and this critic both so set in their ways had difficulty coming to terms with texts that disturbed such a fine orderly existence and promoted the scattering of the mind. The memory lapse feared by Kant is the loss of self-control and the failure to control the world, or else the wind blowing through the open windows into a neat and tidy Prussian home: yet how beautiful it can be when literature blows your papers all over the place.

LITERATURE (in the widest sense, as the practice of texts) is harmful to the body: doctors recognized as much even in Antiquity; it had already become a commonplace.[98] In the first century CE, for instance, Celsus considered that the study of literature (*litterarum disciplina*) was "necessary for the mind, and at the same time bad for the body."[99]

"Weak people," he adds, "among which one must include a large proportion of city-dwellers as well as nearly all those who take an interest in letters, require more [medical] examination, so that care can restore what their physical constitution and their place of residence or study deprives them of."[100] Indeed, the development of cities and the literary lifestyle made the invention of medicine inevitable;

knowledge of medicinal plants and traditional remedies had previously been sufficient to maintain one's health.[101]

Does the Roman doctor recommend returning to a state of nature, as Rousseau later did? Far from it, for miraculously, the remedy is found in the ailment: according to Celsus, we owe the development of medicine to literary studies, not only because medicine aims to cure men of letters of their specific ailments, but because medicine itself takes root in the study of texts, in reflection and contemplation: the best doctors have always been men of letters.[102]

Even more surprising is that while literature invented the medical arts, it sometimes also serves as medicine: Celsus refers to numerous medical problems that can be treated by the prescription of readings, either to be read aloud by the patient, in the case of respiratory or digestive pathologies, or to be read to the patient by someone else, in the case of certain types of madness—the reader in the latter case must deliberately include errors while speaking, in order to arouse the patient's attention and provide a distraction from the mania.[103]

In the eyes of this great doctor, letters are the perfect *pharmakon,* in the full ambiguity of the term—sometimes a poison, sometimes a remedy—a reasonable position one would like to find more often among the denigrators of literature, rather than their complacent definitions of the ideal opponent. But it is true that to file an indictment on moral charges, a tendency to simplification and dubious intellectual ethics are great advantages.

Fourth Trial
Society

Dreams of book-burning. What mandate for writers? The ticket clerk and The Princesse de Clèves. *Against obligatory reading of master-pieces. When a princess made a president suffer. An enigma of literary history. Cultural knowledge questions.* De minimis non curat praetor. *Madame de La Fayette, here we are! France, a literary nation.* Mea culpa. *Five unhappy Proustians sitting at a table. The hatred of literature! "The bigwigs shun it." The poet and the soldier-king. The vengeance of a king. A brief appearance by the emperor. Variations on "If I had children." Ban on studying grammar. The hatred of books and the scribbler's trade. An uneducated riding master. Goodbye to poetry and the anti-novel. Green hat of the poets and yellow star. A final solution. Anti-literature pokes fun at anti-literature. The attack of the sociologists. Birth of cultural studies. An objective anti-literary collusion. Literature as a tool for segregation. Critique of the school of the republic. Democratic and aristocratic anti-literature. Literature is always wrong.*

It is easily conceivable that the trial of literature in the name of truth or morality could, as a last resort, lead to its removal from society, if what is real and what is good are considered important.

Thankfully, book-burnings and the exiling of poets have more often been fantasized about than put into practice. Anti-literature is most of the time merely an intellectual exercise or a knee-jerk rehearsal of platitudes handed down through a multi-millennial tradition. The stakes rarely go beyond the dividing up of territory between competing disciplines and art forms; the social impact of these debates is ordinarily limited to how much room literature is given in institutions or in education. Taken individually, these consequences are minimal. In the long term, however, the effects accumulate, and they are liable to lead to large-scale developments.

EVERY TRIAL BROUGHT against literature is bound to have a social element. In this final chapter, however, the angle of attack changes, as does the nature of the trial. Literature's social function is no longer marginal; it is questioned head-on. The subject of debate here is the ability of writers to express the aspirations, needs, and ideals of their society, to serve as its voice and faithfully represent it, in its complexity and diversity, or, in a narrower sense, their aptitude to incarnate the interests and values of a specific category or class of the population.

This purely social dimension of literary activity varies according to period, country, and regime. As demonstrated by Tocqueville, it adapts to various conceptions of society, whether democratic or aristocratic.[1] But, whatever the political regime concerned, the crux of the matter is the expressive or representative value attributed or not attributed to the literary arts, and whether the role of writers as the voice of the people is recognized or rejected.

Literature faces great expectations in this department; the disappointments are no less sizable.

ON FEBRUARY 23, 2006, in Lyon, Nicolas Sarkozy, then France's minister of the interior and a candidate for president, took the stage at a political rally:

> The other day, I was entertaining myself—you get your entertainment where you can—by looking at the syllabus for the examination for administrative officers. Some sadist or imbecile—I'll let you be the judge—had included among the requirements that candidates would be tested on *The Princesse de Clèves*. How often have you asked a ticket

clerk what she thinks of *The Princesse de Clèves*? What a spectacle that would be.[2]

Sarkozy went on to conclude that the recruitment and promotion of civil servants should be based on experience and merit rather than on their ability to stuff their heads with useless cultural knowledge.

On June 10, 2006, while addressing new members of his party in Paris, Nicolas Sarkozy told the story a little differently:

> The other day I was looking at something fascinating: the syllabus required to be promoted from an administrative clerk to a chief officer. Would you believe that some sadist had included a question in the syllabus asking whether the candidate had read *The Princesse de Clèves*?
>
> How often have you gone up to the counter in a government building and asked the clerk if she's read *The Princesse de Clèves*? At any rate, I read it so long ago that there's a good chance I would have failed the exam.
>
> But put yourself in the shoes of this forty-year-old man or woman who has a job and a family, and on top of that has to study for exams to be promoted to a superior rank—do you think they have time for that?[3]

This heart-wrenching picture is enough to bring tears to your eyes: the forty-year-old mother reading Madame de La Fayette in one hand while preparing a meal for her children with the other—a twenty-first-century version of Victor Hugo's *Les Misérables*. Surely, international conventions will soon ban obligatory reading of masterpieces as inhumane and degrading treatment.

Two years later, having been elected president of the republic, Nicolas Sarkozy delivered a statement on the modernization of public policy and reform of the state. Once again, he emphasized the importance of being able to obtain a professional promotion without having to "recite *The Princesse de Clèves* from memory."[4]

That summer, while addressing a group of young people during a visit to a summer camp, he proposed that civil service examinations recognize volunteer experience:

> In terms of human richness, of commitment to help others, why shouldn't it be taken into account? It's just as valuable as knowing *The Princesse de Clèves* by heart.
>
> I mean, I have nothing against it . . . I mean . . . OK, I mean . . . (*Embarrassed.*) The fact is, *The Princesse* really made me suffer. (*Big smile, beaming with satisfaction.*)[5]

The room erupts into laughter—though, it must be said, only the adults laugh, for the young people visible in the background do not seem to have the slightest idea what Sarkozy is talking about, either because they aren't aware of the president's obsession with the novel, or, more likely, because its title, mentioned at random, means nothing to them.

In this strange statement about youth and popular education, the speaker paradoxically proposes to scale back on the transmission of knowledge before an audience of people who don't know a thing about the culture they might be deprived of and therefore do not understand what they are being asked to relinquish. Yet this remark established *The Princesse de Clèves* as a commonplace of the president's discourse, a rallying symbol and a sign of tacit political consent that would enable the orator to express confessions and comments to his audience in theatrical asides.

To listen to Nicolas Sarkozy, one would think the civil service examination requirements regarding Madame de La Fayette's novel had grown inordinately over a two-year span. Early in 2006, candidates were vaguely asked about the novel. Four months later, they were asked if they had read it. By 2008, it was lock, stock, and barrel: candidates had to recite all two hundred pages by heart. This was the product of a purely rhetorical snowball effect, with each allusion to *The Princesse de Clèves* going one better than the last in a deliberately self-referential gesture aimed at building rapport with the public: another two years and the examination juries would probably have required each candidate to produce a four-hundred-page exegesis and recite the novel forward, then backward, while hopping on one foot.

Meanwhile, the secretary of state for public service discreetly played along in the background. On November 20, 2007, during a televised interview, he explained that one of Nicolas Sarkozy's assistants had been asked: "Who wrote *The Princesse de Clèves*?" And added: "That's humiliating for all low-level civil servants."[6] (It was apparently not a problem that his statement automatically defined an entire category of the population as uncultivated.)

Speaking directly to the interviewer, who had just been identified as a recent graduate of the prestigious École Normale Supérieure, the secretary of state concluded: "You may be the only Frenchman able to answer that question"—a sentence fated to remain deeply enigmatic, for the interview immediately shifted to another topic.

At this point, the television audience and my readers might ask themselves whether the crisis in the French education system was so severe that one had to have studied at the École Normale Supérieure— or even then, to be that one special graduate—to know that *The Princesse de Clèves* was written by Madame de La Fayette, a fact found in every encyclopedia and literature textbook.

The answer to this nagging question would come three months later: in February 2008, on the same television station, speaking to the same journalist, the same secretary of state was serving up the same fare and taking advantage of the opportunity to explain his indignation. According to him, historians do not agree on the actual identity of the author of *The Princesse de Clèves:* they aren't sure whether it was Madame de La Fayette or Monsieur de La Rochefoucauld. Isn't it appalling to ask a mere assistant her opinion on the matter?[7] The secretary of state would later add that these are "pathetic questions,

questions of pure elitist knowledge,"[8] that do not belong in an examination for public service. This was the real "scandal," the real "waste."[9]

At the same time, a report was commissioned on "the content of civil
service entrance examinations," the primary aim of which was to criticize the principle of testing general culture. To prove they had a sense
of humor, the report's authors dedicated it "to Marie-Madeleine
Pioche de la Vergne, comtesse de La Fayette (1634–1693), and to *The
Princesse de Clèves* (1678), without whom this report would never have
seen the light of day."[10] These authors obviously did not share the secretary of state's doubts regarding the identity of the novel's author.

And how could they, given that this is a discussion in which only
specialists are involved? No examiner in her right mind would ask
a question about *The Princesse de Clèves* that required a candidate
in a civil service examination to be aware of a scholarly debate on
whether or not La Rochefoucauld participated in writing the novel.
The secretary of state had had to draw on the full resources of his
hypocrisy to pretend to interpret the question to Sarkozy's assistant
this way, with the single aim of coming to the head of state's rescue
in the *Princesse de Clèves* controversy and providing his indignation
with the legitimacy it so sorely lacked.

FUNDAMENTALLY, the entire debate focused on a single question:
what body of knowledge and experience should a French citizen share
with other citizens in order to hold a position as a civil servant with
dignity and without misunderstanding, whether as a mere clerk or as
an administrative assistant?

It would be difficult to live in a country or a community of any type
and hold any professional position without a modicum of the kind
of cultural grounding that makes it possible to live together, without
a body of shared references that allow dialogue and mutual understanding. No one would deny that practical knowledge and experience
should come first; the examinations emphasize them. Yet is that what
we should limit ourselves to?

An ancillary question: Can literature itself be extracted from this common frame of reference?

Minimal knowledge of French history—such as knowing the date of the French Revolution—does not seem like an extravagant stipulation. Would a president of the republic dare to take umbrage at that? And if knowing the date of the French Revolution seems like an acceptable requirement, why shouldn't one have to know the great works of literature that reflect the republic's values, such as those by Voltaire and Hugo?

Is Proust too difficult or too elitist? Rabelais and Montaigne too distant? One can hardly imagine France without them. And if Rabelais and Montaigne are acceptable, why not Madame de La Fayette, whose only novel influenced the history of the genre, and whose universe, characterized by psychological sophistication, refined manners, and relatively open moral standards, coincides with a certain idea of France that lives on throughout the world?

Beyond that, everything is a question of limits. Where do the requirements stop? How detailed should we get? Knowledge of names and dates isn't much; it is nothing compared with actually reading the works, but it has the advantage of maintaining points of reference as well as the possibility of a national memory, or even a European or global memory.

This is all fodder for public discussion, but such a debate, while not without interest, remains rather technical, applying as it does to the content of civil service examinations, and should not concern a presidential candidate, let alone a sitting president.

De minimis non curat prætor, says the Latin adage: the praetor does not concern himself with details. A wise recommendation. One can only assume that in the twenty-first century a president of the Republic of France has a less overarching view than a mere magistrate of the city of Rome two thousand years earlier. But could it be that if the praetor does concern himself with a detail—or what appears to be one—and does so insistently, it is no longer a detail?

This is exactly what happened: the technical debate about the recruitment and promotion of civil servants was soon overshadowed by a growing controversy, for Nicolas Sarkozy's attack on *The Princesse de Clèves* had been understood, rightly or wrongly, as an attack on literature as a whole.

This was partially inaccurate, given that literature was not targeted as such in the first statement on February 23, 2006. However, the candidate to the presidency revealed with this declaration that he was ill-informed regarding the importance, in educational tradition and in the national memory, of a work like that by Madame de La Fayette— assuming, of course, that she was indeed the author. Such ignorance, quickly spotted by the candidate's opponents, was presented as evidence of Nicolas Sarkozy's unsuitability for the office he was seeking.

The rest is history: *The Princess de Clèves* became the symbol of opposition to the president-elect; its print run increased by unprecedented amounts; discussions were organized by the media; public readings were held on the street, in theaters, and at universities; books were published; the novel was transposed to the present day in a good film adaptation; and Madame de La Fayette was added to the prestigious Bibliothèque de la Pléiade, the ultimate recognition for a French author.[11]

The paradoxical effect of the remarks made by Nicolas Sarkozy and his secretary of state is that it would now be unlikely that any candidate to a civil service examination would not have heard of this novel or would be unable to identify its presumed author, though perhaps the candidate would not be able to recite it by heart. Reason enough for examiners to avoid asking questions about such an easy topic—wasn't that the president's goal, after all?

SARKOZY'S stubborn insistence on repeating the initial anecdote ultimately turned *The Princesse de Clèves* into a martyr to a populist-inclined policy dominated by mistrust of intellectuals—a reciprocal mistrust, admittedly.

The worst thing—and the strangest—is that a president so concerned with the question of national identity could not understand that this identity was in part defined by the particular importance accorded to literature. In 1930, the German philologist Ernst Robert Curtius defined this singular French identity as follows:

> Literature plays a far larger part in the cultural and national consciousness of France than it does in that of any other nation. In France, and in France alone, can the national literature be regarded as its most representative form of expression.... France ... cannot be understood at all politically, socially, or even from the purely human point of view if literature is left out of account; if we fail to grasp the central, uniting part it plays in every sphere of the life of the nation. Further, unless we read the French classics, and read them in the way the French read them, we cannot possibly understand France. All the national ideals of France are colored and shaped by literary form. In France if a man wishes to be regarded as a politician he must be able to express himself in some form of literature. If he desires to exert influence as a speaker he must have a thorough knowledge of the collective literary treasure of the nation. No man who is not master of the spoken or of the written word can exert any influence in public life.[12]

Whether this is myth or fact does not much matter here. This type of discourse, the beginnings of which can be traced back to at least the eighteenth century, was particularly enduring in the first half of the twentieth century, notably in the writings of Albert Thibaudet. Curtius was regularly exposed to contemporary examples of writers heavily involved in political life, such as Maurice Barrès, Charles Maurras, Anatole France, and the Surrealist group.

Seventy years later, the situation was clearly not the same: to a government minister running for president of France, later a sitting president, the image of France as a literary nation had become foreign enough that he could allow himself to steadfastly attack one of the major works of French literature and generally call into question literature's place in culture and professional training, without regarding it as unbecoming for a president.

This was nothing less than a clash between two types of legitimacy: one resulting from universal suffrage, aiming to represent, even ape, a population considered to be ignorant and hostile to literature out of principle; the other the product of the pen, a power that literary works and writers are sometimes granted in order to represent the nation and to speak in its name, at least to some degree.

A few years later, it would be a totally different story: now himself a member of the opposition and trying to regain presidential stature in view of getting reelected, Nicolas Sarkozy would deliver his *mea culpa*, admit he had a passion for literature, comment on Tolstoy, Balzac, and Maupassant, and regret that he had not "corrected that wisecrack" earlier.[13]

Was this a sincere conversion or a mere tactical switch? The question is all the more difficult to answer given that a politician's reality is today limited almost entirely to the image he wants to project—until the next time he changes communications consultants. What does appear genuine is Sarkozy's regret that he had chosen a bad strategy—unless his regret was itself a strategic move.

The *Princesse de Clèves* affair was probably the product more of a lack of thought and poorly calculated opportunism than an actual desire to do harm, but in itself this lack of thought signaled that literature's status was fragile and that its social and political legitimacy was no longer assured, that it seemed negligible and easily overlooked.

Anti-literature is often the fault of people who do not know what they are doing.

ANOTHER ERA, another government, another political party, but nearly the same attitude. In March 2013, the minister of higher education presented a draft bill to authorize classes in French universities to be taught in English. She explained:

> If we do not authorize classes in English, we will not attract students from emerging countries like South Korea and India. And we'll wind up with five people sitting around a table talking about Proust, though I do like Proust . . . [14]

"Though I do like Proust" was clearly aimed at warding off bad luck and avoiding a repeat of Nicolas Sarkozy's mistake with *The Princesse de Clèves*. The minister was wasting her breath: she was still using literature as a foil and an illustration of failure—as an insignificant activity, ultimately.

The example was particularly poorly chosen. In a reply to the minister, Antoine Compagnon reminded her that his seminars on Proust at the Collège de France attracted crowds from all over the world, including South Korea, and that many foreigners decided to learn French with the sole purpose of reading *In Search of Lost Time* in the original. In other words, literature "is a powerful export of French culture and industry," which many politicians had the unfortunate habit of forgetting.[15]

This seems to indicate that some people have a persistent problem with literature, and only literature. Can one possibly imagine the minister speaking this way about the visual arts or cinema? "And we'll wind up with five people sitting around a table talking about Picasso or the New Wave": such a statement is all the more inconceivable given how aware the elites are of the tremendous financial stakes in the visual arts. Next to that, literature is seen as a poor relation.

Even if France's relative preeminence in "the global republic of letters"[16] remains a reality, as is quite clearly indicated by the statistics for foreign translations of French works and the fact that two French writers were awarded the Nobel Prize in Literature six years apart,[17] today's politicians still struggle to see literature for what it was for centuries: the preferred means of expression of the French nation, the one by which it becomes aware of its destiny.[18]

IT IS ENTIRELY possible that such unawareness is a sign of a displacement of legitimacy or a drop in literary activity's status in the scale of values.[19] But it has always been difficult and risky for literature to speak in the name of the people. When the power to do so exists, it is fragile and bound to lead to censorship and dissent. When it is illusory, the critics record its failure. In both cases, anti-literature remains in the news.

Though their principal players did not know it, the most recent controversies were in direct continuity with previous anti-literary discourse and repeated some of its most persistent leitmotifs: there is a long tradition of politicians scorning or taking no interest in literature, and the struggle for political and social legitimacy is one of the oldest that literature has faced.

Could one possibly imagine that the Third Republic, that republic of professors, was exempt from such conflicts? That would be pure rose-tinted nostalgia. Let's reread Zola on Flaubert:

> Literature, in his eyes, was a higher calling, the only important calling in the world. And so he wanted people to be respectful toward it. His big grudge against people was largely due to their indifference to art, their muted defiance, their vague fear before elaborate and brilliant style. There was a phrase he often repeated in his terrible voice: "The hatred of literature! The hatred of literature!" That hatred he found everywhere, among politicians even more than among the bourgeois.[20]

In a chapter of *The Experimental Novel* appropriately entitled "The Hatred of Literature," Zola attacks politicians who put on airs in front of writers:

When you have failed in everything and everywhere, when you have been an unsuccessful lawyer, an unsuccessful journalist, an unsuccessful man from head to feet, politics will take you in hand and make you a minister as good as another, reigning, from the position of a more or less modest and amiable upstart, over the French intelligence. These are the facts.

My God! The facts are still acceptable, for there are strange things happening daily around us. The observer becomes accustomed to it, and contents himself with smiling. But it makes me sick when these men pretend to despise us and patronize us. We are only writers, we hardly count; they limit our share in the sunshine, they place us at the foot of the table. Ah! When the situations are finally determined, gentlemen, we intend to pass in first, to have the whole table and all of the sunshine.[21]

Written accounts of this caste-based anti-literature are most often second hand. This is only logical: those who proclaim their contempt for writers are generally loath to become writers themselves and to fill entire pages with expressions of their scorn; they have other things to think about, luckily. What is new today is that the slightest statement is recorded: a blow against literature has less chance of going unnoticed and remaining without a response.

Conversely, the punching bag already has pen in hand, and social resentment provides the opportunity—why not?—for a poem:

Apollo's art is not for the vulgar herd.
It's hardly a way for the greedy to make big money.
Ambitious men think of poetry as a funny

waste of their time. In a soldier's pack, it's absurd
to expect a book of verse. The bigwigs shun it.
The clever are clever enough to keep their distance.
It's a sorry business. Take Du Bellay, for instance,
to demonstrate the scorn people heap upon it.

Courtiers think it is profitless and dumb.
Artists want to be paid in advance—if they come.
The Muse is a bad mistress, a worse wife.

I remain, nonetheless, faithful. I will not quit.
It's only my writing that comforts me a bit,
and I thank the Muse for the last six years of my life.[22]

Three centuries before Flaubert and Zola, the arguments sound strangely similar; only the posture is different, this resignation before the fate in store for poets, which Joachim Du Bellay makes the subject of his poem and the source of his inspiration. Ignored by the vulgar, mocked by the great, neglected by courtiers, lacking any use in social exchanges in general, poetry is reduced to occupying a no man's land that is all the more celebrated because it receives so little recognition—a symbolic compensation that takes on its full meaning in an art that is, precisely, devoted to symbols.

THE ANTI-LITERATURE of democratic societies has kept many of the traits that already existed under the Ancien Régime: power, whatever its origins, produces its elites and its outcasts—even more so in a monarchic and aristocratic state.

Frederick William I of Prussia, the aptly named "soldier-king," had a particular detestation for anything related in any way to poetry. "Any poet was an odious object to him," reported the Abbé Irail.[23] One day, Frederick noticed characters written above the main door of his palace in Berlin and asked what they were. He was told that this was Latin verse composed by a poet from the city. The king summoned him at once. The poet appeared, expecting a reward; the king ordered him to leave the city and the entire realm without delay. He did so immediately.

Frederick William I also forbade his son to learn Latin and read poetry. In this case, he was less successful: the son continued to educate himself in secret. He was found out and publicly punished. He rebelled and ran away. He was arrested and imprisoned, and so on and so forth—which did not prevent this lettered son from openly devoting himself to his love of poetry and literature once he acceded to the throne, nor from turning his kingdom into one of the most enlightened in Europe, to which he invited the greatest scholars and most brilliant writers. For every poet exiled, ten were rediscovered: this would be Frederick II's revenge on his father.

FREDERICK WILLIAM I did not need to read Plato to hate poetry. His taste for all things military was reason enough. Napoleon I did not have much regard for literature either. He was exclusively partial to science, for it seemed to him that science alone was useful and worthy of respect; writers, by contrast, whom he called "phrasemakers," earned only his "disdain" and "disgust," according to Napoleon's one-time secretary Louis-Antoine Bourrienne. Napoleon's insensitivity "to beautiful poetry and beautiful prose" was so total that fine books seemed to him a pure "arrangement of sonorous words empty of meaning and which, according to him, only struck the ear."[24] Besides, he lacked the time to read literature (just like a recent minister of culture[25]): "[Time] was so precious to him that he would have liked to find a shorter route than a straight line, so to speak; he only liked men who dealt with positive, exact things," without direct political impact.[26]

Here we recognize the legacy of the anti-literary discourse about the futility and frivolity of poetry (as described in the Third Trial), combined with considerations of the political danger posed by writers, and the military man's traditional contempt for the writer.

THIS CLASSIST contempt was conveyed early on even by men of letters: there are abundant accounts of it among the greatest humanists of the sixteenth century. Justus Lipsius stated: "If I had children, I would certainly prevent them from studying."[27] Joseph Justus Scaliger had similar ideas: "If I had ten children, I would not let even one of

them study: I would present them in the courts of the princes."[28] Both
examples are cited by François de La Mothe Le Vayer in a work whose
title says it all: *Doute sceptique si l'étude des belles-lettres est préférable
à toute autre occupation* (Skeptical doubt as to whether the study of
literature is preferable to any other occupation).[29] Here, La Mothe
Le Vayer comments on the regrets expressed by his two illustrious
precursors:

> All those great Palamedes, who loved letters so much that they increased
> their number, at the end are reduced just as the Greek himself was—
> which is why I give them his name—to making constant complaints that
> they lost so much time acquiring something that made them unhappy
> and that they had imagined entirely differently from how they experi-
> enced it. This may be what led certain emperors to persecute men of
> letters by very strict edicts, and popes to mistreat those they referred
> to as *Terentianos,* as being too attached to the beautiful diction of the
> classical authors.[30]

La Mothe Le Vayer reports that in 1622 "the study of grammar
was prohibited in Spain" in order to prevent the proliferation of "a
laziness that is harmful to the state, as well as being the ruin of those
who become accustomed to it."[31] At a time when the separation of
discourses was not what it is today, it was all of learning that was targeted under the name of belles-lettres or grammar, and not only poetry
or what we now call *literature;* as for actual poetry and literature, the
courts and princes considered them, at best, purely servile arts and, at
worst, useless, if not harmful activities. They were universally scorned.

La Mothe Le Vayer wrote his *Doute sceptique* in 1667. It was a distant
echo, in the heart of the seventeenth century and the classical period,
of the anti-literary question earlier raised by Montaigne regarding
education—as always, the central issue. Indeed, one finds a surprising passage in Montaigne's *Essais* in which the philosopher, referring to himself as an exception, gives thanks to his tutor for having

developed his taste for Roman poets, without which, he adds, "I should have gotten nothing out of school but *a hatred of books,* as do nearly all our noblemen."[32] This striking expression describes a sociological reality of the period: in the sixteenth and seventeenth centuries, the hatred of books was a class hatred—founded in social class no less than classrooms—combined with a caste-based contempt for schoolteachers and writers.

Paradoxically, Montaigne himself does not always avoid this contempt—he who prefers the charms of conversation to those of text. He makes fun of "scribbling," a "symptom of an unruly age"; rejects pedantry, arrogance, and vain subtleties; and praises the simple language and natural style that are the antithesis of lettered artifice.[33]

The model of the *honnête homme* thus emerges from the *Essais* as it would be disseminated throughout the entire next century: an aristocratic socialite, free of the dishonoring yoke of studies, accustomed to physical exercise and the government of his land, and professing nothing but disdain for books—other than the *Essais* themselves, his only breviary.[34] The time had come for the triumph of the *esprit,* the kind of wit that allowed one to shine in salons, the sign of a natural nobility that would inevitably be spoiled by excessive familiarity with literature. Pedantry of any kind is execrated.

A FEW YEARS after Montaigne's death, the author of the first French treatise on horseback riding, a Gascon like the late philosopher, admitted at the beginning of his book that he had always preferred "vigorous exercise" to "fine letters" and that he had been born, "to my great regret, with the shortcoming of never dedicating myself to reading." Emboldened by this confession, he went so far as to take pride in his volume's lack of art:

> My writings, however poorly polished, will bring more usefulness and contentment to noble and generous minds than the stack of books they usually have in their hands, though their language is more eloquent and

affected, for the virtue in action is far worthier than that in contemplation, and beautiful actions are to be prized above beautiful words.[35]

An attitude typical of the aristocrat who values action at the expense
of beautiful language.

CURIOUSLY, this anti-literary discourse, through which the aristocratic caste proclaimed its own values, did not prevent the writing
of books, or even the development of a new literature, whose distinguishing feature was mockery of belles-lettres. This was the case
with Charles Sorel's novel *Le Berger extravagant* (The extravagant
shepherd), whose subtitle was distinctly anti-literary: *où parmi des
fantaisies amoureuses on voit les impertinences des romans et de la
poésie* (wherein, among fantasies of love, one sees the impertinences
of novels and poetry). The novel even includes a poem entitled "Adieu
à la poésie" (Farewell to poetry).[36] A few years later the author pseud-
onymously published *L'Anti-roman,* plainly appropriating anti-literary
discourse to produce a work of literature.

Over the course of the seventeenth and eighteenth centuries, the
promotion of a style of writing intended to be closer to nature and
ordinary usage and free of showy devices eventually invested literature
with a new legitimacy and a force of expression, if not of sincerity, that
would ultimately be fulfilled in the romantic revolution—which was
less a revolution, from this perspective, than an evolution: ironically,
the aristocratic posture of anti-literature led to a more democratic
regime of literary expression.

AS IS OFTEN the case, Italy was in the vanguard of this movement. In
1526, the satirical poet Francesco Berni published a *Dialogue against
Poets,* in which he officially renounced the very title of poet—"I de-
poeticize myself" (*mi spoeto*)—after having poured out every possible
insult at his colleagues and ostracized them from society:

SANGA: Just as the Christians mark the Jews as a despicable and odious people by making them wear a yellow hat or a red roundel, poets must in the same manner wear a green hat, both as a sign of infamy and to enable people to keep away from them and not let them get close.

BARBI: As for me, I say a white band, like for those who are sick! And I think I would also organize a specific inquisition against poets, as they do for heretics and *marranos* in Spain, which, you should be aware, is all the more necessary now that we no longer know whom we have to protect ourselves against.[37]

White bands and green hats, as for the sick and the insane, and ostracism, as for the Jews: an anti-poetic police force and another ghetto have seen the day. And why stop while you're ahead? Follow through with the comparison and allow poets to enjoy the same fate that Christian society, in its goodness, reserved for Jews and heretics:

Poets appear to me to be the kind of animal that Piovano Arlotto preached was only good dead: he meant pigs. Well, poets are like pigs: if I like them at all, I only like them when they're dead; this is why I wish they were all dead.[38]

Though one must allow for burlesque exaggeration in this dialogue, the expression is radical and the solution brutal and proven to be effective: a death sentence for poetry, if not poets. All types are included; every model of humanist poetry is considered fit for the bonfire, from Homer to Virgil, from Hesiod to Horace, and from Aeschylus to Catullus.

The only ones to escape the slaughter are the lords who poeticize in their spare time, such as Pietro Bembo, Giovanni Pontano, and Jacopo Sannazaro: "Those ones, we know who they are, and that they can do something other than write verse if they want to. They do not make poetry their profession."[39] The condemnation is thus revealed to be socially discriminatory—reserved for a particular class of professional poets who are poor and dependent, useless to the state, licentious, even dangerous, and who are perpetuating the autonomous tradition of a lettered and artificial poetry.

By publicly de-poeticizing himself and making amends, Berni obeyed the moral injunction of his protector, the austere and powerful bishop Gian Matteo Giberti, who championed a strict reform of the church.[40] However, one cannot rule out the hypothesis that with this startlingly earthy and violent, deliberately grotesque and contradictory dialogue, Berni sought to parody the anti-literary and anti-poetic imprecations then being hurled from the pulpit, as had been memorably demonstrated by Savonarola and his acolytes thirty years earlier in Florence.[41] This dialogue was another paradoxical example of celebrating the power of poets, commensurate with the severity of the crimes they were accused of.

In this case, the project was of a fundamentally ironic nature: the ingenuity of Berni's rhetorical device is that we will never know whether we are dealing with the real thing. But this uncertainty does not prevent his words from making one shudder at the thought of the social violence they imply: even when anti-literature pokes fun at anti-literature, the symbolic force of its discourse remains intact.[42]

IN ARISTOCRATIC SOCIETY, the lords have nothing but contempt for literature; in democratic society, it is the people—or their representatives and those who claim to speak for them—who constitute the greatest political danger to literature. With the end of the dominant bourgeois culture and the spread of a mass culture shared by all social classes, the second half of the twentieth century witnessed the expression of increasingly virulent criticisms of literature's status in official culture.

In this new trial inspired by democratic impulses, sociologists imposed themselves as the spokespeople for those who had until then not had a voice, taking over this function from writers such as Hugo, Zola, and Jules Vallès. Claiming to speak in a more neutral, objective, and supposedly less self-interested voice, they studied the actual forms of popular culture, which had up to this point been neglected by the academy.

The seminal work was Richard Hoggart's 1957 book *The Uses of Literacy*, which brought to light, for the first time, the particular way in which the English working classes experienced their relationship to the written word, as well as the place it occupied among a larger group of distractions.[43] The inspiration for this research, carried out by an academic from the same background as his subjects, was eminently empathetic, and the book rose almost to the level of literary fiction in its manner of describing and representing typical figures, objects, and scenes of popular life: the ascent of the scholarship student, the reading of illustrated magazines, the songs sung by neighborhood choirs, and so on.

One year later, in *Culture and Society (1780–1950)*, Raymond Williams described the emergence of the concept of culture in England during the Industrial Revolution and raised the question of how one would define a "common culture" in the contemporary world.[44] The use of historical perspective opened a debate: by showing that the very idea of culture had undergone significant changes over the previous two centuries, Williams suggested that it could be subject to further change.

This approach gave rise to the new discipline of cultural studies. Initially centered at the University of Birmingham, where Hoggart had been appointed a professor, cultural studies spread throughout the English-speaking world in the 1970s and 1980s. In many institutions, English departments took on this new name. This change went hand in hand with a marginalization of the field of literary studies, which was now considered just one element in a larger whole, on a par with cinema, television, and pop music.

Naturally, voices were raised in protest against this dilution of literature in culture, which was seen as the loss of a privileged status.[45] Objectively speaking, it cannot be denied that the development of cultural studies has had an anti-literary effect, by reducing the representation of literature in academic curricula and research.

Yet this had not been the original intention: neither Hoggart nor Williams was calling into question the significance of literature in the common culture or seeking to reduce it. Both were professors of English literature, devoted to passing on their knowledge of and appreciation for the great works of the canon under the best conditions and to all their students, no matter their social background.[46] In fact, it was precisely because of the difficulties they were encountering in this endeavor that they began to take a specific interest in the forms of popular culture. For Hoggart, the most complex figures of literary modernity—Yeats, Eliot, Joyce—were unsurpassable beacons. According to Williams, recognizing the existence of a historical "bourgeois culture" should under no circumstances lead the new rising classes either to neglect what he called, significantly, a "common human inheritance," or to attempt to pare it down.[47]

In fact, the attacks against literature in the academy came from several fronts at once: during the same period that witnessed the publication of Hoggart's and Williams's major books, the late 1950s, Snow gave his famous speech on "the two cultures," with the great success we have noted. We have also seen how Snow then used sociology as an argument against the defenders of literary culture.[48] The coincidence between the appearance of a sociology of culture, on one hand, and the demand for a more scientific university education, on the other, functioned like a concerted attack, with literary studies as the principal victim.

A subject does not need to explicitly express the discourse of anti-literature for anti-literature to exist: all that is necessary is a social groundswell, the multiple causes of which are to be found everywhere, including sometimes in literature itself.[49]

THE DISCOURSE of French sociology, while equally ambiguous, was something different, something perhaps more dangerous. In 1970,

Hoggart's seminal volume was published under Pierre Bourdieu's imprint with Éditions de Minuit, "Le Sens Commun," with a preface by Jean-Claude Passeron and a title surprisingly different from the original: *La Culture du pauvre* (The culture of the poor person). For several years, Bourdieu and Passeron had been collaborating on studying "the uses of literacy'" (to use Hoggart's original title) in different situations and different places—schools, universities, museums—following an approach that cut across the social classes. By substituting the simplifying and categorizing singular ("the poor person") for a plural liable to misunderstanding or even to a potentially pejorative interpretation ("We taught them to read and this is how they've used . . . this instrument of liberation!"), the French title made it possible to pigeonhole Hoggart's book, to slant its reception, and to more effectively integrate the contributions of English cultural sociology with French research.[50] In short, to make it a complement rather than a competitor.

Yet there was quite a distance between the method followed by the English sociologist, which was subjective, empathic, intuitive—literary, as it were—and that of Bourdieu and Passeron, who claimed to achieve uncompromising objectivity and scientific rigor by using academic rhetoric, a specialized vocabulary, and charts and statistics based on apparently exhaustive surveys—all features of a technical nature that were totally absent from Hoggart's work.

This was a question of a difference not only of method, but of content. Neither Hoggart nor Williams had called into question the preeminent value of literary high culture, to which, on the contrary, they explicitly paid tribute. The situation is entirely different with Bourdieu and Passeron: they say nothing about literature's own value or what it represents to them, in this respect keeping perfect axiological neutrality and epistemological distance. On the other hand, their entire discourse aims to show that this literary culture that is so highly praised is ultimately an instrument of power in the hands of the dominant social classes. It has no value in and of itself (or at least this value has no impact on the process described); it does not serve to shape students' sense of aesthetics and morals in one way or another; it does not enrich their lives; it does not aim to give meaning to the world in which they live; it does not serve to give them the language and common references that will allow them to become integrated into society.

In fact, it is the opposite: literature only serves as a tool of distinction between the social classes; it is only the shibboleth by which elites reproduce themselves, the sign of recognition by which well-off students find their way in the system, the instrument of cultural segregation, the most manifest proof of the hypocrisy or failure of the democratic ambitions of the French republican school:

> But one cannot account for the pre-eminent value the French system sets on literary aptitude and, more precisely, on the capacity for turning all experience, not least literary experience, into literary discourse; in short, everything that goes to make up the French way of living the literary—and sometimes even the scientific—life like a Parisian life, unless one sees that this intellectual tradition nowadays still fulfills a social function in the functioning of the educational system and in the equilibrium of its relations with the intellectual field and the different social classes.[51]

Literature is an empty object, without content; a pure stylistic effect, as it were, which has remained useful in the educational system only as the distinguishing feature of an inherited linguistic and cultural capital. One piece of evidence is that teachers have a tendency, paradoxically, to value aspects of their students' work that do not directly relate to school and are not taught there: when they write "academic" in the margin of a student's essay, it is anything but a sign of approval; the disdain expressed by the institution for what relates to the institution itself ratifies its own defeat as an instrument of social mobility, in so far as, in a pernicious and painful way for the student concerned, it only considers that this student has "complete possession" of the culture when this culture "has been acquired by familiarization," namely not at school but in the context of a family belonging to the "dominant classes."[52] The institution is thus enlisted to perpetuate a preexisting order, and the aesthetic of the pure work of art, as it was promoted in the nineteenth century, is the preferred ideological tool of this recruiting, since it turns literature into an autotelic object that has no other aim than to formally distinguish itself from other discourses. Literature is the ultimate sign of distinction, as well as its symbol.

Admittedly, Bourdieu and Passeron sometimes recognize that other bodies of knowledge can, in certain circumstances, take on this "function of social distinction": for example, "econometrics," "computer science," and "the latest thing in structuralism." But the primacy that the French education system gives to "the social function of culture (scientific as well as literary culture) over the technical function of competence" ensures literature an eminent position as the very symbol of gratuitous knowledge, and it is to literature, as well as to the arts in general, that the two sociologists devote most of their analyses.[53]

In this line of reasoning, they prove to be no less the heirs than the victims of the aesthetic discourse that empties literature of any content. It is true that without content, literature no longer has a literal sense and that, without a literal meaning, its relevance can only be measured on a higher level, that of society considered as a whole, as a distinguishing feature inside the system of social signs.[54] "What would become of the literary world," Bourdieu asks, "if one began to argue, not about the value of this or that author's style, but about the value of arguments about style? The game is over when people start wondering if the cake is worth the candle."[55]

Yes, of course—but this would only be true if literature were *just* a game, if it did not express a vision of the world, a particular celebration or denunciation of the gods, humankind, existence, what have you, and if it did not take on a hygienic or medical function.[56] If literature should prove to have a purpose other than a purely aesthetic function, a good part of the argument against it would collapse, and sociologists would have as little interest in it as a sign of distinction as they do in econometrics or computer science.

Strictly speaking, Bourdieu and Passeron's discourse is not anti-literary; Bourdieu even occasionally felt the need to express his wariness of politicians who confine "the dispossessed" to their cultural enclaves, as well as his personal admiration for the great works and their capacity to transform society.[57] But aesthetic value as a value (which is not the same thing as its value as a sign) and the very meaning of literary works are simply eliminated from his sociological system of explanation, or considered at best a negligible quantity, and he supplies all the tools for literature to be sidelined in education.[58]

This was obviously not the objective: Bourdieu and Passeron's project was primarily focused on a critique of so-called democratic schools.[59] But since they do not provide the slightest hint of a possible solution or reform; since they reduce the multiple, complex relations of domination permeating society to a single one that operates unilaterally; since their fundamentally pessimistic discourse describes static situations, with no evolution and without exception, without showing the marginal successes that nevertheless confer a modicum of legitimacy on the system and contribute to modifying the composition of society and the distribution of cultural capital in the long run, there seems to be no other way out than the complete abrogation of the system and the disappearance of literature as an academic subject, in order to put an end to the unfair discriminations that it causes. This argument provides literature's opponents with powerful weapons.

THE MORAL OF THE STORY is that literature does not adequately reflect the whole of society. When the regime is aristocratic, literature is criticized for not being aristocratic enough and not belonging to the clan of the powerful; when it is democratic, it is accused of being elitist and contributing to the system's flaws. In short, it always seems inadequate relative to some political demand: not aristocratic enough, not democratic enough. Everywhere, under every regime, the writer is scorned, or is considered dangerous, or is denounced as the blind servant of a reprehensible system. In any case, this proves that the problem is not so much an essential or permanent lack of democracy on the part of literature as its lack of power: its powerlessness makes it the ideal scapegoat.

Plato recommended that the guardians of the republic not devote themselves to imitative poetry, that is to theater, which would lead them to play parts unworthy of them: he considered that poetic fiction carried an uncontrollable subversive charge, liable to topple the order on which society was founded—the opposite of the accusation made by Bourdieu and Passeron, who see it as a conservative tool for perpetuating social inequalities, because, unlike Plato and his contemporaries, they do not believe in the content of fictional works.[60]

However, the conclusion is one and the same: poetry (or *The Princesse de Clèves*) is useless. No city ever tried to keep within its walls Homer, Hesiod, or the other poets who were circulating throughout Greece, unlike the sophists and wise men, for whom fortunes were paid.[61] No one in a government building has ever asked the ticket clerk what she thinks of Madame de La Fayette. It is as if the arguments against literature have less weight than the conclusion, and that the conclusion is always predetermined: literature's social fragility and its status as an unprofitable activity in the republic expose it to every accusation and every proscription.

Yet two thousand five hundred years have passed and literature is still here, different, of course, and endowed with incomparable forms and functions, but present, alive, and current. Anti-literature is also here, in perfect symbiosis, to limit literature's powers and uses, define its outlines, suggest the dangers it poses, and lament its failures. The trial brought against literature in the name of society less often underlines its strength than its weakness and impotence: a good reason to keep reading and writing it—differently.

Conclusion
The Hidden Face of Literature

Is it worth giving anti-literature so much attention and building a monument to it, in the fashion of Bouvard and Pécuchet? It might be a mistake to give too much credit to what are most often minority discourses, which stand out against the general acceptance of literature.

However, one should also not underestimate the importance of anti-literary discourses: they reveal something about the opposite camp by exposing the dynamic of tensions and conflicts within literary discourse, the expectations it arouses or disappoints, the antagonisms it creates, and the limits that some would like to place on it. This is the hidden face of the history of literature, in which the stirrings of other competing discourses appear: philosophy, the natural sciences, the social sciences.

Additionally, one should not be deceived by the relatively small number of these anti-literary statements. Their mere existence is evidence of hostility against literature that has most often remained silent, and for good reason: anti-literature is not designed to be expressed in books and texts; it is silent out of principle or necessity (when the attacker is illiterate); its most general form is a plain refusal to read. Anti-literary discourse reveals the tip of an iceberg whose actual size will probably remain forever unknown.

There is more continuity in anti-literature than in literature. An understanding of the historical meaning of this kind of discourse is complicated by the fact that it often repeats old topics and arguments, the vast majority of which can already be found in Plato: real innovation is rare in anti-literature. Its discourse is difficult to interpret when it repeats out of their original context accusations that only made sense in Athens in the fourth century BCE. The anti-literary tradition inaugurated by Plato has lingered on, while at the same time literature has been completely transformed, along with its functions, responsibilities, and status.

This nearly insurmountable gulf reveals both the specificity of the ancient discourses and our modern singularities. Whence that frequent, persistent feeling that anti-literary arguments fall flat, that they tilt at windmills—or at an entirely fabricated opponent. The fact is that they were not conceived for the object that they are supposed to address.

All the more reason to avoid trying to systematically detect the objective reflection of the literature of a period in its anti-literature. Yet since the choice of arguments is often arbitrary, it is also a reason to look at the motivations for selecting one of these arguments over another.

ANTI-LITERATURE is not impervious to the expectations, fears, and obsessions of the various periods in which it asserts itself. This is the case with the charge of homosexuality (or sodomy), which sometimes presents itself in an attenuated form as a reproach against individual or collective effeminacy: recall C. P. Snow and his praise for the hetero-sexual ruggedness particular to scientists, or Rousseau, who believed all of society was at risk of becoming soft and losing its virile virtue every time it yielded to the temptations of literature and the arts.

Orpheus, who was simultaneously the first poet and the first sod-omite, serves as the founding myth of this accusation. Paradoxically, this charge appears nowhere in Antiquity: the first traces of it are found in the fifteenth century, and it persists through the twentieth century, covering the major period of modern homophobia. Yet the suppression of homosexuality had begun centuries earlier; other factors probably needed to come into play to seal the holy alliance between anti-literature and homophobia, including the crisis of the lettered class in the fifteenth century and the emergence of a new status of the literary text and of the author.

In any case, the history of anti-literature cannot be reduced to the interplay of simple deterministic factors.

DESPITE THE FACT that the four trials perpetually faced by literature are repeated century after century, the same arguments being rehashed with infinite, minor variations, they are not evenly distributed throughout history: there are specific time periods in which a certain trial, a certain argument, or a certain indictment is more likely to be heard, though not to the exclusion of the others.

It is possible to suggest, in an exploratory and experimental way, that the four trials could therefore be said to correspond with four historical phases or four ideological environments, each of which highlights a different function or possible aspect of literature:

—literature as authority: in these periods, in these cultures, certain usages of language, even language as a whole, retain their sacred aura. Remember that the poets were in contact with the Muses; certain texts, such as the Bible or the oracles, are transcendent. This is how ancient Greece, Late Antiquity, and the Early Middle Ages appear to us.

—literature as vision: this is the secularized version of the previous phase. The works—such as plays, epic poems, and novels—are supposed to produce a copy of reality, at the risk of the copy taking the place of reality; philosophy and the sciences develop. This is classical Greece, modernity in the widest sense, the positivist nineteenth century, the technocratic twentieth century.

—literature as action: these are the great eras of the development of religious rhetoric or reform; the typical texts are the epigram and the sermon. A notable example is the period from the Renaissance to the eighteenth century.

—literature as individual or collective expression: the typical texts are the essay in the style of Montaigne and the memoir, even the autofiction, in which aristocratic or democratic subjectivity asserts itself. This period stretches from modernity to the contemporary era.

THE VAGUENESS of this chaotic classification and these descriptions sketched in broad outline, as well as their open-ended, schematic, and heterogeneous character, should serve as a deliberate warning against any temptation to believe that these four idealized periods are mutually exclusive or to consider that they occur in a strict chronological succession. The periods are all the more difficult to define given that anti-literary discourse is sometimes aimed at an earlier, obsolete state of literature: this was even the case with Plato, who attacked a state of poetry that was already partially outdated when he was writing, and that he mythologized in order to create an opponent worthy of himself.

The danger would be to solidify these various conceptions and ignore the intersections, continuities, reverberations, afterlives (the *Nachleben* of Aby Warburg), and revivals that are always at work.[1] What we are considering here are potentialities of literature that are more or less exploited in the discourses that deal with it.

THESE POTENTIALITIES are all the more numerous given that literature does not have a proper definition.

Our current conception of literature, focused on the novel, poetry, theater, and the essay, is relatively recent. It was not until toward the end of the eighteenth century that the word *literature* (or its equivalents) finally eliminated its rivals in the European languages and began to be used in reference to such a heterogeneous body of texts. Previously, the appellations *letters* and *belles-lettres* were used; even earlier, that of *poetry;* but most of the time there was no general term to refer to so many different kinds of texts as a clearly identified group: at the time, writing was thought of as falling into distinct categories, or genres, and included the sciences.

It is more than likely that the reason there was no such overall designation is that people did not feel a need for it. The end of the eighteenth century coincided with the emergence of the different fields of knowledge as distinct territories. This endeavor in definition led to the sudden need to name what did not have a real name.

In Latin, *litteratura* initially meant *writing* (*littera* refers to the letter); by extension, the word was then used to refer to the science of writing, that is to say, grammar or philology; by another kind of extension, it also referred to what had been put down in writing or what could be drawn from a written text—in other words, knowledge and erudition, including the sciences. This very broad sense of the term endured until the modern era.

At the end of the eighteenth century, the term *literature* could therefore refer to writing par excellence, with a capital W. Yet fundamentally, *literature* was a name used by default because no more specific word was available. Its meaning was even more general than that of its predecessor, *belles-lettres,* which was itself more general than *poetry. Belles-lettres* emphasized the aesthetic dimension, with the idea of a more or less precise consensus about what was beautiful. *Literature* did not involve any idea of this type, or any real definition.[2]

TODAY, the impossibility of being assigned a positive definition seems to be literature's strength, if not its raison d'être. It is the result of the particular history it has followed since its very beginnings, which can be summed up as an enterprise that is perpetually renewed through dispossession[3] or through a conceptual hollowing-out. This does not date back to the triumph of the term *literature* in the eighteenth century; its beginnings can be found much earlier, when the first critical treatises were published.

In the *Poetics,* for example, Aristotle wanted to exclude from poetry proper all works, including those in verse, that fell within particular fields of knowledge, including medicine, natural science, philosophy, and history; even though Empedocles wrote in verse, he was no longer to be called a poet, but a naturalist. Had Herodotus chosen to write his *Histories* in verse rather than prose, he should nevertheless be known as a historian, not a poet.[4] Admittedly, Aristotle was seeking to give poetry a positive definition, based on mimesis, but in his case, this attempt seems much less convincing than his wish to define poetry from the exterior, from its boundaries. Outside of poetry, according to Aristotle, lies the territory of exact knowledge and real events; inside, well, there is just the remainder, which is indefinable.

In a similar way, the entire history of Western literature since its beginnings is characterized by successive restrictions and limitations applied to literature, which finds itself regularly expelled from territories it had previously occupied. Anti-literature has been a driving force in this process by its effect not so much on literary production in and of itself as on the reading and reception of works: when texts are reputed to have no claim to authority, truth, or morality and to no longer represent society, what do they have left to offer? Nothing more than words, language, sentences, writing.

Literature is what remains when everything has been removed, an irreducible residue that endures because there is always scrap—discourse that no one knows what to do with. Cold comfort.

SO GOES THE OFFICIAL HISTORY, the apparent history of literature, the one that centuries of anti-literature would have us believe, the one many thinkers and many critics have believed in up to the present day: literature as a pure use of language. People speak of *poetic function, literality,* and *formalism.* In this scenario, literature has been reduced to its essence.[5]

Yet there is no chronology that points toward a uniform impoverishment of the literary fact: history goes through ups and downs.[6] There is no reduction to any kind of essence: the essence is an illusion. Yes, the will to root out every possible essence, every power from literature has undoubtedly existed at times and probably still does. But literary works nonetheless continue to speak with authority, to present truths, to put forward ethical models, to express the will and the opinions of individuals and peoples.

These works speak of the world, of humans, gods, politics, hearts and feelings, memories and the future, what did not and will never take place, and what might happen after all. They invoke the gods and make them appear, they transport us through time, space, and the mind, heal the sick, cure the possessed, poison the healthy, send the rich home empty-handed and enrich them, overthrow the powerful and keep them in power, elevate the humble or belittle them. They create new universes and new cities, rename the real, transform it, abolish it, idealize it, leave it intact. They make me exist, bring me into the private world of a reader one thousand leagues and one thousand years away, create and destroy both invisible communities and real friendships. They immortalize this bare tree outside my window, the birdsong I hear in the depths of winter, the cold blue of the sky, the clicking of the keyboard on which I type in the frenzy of the man reaching the end of his book. They express fatigue and energy, black and white, light and dark, good and evil, soft and hard, high and low, love and hate, everything and its opposite. In short, they continue to do everything that they were forbidden to do for centuries, through endless trials; and they do far more beyond that, which we have not the slightest idea of and won't discover until much later—if ever.

They do this as they have always done, that is to say without legitimacy, without method, without a fuss.

Literature is the ultimate illegitimate discourse.

EVEN IF ABSURD, unjust, or anachronistic, anti-literature affirms the existence of that which it opposes; it demonstrates literature's strength and power, whatever they may be, and pays it a paradoxical form of homage.

Far worse indeed than the hatred of literature would be indifference: may the gods prevent that day from ever arriving.

Notes

Introduction

1. At least if one is to believe Plato.

2. William Marx, *L'Adieu à la littérature: histoire d'une dévalorisation (XVIIIe–XXe siècles)* (Paris: Éditions de Minuit, 2005). See also Reinhard Baumgart, *Addio: Abschied von der Literatur: Variationen über ein altes Thema* (Munich: Hanser, 1995); Laurent Nunez, *Les Écrivains contre l'écriture (1900–2000)* (Paris: Corti, 2006), and *Si je m'écorchais vif* (Paris: Grasset, 2015). Often, the use of the term *anti-literature* has been restricted to discourse originating in literature itself (see, for example, Adrian Marino, "Tendances esthétiques," in Jean Weisgerber, ed., *Les Avant-gardes littéraires au XXe siècles*, 2 vols. [Amsterdam: John Benjamins, 1984], 2:678–685). This will not be the case in this volume, which deals nearly exclusively with nonliterary anti-literature.

3. Admittedly, one can find acoustic anti-music (musique concrète, for instance) or visual anti-painting (Marcel Duchamp), but these fall within the realm of art, or are at the very least eventually reintegrated into art. The medium of language raises the modern question of art with much sharper contrast.

4. The first to attempt a systematic survey of these anti-literary discourses is Adrian Marino in his *Biography of "The Idea of Literature" from Antiquity to the Baroque*, trans. Virgil Stanciu and Charles M. Carlton (Albany: State University of New York Press, 1996), to which this volume owes a great deal; each historical part ends with a section entitled "Denying Literature." I must also not forget to mention the great precursor, Abbé Simon-Augustin Irail, and his *Querelles littéraires ou mémoires pour servir à l'histoire des révolutions de la république des lettres, depuis Homère jusqu'à nos jours* (Paris: Durand, 1761), published in four methodically organized volumes.

5. On the dispute against theater, see Laurent Thirouin, *L'Aveuglement salutaire: le réquisitoire contre le théâtre dans la France classique* (Paris: Champion, 1997). A symposium organized by François Lecercle and Clotilde Touret on "the hatred of theater" from Antiquity to the nineteenth century was recently held at the Université Paris-Sorbonne (October 23–25, 2014); the proceedings are forthcoming from Garnier. On the polemic over fiction, see Teresa Chevrolet, *L'Idée de*

fable: théories de la fiction poétique à la Renaissance (Geneva: Droz, 2007); Anne Duprat and Teresa Chevrolet, "La Bataille des fables: conditions de l'émergence d'une théorie de la fiction en Europe (XIVᵉ–XVIIᵉ siècles)," in Françoise Lavocat and Anne Duprat, eds., *Fictions et Cultures* (Paris: Société française de littérature générale et comparée, 2010), 291–308.

Words from Elsewhere

1. *The Iliad of Homer,* trans. Richmond Lattimore (1951; Chicago: University of Chicago Press, 2011), 8.293–299. This is the translation used for quotations from *The Iliad* throughout this chapter. Lattimore's spellings of proper names are retained in quotations. Unless otherwise noted, all other translations were translated into French by the author and subsequently into English by the translator.

2. A scene from Alfred Hitchcock's 3D film *Dial M for Murder* (1954). On the role of deictics and enunciative effects in Greek poetry, see Egbert J. Bakker, "Homeric *Hoûtos* and the Poetics of Deixis," *Classical Philology* 94, no. 1 (January 1999): 1–19, and *Pointing to the Past: From Formula to Performance in Homeric Poetics* (Cambridge, MA: Center for Hellenic Studies, 2005), 71–91, 154–176; see also Claude Calame, "Deictic Ambiguity and Auto-Referentiality: Some Examples from Greek Poetics," *Aruthesa* 37, no. 3 (2004): 415–443, and *Masques d'autorité: fiction et pragmatique dans la poétique grecque antique* (Paris: Belles Lettres, 2005), esp. 13–40.

3. *Iliad* 8.300–301.

4. See William Marx, "Valéry, Flaubert, et les oiseaux qui marchent: généalogie d'une image," *Revue d'histoire littéraire de la France* 103, no. 4 (2003): 919–931. Translation by Cecil Day-Lewis in *Le Cimetière marin / The Graveyard by the Sea* (London: Secker & Warburg, 1946).

5. *Iliad* 3.166–170, 178–179.

6. *Odyssey* 8.489–492. Translation by Richmond Lattimore, from *The Odyssey of Homer* (New York: Harper & Row, 1965). Subsequent English translations are also from this edition.

7. *Odyssey* 8.487–488, 496–500.

8. *Translator's note:* Rimbaud's original phrase was "Je est un autre."

9. The reader will have recognized a variation on the myth of the invention of literature as so engagingly told by Nabokov: the Neanderthal child crying wolf

without having a wolf on his trail. See *Lectures on Literature* (New York: Harcourt Brace Jovanovich, 1980).

10. Stéphane Mallarmé, "Avant-Dire" au *Traité du verbe* par René Ghil (1886). *Translator's note:* English translation from "Stéphane Mallarmé," Poetry Foundation website, https://www.poetryfoundation.org/poems-and-poets/poets/detail /stephane-mallarme#poet.

11. Mallarmé, "The Tomb of Edgar Poe," trans. Mary Ann Caws, in *Selected Poetry and Prose,* ed. Mary Ann Caws (New York: New Directions, 1982).

12. *Iliad* 1.1; *Odyssey* 1.1.

13. *Iliad* 2.485–492.

14. Hesiod, *Theogony* 27, 32.

15. Homeric hymns to Hermes, Aphrodite, Artemis, to the mother of the gods, and to Pan.

16. *Iliad* 1.1–7.

17. For a detailed analysis of the various situations of utterance, see C. Calame, *Le Récit en Grèce ancienne: énonciations et représentations de poètes* (Paris: Méridiens Klincksieck, 1986), 37–43.

18. See Penelope Murray, "Poetic Inspiration in Early Greece," *Journal of Hellenic Studies* 101 (1981): 87–100.

19. See Ann Banfield, *Unspeakable Sentences* (London: Routledge & Kegan Paul, 1982).

20. *The Shadow over Innsmouth* (1936).

21. See Pausanias, *Description of Greece* 9.29.2–3, and more generally, on the Muses as bearers of truth, Marcel Detienne, *Les Maîtres de vérité dans la Grèce archaïque* (1967; Paris: Livre de Poche, 2006), 59–84; Roberto Calasso, *La Folie qui vient des nymphes,* trans. Jean-Paul Manganaro (Paris: Flammarion, 2012).

22. Plutarch, *The Oracles at Delphi No Longer Given in Verse* 24.406c. Translation by Frank Cole Babbitt, in *Moralia, Volume V,* Loeb Classical Library 306 (Cambridge, MA: Harvard University Press, 1936).

23. Paul Valéry, *The Pythoness,* in *Charms* (1922). Translation by David Paul in *Collected Works of Paul Valéry,* vol. 1 (Princeton: Princeton University Press, 1971), 177.

24. *Odyssey* 22.347–348. Adapted by the author from the translation by Richmond Lattimore.

First Trial: Authority

1. Homeric *Hymn to Selene*, line 20.

2. See the Prologue. Plato, *The Republic* 3.398a.

3. Epistle to the Romans 7:7.

4. Let us recall here what was said in the Introduction, namely that for the sake of linguistic convenience, in this volume the word *literature* refers to what was historically referred to as such as of the late eighteenth century, a term that was also applied retroactively.

5. Xenophanes of Colophon frag. 1, in *Fragments,* ed. J. H. Lesher (Toronto: University of Toronto Press, 2001).

6. Frag. 10 and 11. See also frag. 12.

7. See Glenn Most, "What Ancient Quarrel between Philosophy and Poetry?" in Pierre Destrée and Fritz-Gregor Herrmann, eds., *Plato and the Poets* (Leiden: Brill, 2011), 4-5.

8. Heraclitus of Ephesus DK 40. Updated from the translation by John Burnet in *Early Greek Philosophy* (London: A. and C. Black, 1920). All quotations from Heraclitus in this chapter are from this translation.

9. Heraclitus DK 57.

10. Heraclitus DK 88, 67, and 60.

11. Heraclitus DK 42.

12. See the inscription of Paros, in Archilochus, *Fragments,* ed. François Lasserre (Paris: Belles Lettres, Collection des Universités de France, 1968), p. cv; Douglas E. Gerber, ed. and trans., *Greek Iambic Poetry: From the Seventh to the Fifth Centuries BC,* Loeb Classical Library 259 (Cambridge, MA: Harvard University Press, 1999), 18-21.

13. See Plutarch's account in Archilochus, *Fragments,* pp. cvii–cviii; Gerber, ed. and trans., *Greek Iambic Poetry,* 40-41.

14. Heraclitus DK 56.

15. See Heraclitus DK 1 and 50.

16. See Alfred and Maurice Croiset, *Histoire de la littérature grecque,* 2 vols. (Paris: Thorin, 1887–1899), 2:469–471.

17. Heraclitus DK 92.

18. See Heraclitus DK 73 and 89.

19. The bibliography on Plato's condemnation of poetry is considerable. In particular, see Thomas Gould, *The Ancient Quarrel Between Poetry and Philosophy*

(Princeton: Princeton University Press, 1990); Penelope Murray, ed., *Plato on Poetry* (Cambridge, UK: Cambridge University Press, 1996); Susan B. Levin, *The Ancient Quarrel between Philosophy and Poetry Revisited: Plato and the Greek Literary Tradition* (Oxford: Oxford University Press, 2001), 127–167; Ramona A. Naddaff, *Exiling the Poets: The Production of Censorship in Plato's "Republic"* (Chicago: University of Chicago Press, 2002); P. Destrée and F.-G. Herrmann, eds., *Plato and the Poets*.

20. Plato, *The Republic* 3.398a. Translation by Allan Bloom in *The Republic of Plato* (1968; New York: Basic Books, 2016). All quotations from *The Republic* below are from this translation.

21. Plato, *The Republic* 3.398a–b.

22. Ibid. 3.389b.

23. Plato, *Ion* 534b. Translation updated from W. R. M. Lamb in Plato, *Statesman, Philebus, Ion,* trans. H. N. Fowler and W. R. M. Lamb, Loeb Classical Library 164 (Cambridge, MA: Harvard University Press, 1925).

24. In *Meno* (99c–d), Socrates defines as "divine" those "who, having no intelligence, yet succeed in many a great deed and word." These include the prophets, soothsayers, poets, and statesmen.

25. See Laurent Nunez's beautiful remark about Plato's "rejection of authorship" in *Si je m'écorchais vif* (Paris: Grasset, 2015), 68.

26. See Marcel Detienne, *Les Maîtres de vérité dans la Grèce archaïque* (1967; Paris: Livre de Poche, 2006), 8.

27. Plato, *The Republic* 10.614b, 10.620c–d.

28. See ibid. 10.620b; and *Odyssey* 11.542–564. The numerical coincidence (despite the fact that the accuracy of the count in *The Odyssey* is debatable) is noted by Bloom, *Republic of Plato,* 436.

29. Leo Strauss, *The City and the Man* (Charlottesville: University Press of Virginia, 1964).

30. Diogenes Laertius, *Life of Plato,* 5, in *Lives of Eminent Philosophers,* vol. 1, trans. R. D. Hicks, Loeb Classical Library 184 (Cambridge, MA: Harvard University Press, 1925).

31. This thesis partially echoes Arthur C. Danto's argument in *The Philosophical Disenfranchisement of Art* (New York: Columbia University Press, 1986).

32. Isocrates, *Evagoras* 11, adapted from the translation by La Rue Van Hook, in *Isocrates,* vol. 3, Loeb Classical Library 373 (Cambridge, MA: Harvard University

Press, 1945). This is a characteristic example of "anticipatory plagiarism," to which Pierre Bayard has devoted a book: *Le Plagiat par anticipation* (Paris: Éditions de Minuit, 2009).

33. Isocrates, *Antidosis* 166.

34. On the absence of a unifying mythology in Greece, see C. Calame's brilliant reflections in *Qu'est ce que la mythologie grecque?* (Paris: Gallimard, Folio, 2015), esp. 23–76.

35. Plato, *Laws,* 7.817 b–d. Translation by Tom Griffith, in Malcolm Schofield, ed. (Cambridge, UK: Cambridge University Press, 2016).

36. This is precisely the paradox of the "gap" between Antiquity and us, as theorized by Florence Dupont: both inside and outside. See F. Dupont, *L'Antiquité, territoire des écarts* (Paris: Albin Michel, 2015), 291.

37. Matthew 11:25 (King James version).

38. 1 Corinthians 1:17; 19–20. Paul quotes Isaiah 29:14. The biblical quote has been revised by the author to be closer to the Greek.

39. On the complicated historical relationship between Christianity and literary culture, see Helmut Richard Niebuhr, *Christ and Culture* (New York: Harper, 1951).

40. Jerome, letter 70, to Magnus; quoted by Michel Zink, "La vérité à la lettre: foi, poésie, vérité," in Olivier Guerrier, ed., *La Vérité* (Saint-Étienne: Publications de l'Université de Saint-Étienne, 2014), 19. Jerome still seems to be trying to exorcise the famous dream in which God had accused him of being "Ciceronian, rather than Christian" (letter 22.30).

41. Augustine of Hippo, *On Christian Doctrine* 2.40.60; quoted by Zink, "La vérité à la lettre."

42. Isidore of Seville, *Sentences* 3.13.2–4. The reference is to the Second Epistle to the Corinthians 4:7.

43. Isidore, *Sentences* 3.13.8.

44. Ibid. 3.13.7.

45. Psalm 70:15–16, quoted by Isidore, *Sentences* 3.13.9.

46. See *La Bible de Jérusalem: édition de référence* (Paris: Fleurus / Cerf, 2001), 1236 note hp.

47. Augustine, *Expositions of the Psalms* 70.19.

48. Isidore, *Sentences* 3.13.11.

49. See the Third Trial.

50. Gregory I the Great, letter to Leander of Seville 5.516b, in *Morals on the Book of Job,* trans. John R. C. Martyn, in *The Letters of Gregory the Great* (Toronto: Pontifical Institute of Mediaeval Studies, 2004).

51. Ibid. 5.516c.

52. Gregory I the Great, *Morals on the Book of Job* 18.46.74. Quoted and translated into French by Claude Dagens in "Grégoire le Grand et la culture: de la *'sapientia huius mundi'* à la *'docta ignorantia,'"* *Revue des études augustiniennes* 14, no. 1–2 (1968): 17–26. English translation from the French.

53. Guibert of Nogent, *On the Relics of Saints* 1. Translated by Joseph McAlhany and Jay Rubenstein in *Monodies and On the Relics of Saints* (New York: Penguin Books, 2011), 217.

54. Pierre Damien, *Letters,* in *Patrologia latina* 144 col. 76 (Reindel no. 21, 2): "mea igitur grammatica Christus est."

55. Ecclesiastes 12:11. This is from the Vulgate.

56. I have borrowed these significant examples of the use of the word "poet" in the Middle Ages from Zink, "La vérité à la lettre," 20–22.

57. Thomas Aquinas, *Summa Theologiae* 1a.1.9 arg. 1. Quoted by Umberto Eco in *The Aesthetics of Thomas Aquinas,* trans. Hugh Bredin (Cambridge, MA: Harvard University Press, 1988). The translation used here and below is by the Fathers of the English Dominican Province (New York: Benzinger, 1947–1948).

58. Aquinas, *Summa Theologiae* 1a.1.9 co.

59. Ibid. 1a.1.9 ad 2. The reference is to Matthew 7:6.

60. Ibid. 1a.1.9 ad 3.

61. Ibid. 1a–2ae.101.2 ad 2. Quoted by Eco, *Aesthetics of Thomas Aquinas.*

62. See the Third Trial.

63. These reflections on Ancient Rome owe a great deal, including in their form, to my exchanges with Florence Dupont, whom I warmly thank for her luminous remarks. I am, however, solely responsible for the opinions expressed.

Second Trial: Truth

1. Charles Percy Snow, *The Two Cultures* (1959; Cambridge, UK: Cambridge University Press, 1993), 13–15.

2. The French translation of C. P. Snow's lecture, by Claude Noël, was not published until 1968, by Jean-Jacques Pauvert, under the title *Les Deux Cultures* (The

two cultures), in the "Libertés nouvelles" collection edited by Jean-François Revel, which notably included works by Tristan Tzara, Henry David Thoreau, and Jean Paulhan. This time-lag in the lecture's reception may have something to do with the fact that this debate was nothing new in France, where the technocratic culture of which Snow was a perfect example had long ago triumphed. From the beginning of the twentieth century, the traditional humanities had been classified in the category of social sciences (see the beautiful text by Jean Starobinski, "Scientific Language and Poetic Language," in Walter Rüegg, ed., *Meeting the Challenges of the Future: A Discussion between "The Two Cultures,"* Balzan Symposium 2002 [Florence: Olschki, 2003], 21–32, 63–64); in schools, the division between literature and sciences had been a reality for decades (perhaps even since the introduction in 1852 of the "bifurcation," a reform that gave science a new prominence in the secondary school curriculum: see Paul Aron and Alain Viala, *L'Enseignement littéraire* [Paris: Presses universitaires de France, 2005], 52–54); and the polemic against literature had been carried out by writers themselves for nearly a century (see William Marx, *L'Adieu à la littérature: histoire d'une dévalorisation (XVIIIe–XXe siècles)* [Paris: Éditions de Minuit, 2005]). Additionally, the conceptual and stylistic vacuity of Snow's argument did not offer much to attract French intellectuals: you can catch more flies with honey than vinegar.

3. See Guy Ortolano, *The Two Cultures Controversy: Science, Literature, and Cultural Politics in Postwar Britain* (Cambridge, UK: Cambridge University Press, 2009), 60; Philip Snow, *Stranger and Brother: A Portrait of C. P. Snow* (London: Macmillan, 1982), 117.

4. See Stefan Collini, "Introduction," in Snow, *The Two Cultures*, vii–lxxiii.

5. Snow, *The Two Cultures*, 11–14, 23.

6. C. P. Snow, "The Two Cultures," *New Statesman and Nation*, October 6, 1956, 413. My italics. Harwell was the center for British nuclear research, Hampstead a bourgeois, intellectual area of London. Los Alamos and New York's Greenwich Village are the U.S. equivalents.

7. Ibid., 414. In the 1959 version, the comparison of Harwell and Hampstead is no longer present as such: with a change in perspective, it is replaced by the correspondence between Greenwich Village and Chelsea; the emphasis is now on the similarities between literary circles on either side of the Atlantic (*Two Cultures*, 2).

8. This argument has a long history: see the Third Trial.

9. Snow, *The Two Cultures*, 7.

10. Ibid., 7–8.

11. Snow, "The Two Cultures," 414.

12. Julien Benda, *La Trahison des clercs* (Paris: Grasset, 1927).

13. Julien Benda, *La France byzantine, ou le Triomphe de la littérature pure: Mallarmé, Gide, Valéry, Alain, Giraudoux, Suarès, les Surréalistes. Essai d'une psychologie originelle du littérateur* (Paris: Gallimard, 1945). C. P. Snow's critique of "Alexandrianism" is in "Challenge to the Intellect," *Times Literary Supplement,* August 15, 1958, iii.

14. Snow, "The Two Cultures," 414.

15. Theodor W. Adorno, *Prisms,* trans. Samuel and Shierry Weber (Cambridge, MA: MIT Press, 1981), 34. See Marx, *L'Adieu à la littérature,* 123–124.

16. T. W. Adorno, *Negative Dialectics,* trans. E. B. Ashton (New York: Continuum Publishing Company, 1973), 367.

17. Snow, *The Two Cultures,* 22.

18. Snow, "Challenge to the Intellect."

19. See Ortolano, *The Two Cultures Controversy,* 95.

20. Edith Sitwell, [untitled], *Spectator,* no. 6977, March 16, 1962, 331.

21. "The Two Cultures," *Spectator,* no. 6979, March 30, 1962, 387–388.

22. Frank Raymond Leavis, "The Two Cultures? The Significance of C. P. Snow," *Spectator,* no. 6976, March 9, 1962, 297. (Reprinted in Leavis, *Nor Shall My Sword: Discourses on Pluralism, Compassion, and Social Hope* [London: Chatto & Windus, 1972], 41.)

23. Ibid. (*Nor Shall My Sword,* 42).

24. Ibid., 297–298 (*Nor Shall My Sword,* 44–45).

25. Ibid., 299 (*Nor Shall My Sword,* 47).

26. See Collini, "Introduction," xx; Snow, *Stranger and Brother,* 35.

27. Snow, *The Two Cultures,* 44. Leavis, "The Two Cultures?" 300 (*Nor Shall My Sword,* 53).

28. Leavis, "The Two Cultures?" 303 (*Nor Shall My Sword,* 61–62).

29. Snow, "The Two Cultures: A Second Look," in *The Two Cultures,* 71. See also Wolf Lepenies, *Les Trois Cultures: entre science et littérature, l'avènement de la sociologie,* trans. Henri Plard (Paris: Éditions de la Maison des sciences de l'homme, 1990), 151–191.

30. Snow, *The Two Cultures,* 9.

31. This debate had been raging in the British academy since the nineteenth century, as described by Lepenies, *Les Trois Cultures.*

32. See the Fourth Trial.

33. Matthew Arnold, "Joubert" (1865), in *Selected Prose*, ed. P. J. Keating (1970; London: Penguin Books, 1987), 172; "The Study of Poetry," in ibid., 341. See, for example, F. R. Leavis, "Luddites? *Or* There Is Only One Culture" (1966), in *Nor Shall My Sword*, 97: "the judgments the literary critic is concerned with are judgments about life."

34. See Marx, *L'Adieu à la littérature*, 68–73.

35. Lionel Trilling, "Science, Literature, and Culture: A Comment on the Leavis–Snow Controversy," *Commentary*, June 1962, 461–477. See Collini, "Introduction," xxxviii–xl; Ortolano, *Two Cultures Controversy*, 198–200.

36. George Steiner, "F. R. Leavis," *Encounter* no. 104, May 1962, 37–45, collected in *Language and Silence: Essays on Language, Literature, and the Inhuman* (1967; New Haven: Yale University Press, 1998), 221–238. The passage quoted is on page 42 (*Language and Silence*, 233, with additional commentary by Steiner). French editions of *Language and Silence*, including the latest (*Langage et Silence* [Paris: Belles Lettres, 2010]), do not include this article, probably because both Leavis and the controversy about the "two cultures" are totally unknown in France—a state of ignorance which this omission does nothing to correct. On Steiner's relationship with Snow, see Ortolano, *Two Cultures Controversy*, 125–126.

37. See Ortolano, *Two Cultures Controversy*, 99.

38. Leavis, "The Two Cultures?" 297 (*Nor Shall My Sword*, 42).

39. Thomas Henry Huxley, "Science and Culture" (lecture delivered on October 1, 1880), in *Science and Culture, and Other Essays* (New York: Appleton, 1882), 7–30.

40. M. Arnold, "Literature and Science" (lecture delivered on June 14, 1882), in *Philistinism in England and America*, ed. R. H. Super (Ann Arbor: University of Michigan Press, 1974), 53–73 (with an abundant critical apparatus, 462–470, 546–554).

41. Trilling, "Science, Literature, and Culture," 461–462.

42. May the spirits of Karl Marx and George Santayana forgive me for grafting these quotes!

43. On these shifts in literature, see Marx, *L'Adieu à la littérature*.

44. On this, see Gilles Philippe, *Le Rêve du style parfait* (Paris: Presses Universitaires de France, 2013), 42–54.

45. Charles Maurras, lecture on Anatole France delivered at the Théâtre de l'Avenue on April 16, 1932, partially reprinted in "Renan (Ernest)" in *Dictionnaire politique et critique*, Pierre Chardon, ed. (Paris: À la cité des livres, 1932), 4:390.

46. Jules Huret, *Enquête sur l'évolution littéraire* (Paris: Charpentier, 1891), 420–421.

47. Ibid., 421–422.

48. Ibid., 422.

49. Arnold, "Literature and Science," 57. The allusion is to Ernest Renan, "Le petit séminaire Saint-Nicolas du Chardonnet" (1880), in *Souvenirs d'enfance et de jeunesse* (1883), reprinted in *Oeuvres complètes*, ed. Henriette Psichari (Paris: Calmann-Lévy, 1947–1961), 2:818. On Renan's criticism of what he calls the "superficial humanism" prevalent at the school, see Jean Seznec, "Renan et la philologie classique," in *Classical Influences on Western Thought, A.D. 1650–1870. Proceedings of an International Conference Held at King's College, Cambridge, March 1977*, ed. R. R. Bolgar (Cambridge, UK: Cambridge University Press, 1979), 349–362.

50. Ernest Renan, *L'Avenir de la science: pensées de 1848* (1890), reprinted in *Oeuvres complètes*, 3:804–805. Quoted by Marius-Ary Leblond (pseudonym of Marius and Ari Leblond), "Le Roman et la Science," *Revue universelle* (1902), 2:425.

51. Ernest Renan, "Probabilités" (1871), in *Dialogues et fragments philosophiques* (1876), reprinted in *Oeuvres complètes*, 1:599–600.

52. Ibid., 1:600.

53. Ibid.

54. Georg Wilhelm Friedrich Hegel, *Lectures on Aesthetics* (1835). Cited from the French edition, *Esthétique* (Paris: Librairie générale française, 1997), 2:401 (part 3, sect. 3, chap. 3, intro., 1). See Marx, *L'Adieu à la littérature*, 52–53.

55. Ernest Renan, "Prière sur l'Acropole" (1876), in *Souvenirs*, 759. See Marx, *L'Adieu à la littérature*, 57–59.

56. Jean Le Rond d'Alembert, "Réflexions sur la poésie, écrites à l'occasion des pièces que l'Académie française a reçues en 1760 pour le concours" (speech delivered on August 25, 1760), in *Oeuvres complètes* (Paris: Belin, 1822), 4:292.

57. D'Alembert personally notified Voltaire of the praise he had given him in his speech (letter dated September 2, 1760, D9184, in Voltaire, *Correspondence*, ed. Théodore Besterman, vol. 22, in *Complete Works* [Banbury: Voltaire Foundation, 1972], 106:88): "On the feast of Saint Louis, I read a piece against bad poets and in your honor at the Académie Française. I only found you to have two unforgivable failings, that of *being French and alive*. That is what I concluded with, and the audience applauded, much less for me than for you."

58. D'Alembert, "Réflexions," 297.

59. Ibid., 292.

60. Ibid., 294–295.

61. D'Alembert, "Discours lu à l'Académie française, le 25 Août 1771, avant la distribution des prix d'éloquence et de poésie," in *Oeuvres complètes,* 4:317–320.

62. D'Alembert, "Réflexions," 294.

63. Ibid., 295–296.

64. In 1675, Father René Le Bossu asked the question in an entirely theoretical manner (*Traité du poème épique* [1675], [Paris: Musier, 1708], 38–29): "If one wrote an epic in prose, would it be an epic poem? I do not think so, because a poem is a speech in verse. Nonetheless, that would not prevent it from being an epic; just as a tragedy in prose is not a tragic poem, and remains a tragedy." In 1731, Jean Soubeiran de Scopon pleaded at length for tragedies to be written in prose in his "Réflexions à l'occasion du *Brutus* de M. Voltaire, et de son discours sur la tragédie," *Mercure de France,* April 1731, 632–655. In the eighteenth century, criticism of versification had become such a commonplace in literary debates that it was sometimes—however paradoxically—expressed in verse, as was the case with Antoine Houdar de La Motte. See Jean Ranscelot, "Les manifestations du déclin poétique au début du XVIIIᵉ siècle," *Revue d'histoire littéraire de la France* 33 (1927): 497–520; Sylvain Menant, *La Chute d'Icare: la crise de la poésie française (1700–1750)* (Geneva: Droz, 1981), 47–110; Guillaume Peureux, *La Fabrique du vers* (Paris: Seuil, 2009), 367–439.

65. D'Alembert, "Suite des réflexions sur la poésie, et sur l'ode en particulier," in *Oeuvres complètes,* 4:301.

66. On Isocrates, see the First Trial in this book. Charles Perrault, *Parallèle des anciens et des modernes en ce qui regarde la poésie* (Paris: Coignard, 1692), 3:123–124. See Ranscelot, "Les manifestations du déclin poétique," 504–505.

67. Walter Benjamin, *The Concept of Criticism in German Romanticism,* trans. David Lachterman, Howard Eiland, and Ian Balfour, in *Selected Writings: 1913–1926* (Cambridge, MA: Belknap Press of Harvard University Press, 1996), 173.

68. Carl Gustav Jochmann, *Die Rückschritte der Poesie* (1828; Hamburg: Meiner, 1982). See Walter Benjamin, "'The Regression of Poetry' by Carl Gustav Jochmann," in *Selected Writings: 1938–1940,* ed. Howard Eiland and Michael W. Jennings (Cambridge, MA: Belknap Press of Harvard University Press, 2003), 356–381; Marx, *L'Adieu à la littérature,* 168–169.

69. "Lettre à M. Fréron sur la sortie que M. d'Alembert a fait le jour de la Saint-Louis à l'Académie Française contre la poésie et les poètes," *L'Année littéraire* (1760), 176.

70. Michel Paul Guy de Chabanon, *Sur le sort de la poésie en ce siècle philosophe* (Paris: Jorry, 1764), 7.

71. D'Alembert, "Réflexions," 292.

72. D'Alembert, "Discours," 315–316.

73. D'Alembert, "Dialogue entre la poésie et la philosophie, pour servir de préliminaire et de base a un traité de paix et d'amitiés perpétuelle entre l'une et l'autre," in *Oeuvres complètes*, 4:374–375.

74. Ibid., 4:380.

75. Plato, *The Republic* 2.378e–383c.

76. Ibid. 2.378a–e.

77. Ibid. 10.595a–607b.

78. Ibid. 10.607e–608b.

79. According to Glenn Most ("What Ancient Quarrel Between Poetry and Philosophy?" in Pierre Destrée and Fritz-Gregor Herrmann, eds., *Plato and the Poets* [Leiden: Brill, 2011], 1–20), the quarrel is not as old as Socrates claims: Plato only sought to give the antagonism between the two discourses an archetypal dimension.

80. *Republic* 10.607b–c.

81. Ibid. 7.521c.

82. Ibid. 7.522c–535a.

83. On this myth, see the First Trial.

84. D'Alembert, "Dialogues," 381.

85. Leonard da Vinci, *Codex Atlanticus*, fol. 327v; quoted by Giuseppina Fumagalli, *Leonardo, omo sanza lettere* (Florence: Sanzoni, 1952), 38. See Adrian Marino, "Tendances esthétiques," in Jean Weisgerber, ed., *Les Avant-gardes littéraires au XXᵉ siècles*, 2 vols. (Amsterdam: John Benjamins, 1984), 2:147.

86. Leonardo, *Codex Atlanticus*, fol. 207r. Translated by Jean Paul Richter in *Leonardo da Vinci: Notebooks*, ed. Irma Richter (1952; Oxford: Oxford University Press, 2008), 264. Adapted where necessary.

87. René Descartes, *Discourse on Method*, trans. Donald A. Cress (Indianapolis: Hackett Publishing Company, 1998), 4–6.

88. Lodovico Castelvetro, *Poetica d'Aristotele vulgarazitta e sposta*, ed. Werther Romani (Rome: Laterza, 1978), 1:45–46.

89. On the opposition between poetry and literature understood as knowledge, see the highly enlightening reflections of Adrian Marino in "Tendances esthétiques," 147–149, 197–200. See also the Fourth Trial.

90. Malherbe as quoted by Tallement des Réaux, *Historiettes,* ed. Antoine Adam, Bibliothèque de la Pléiade (Paris: Gallimard, 1960), 1:115.

91. Gregory Currie, "Let's Pretend: Literature and the Psychology Lab," *Times Literary Supplement,* no. 5657, September 2, 2011, 14–15.

92. This is Daniel Wegner's thesis, as described by Currie, "Let's Pretend," 15.

93. Marcel Proust, *Swann's Way,* trans. Lydia Davis (New York: Viking Penguin, 2003), 396.

94. Paul Valéry, *The Young Fate,* in *Collected Works of Paul Valéry,* trans. David Paul (Princeton, NJ: Princeton University Press, 1971), 1:69.

95. Currie, "Let's Pretend," 15.

96. Gregory Currie, "Does Great Literature Make Us Better?" *New York Times,* June 1, 2013, available at http://opinionator.blogs.nytimes.com/?s=Gregory+Currie. A version of this article was published in the print edition of the *New York Times* with the headline "Does Fiction Civilize Us?" February 6, 2013, SR12.

97. Carol Tavris, "Porch Companions" (review of David Brooks, *The Social Animal: A Story of How Success Happens*), *Times Literary Supplement* no. 5657, September 2, 2011, 13.

Third Trial: Morality

1. Bernard Lamy, *Nouvelles Réflexions sur l'art poétique* (Paris: Pralard, 1668), 108.

2. Tanneguy Le Fèvre, "Préface," in *Le Premier Alcibiade de Platon traduit en Français par M. Le Fèvre* (1666; Amsterdam: Rey, 1776), xi.

3. Ibid., xi–xii.

4. Romans 7:15. See Euripides, *Medea* lines 1074–1080.

5. Le Fèvre, "Préface," xiii–xiv.

6. Tanneguy Le Fèvre, *Méthode pour commencer les humanités grecques et latines* (1672; Paris: Brocas et Simon, 1731), 6–8.

7. Ibid., 66. The poems are on pages 66 and 71.

8. Ibid., 67.

9. Ibid.

10. François Graverol, *Mémoires pour servir à la vie de Tanneguy Le Fèvre* (1686), in Albert-Henri Sallengre, *Mémoires de littérature* (The Hague: Du Sauzet, 1717), vol. 2, part 2:16.

11. This debate is further discussed later in the chapter. See also Giovanni Saverio Santangelo, *Madame Dacier, una filologa nella crisi (1672–1720)* (Rome: Bulzoni, 1984).

12. See Santangelo, *Madame Dacier,* 41–42n26; Jean Ranscelot, "Les manifestations du déclin poétique au début du XVIIIᵉ siècle," *Revue d'histoire littéraire de la France* 33 (1927): 502–504.

13. Tanneguy Le Fèvre fils, *De futilitate poetices* (Amsterdam: Desbordes, 1697), table of contents (*Index capitum,* non-paginated). These quotations and the following are translated from the Latin.

14. Ibid., 2–3.

15. Ibid., 3.

16. Ibid. The passage from Juvenal is from *Satires* 1.1–4. Translated by Susanna Morton Braun, in *Juvenal and Persius* (Cambridge, MA: Harvard University Press, 2004), 131.

17. Le Fèvre fils, *De futilitate poetices,* 30–31.

18. See the Second Trial.

19. Le Fèvre fils, *De futilitate poetices,* 47. Condemnation of immoral poetry is a very old theme. In the Renaissance, the Carmelite Battista Spagnoli (or Baptist of Mantua) provides an interesting example in his poem *Against Poets Shameless of Speech* (*Contra poetas impudice loquentes,* 1489): expressed in verse, the accusation is leveled only at certain poets, not at poetry in general, for the blessed Baptist champions the existence of a Christian poetry. See the edition by Mariano Madrid Castro, in *Humanistica Lovaniensia,* vol. 45 (Leuven: Leuven University Press, 1996), 93–133.

20. Le Fèvre fils, *De futilitate poetices,* 62.

21. Ibid., 62–63.

22. Cicero, *Orator* 20.67. Quoted by Le Fèvre fils, *De futilitate poetices,* 63.

23. Le Fèvre fils, *De futilitate poetices,* 63–64.

24. See Pausanias, *Description of Greece* 9.27.6.

25. Le Fèvre fils, *De futilitate poetices,* 67–68. The phrase "weakens the spirits and crushes all the nerves of masculine virtue" is inspired by Cicero, *Tusculan Disputations* 2.27.

26. See Gregory S. Johnston, *A Heinrich Schütz Reader: Letters and Documents in Translation* (Oxford: Oxford University Press, 2013), 260–261.

27. Friedrich Wilhelm Schütz, *Disputatio prior eaque historica de combustione librorum haereticorum* (Leipzig, 1696); F. W. Schütz and Johann Christoph Schwedler, *Disputatio posterior eaque moralis de combustione librorum haereticorum* (Leipzig, 1697).

28. Schütz and Schwedler, *Disputatio posterior*, sec. 3. Quote from Seneca, *De tranquillitate animi* 11.8.

29. Giglio Gregorio Giraldi, *De historia poetarum tam Graecorum quam Latinorum ialogi decem* (1545), in *Opera* (Leiden, 1696), vol. 2, col. 31f. Quoted as the epigraph of F. W. Schütz, *Exercitatio adversus Tanaquilli Fabri librum de futilitate poetics* (Leipzig, 1698), unpaginated.

30. Schütz, *Exercitatio,* introduction. I have kept the author's italics, which generally identify quotes, including those from Le Fèvre fils, *De futilitate poetices,* preface.

31. Schütz, *Exercitatio,* introduction.

32. Ibid., corollaries (last page).

33. Ibid., chap. 13.

34. Ibid., chap. 15. The image of the poet touching the stars with his forehead is taken from Horace, *Odes* 1.1.5.36.

35. Paul Valéry, "Propos sur la poésie" (1927), in *Oeuvres,* ed. Jean Hytier, Bibliothèque de la Pléiade (Paris: Gallimard, 1957), 1:1373–1374; "Poésie et pensée abstraite" (1939), ibid., 1331–1333.

36. The recommendation is explicit in the marginal commentary by Marie de Gournay in her edition of the *Essais,* which was the one used by F. W. Schütz: "Fables of Ovid's *Metamorphosis,* highly recommended in childhood" (Michel de Montaigne, *Essais* [Paris, 1652], 113). Schütz refers to it, without an explicit citation, in a marginal bibliographic note in chap. 15 of his *Exercitatio.* See Michel de Montaigne, *Essais,* ed. Jean Balsamo, Michel Magnien, and Catherine Magnien-Simonin, Bibliothèque de la Pléiade (Paris: Gallimard, 2008), 182 (book 1, chap. 25 ["De l'institution des enfants"]).

37. See Schütz, *Disputatio prior,* dedication to his father (Christoph Georg Schütz); *Exercitatio,* dedication to the town councilors of Leipzig (his father having died in the meantime, in 1696).

38. In 1761, the Abbé Simon-Augustin Irail somewhat underestimated the fame of *De futilitate poetices,* but thoroughly recognized its dangerousness (*Querelles littéraires ou mémoires pour servir à l'histoire des révolutions de la république des lettres, depuis Homère jusqu'à nos jours* [Paris: Durand, 1761], 2:234–235): "Among

the greatest enemies of poetry, one must include a brother of Madame Dacier, a scholar like her, though less famous, with a mind stubbornly dedicated to reform. He wanted to extend it to literature, as well as religion. After having abjured the Calvinism to which his father had remained devoted out of philosophical indifference and excessive religious tolerance, he displayed rigorous and singular ideas. He found poetry scandalous, applied himself to decrying it, and produced a book in which he deemed it not only useless, but very dangerous. The book is in Latin; it at least had the advantage of being little known."

39. Louis Racine, *Réflexions sur la poésie* (1747), in *Oeuvres,* vol. 2 (Paris: Le Normant, 1808), 141, 144.

40. Ibid., 140–141. The quote, which is not completely accurate, is taken from Jacques-Bénigne Bossuet, *Traité de la concupiscence* (posthumous), chap. 18, in *Oeuvres,* ed. Jules Simon (Paris: Charpentier, 1843), 327.

41. Plato, *Ion* 534b.

42. Racine, *Réflexions sur la poésie,* 138.

43. See Pamela Hunt Steinle, *In Cold Fear: "The Catcher in the Rye," Censorship Controversies, and Postwar American Character* (Columbus: Ohio State University Press, 2000).

44. See Gregg Camfield, *The Oxford Companion to Mark Twain* (New York: Oxford University Press, 2003), 76.

45. See, for example, John H. Wallace, *"Huckleberry Finn* Is Offensive," *Washington Post,* April 11, 1982; David L. Smith, "Huck, Jim, and American Racial Discourse," *Mark Twain Journal* 22 (fall 1984): 4–12. Both articles have been collected in Stuart Hutchinson, ed., *Mark Twain: Critical Assessments,* 4 vols. (Mountfield, UK: Helm Information, 1993), 3:399–416.

46. Mark Twain, *Adventures of Tom Sawyer and Huckleberry Finn,* ed. Alan Gribben (Montgomery, AL: NewSouth Books, 2011).

47. See Michael E. Miller, "Columbia Students Claim Greek Mythology Needs a Trigger Warning," *Washington Post,* May 14, 2015.

48. Ralph Waldo Emerson, "The American Scholar" (1837).

49. Jean-Jacques Rousseau, *Émile ou de l'éducation* (1762), in *Oeuvres complètes,* vol. 4, ed. Bernard Gagnebin and Marcel Raymond, Bibliothèque de la Pléiade (Paris: Gallimard, 1969), 353. English translation by Allan Bloom, *Emile: Or, On Education* (New York, Basic Books, 1979), 113. This is the translation used throughout the chapter, with occasional revisions.

50. Rousseau, *Émile,* trans. Bloom, 114.

51. Ibid.

52. Ibid.

53. Ibid., 115.

54. Ibid., 115–116.

55. Ibid., 184.

56. Ibid., 168.

57. Denis Diderot, *Réfutation suivie de l'ouvrage d'Helvétius intitulé "L'Homme,"* in *Oeuvres complètes,* vol. 2, ed. J. Assézat and M. Tourneux (Paris: Garnier, 1875–1877), 285; quoted by François Bouchardy in Rousseau, *Oeuvres complètes,* 4:xxix.

58. See above in this chapter. From the beginning of the eighteenth century, numerous criticisms were made in Europe regarding the harmful effects of progress: see Alexander Wenger, *La Fibre littéraire, le discours médical sur la lecture au XVIIIᵉ siècle* (Geneva: Droz, 2007), 207.

59. Jean-Jacques Rousseau, *Discours sur les sciences et les arts* (1750), in *Oeuvres complètes,* 4:10. English translation by G. D. H. Cole, *A Discourse on the Arts and Sciences,* in *The Social Contract & Discourses* (London: J. M. Dent & Sons, 1920), 134. This is the translation used throughout the chapter, with occasional revisions.

60. Rousseau, *A Discourse on the Arts and Sciences,* trans. G. D. H. Cole, 135.

61. Ibid., 147.

62. Ibid., 152.

63. Rousseau, *Dernière réponse* (1752), in *Oeuvres complètes,* 4:95. English translation by Victor Gourevitch, *Last Reply,* in *The Discourses and Other Early Political Writings* (Cambridge, UK: Cambridge University Press, 1997), 84. This is the translation used throughout the chapter, with occasional revisions.

64. Rousseau, *Discourse on the Arts and Sciences,* 145.

65. Ibid., 151.

66. Rousseau, *Last Reply.*

67. See William Marx, *L'Adieu à la littérature: histoire d'une dévalorisation (XVIIIᵉ–XXᵉ siècles)* (Paris: Éditions de Minuit, 2005), 60–80.

68. See Jean-Jacques Rousseau, letter to Voltaire, September 10, 1755.

69. Pacifico Burlamacchi (Pseudo-Burlamacchi), *La vita del Beato Ieronimo Savonarola,* ed. Piero Ginori Conti (Florence: Olschki, 1937), 131; quoted by Franco Cordero, *Savonarola,* vol. 3: *Demiurgo senza politica (1496–1497)* (Rome: Laterza, 1987), 506. On the events of February 7, 1497, see Cordero, 504–507.

70. See also the First Trial.

71. Ermolao Barbaro the Elder, *Orationes contra poetas,* ed. Giorgio Ronconi, (Florence: Sansoni, 1972), 1, sec. 103, 104.

72. Ibid., 1, sec. 23, 87. According to Ovid's *Metamorphoses* (10.78–85), Orpheus converted to the love of boys after the death of Eurydice, either out of bitterness or in order not to betray her with another woman. This myth was much commented upon in the Middle Ages. In 1494, Dürer published an engraving after Mantegna representing the death of Orpheus under the blows of the maenads, with the inscription: "Orpheus, the first pederast" (*Orpheuß der Erst Puseran*).

73. See the First Trial.

74. To this already long though incomplete list, one could add the Spanish humanist Juan Luis Vives (1492–1540), whose influential pedagogical treatise *De disciplinis* (1531), which uses Plato as a constant reference, critiques the immorality of poetry and the poets and suggests reducing their importance in education. See Juan Luis Vives, *De disciplinis / Savoir et enseigner,* ed. Tristan Vigliano (Paris: Belles Lettres, 2013). English edition: Juan Luis Vives, *On Education,* trans. Foster Watson (Cambridge, UK: Cambridge University Press, 2014).

75. Plato, *The Republic* 2.377e–378e.

76. Ibid. 2.378d–e.

77. Ibid. 3.387b–389a, 389e–392a.

78. Ibid. 3.386a–387c.

79. Ibid. 3.401b.

80. Ibid. 3.387b.

81. Ibid. 10.604e.

82. Ibid. 10.605b–c.

83. Ibid. 10.606d.

84. Ibid. 10.607a.

85. See Andrew Ford, *The Origins of Criticism: Literary Culture and Poetic Theory in Classical Greece* (Princeton, NJ: Princeton University Press, 2002), 225–226.

86. Plato, *The Republic* 3.392b.

87. See Aristotle, *Poetics* 13.1452b27–1453a22. On this question, see William Marx, *Le Tombeau d'Oedipe. Pour une tragédie sans tragique* (Paris: Éditions de Minuit, 2012), 99.

88. As discussed earlier in this chapter.

89. Aristotle, *Poetics* 6.1449b.24–28.

90. For more information on tragic catharsis according to Aristotle, see chap. 3 of Marx, *Le Tombeau d'Oedipe*, 87–122, which is entirely devoted to it.

91. Aristotle, *Rhetoric* 3.4.1406b.24, 32–35.

92. Plato, *The Republic* 10.601b. The reader will recognize Isocrates's argument (see the First Trial).

93. The phrase, which has become proverbial, was inspired by the *Nicomachean Ethics* 1.4.1096a.13.

94. See Wenger, *La Fibre littéraire*.

95. Immanuel Kant, *Anthropologie in pragmatischer Hinsicht* (1798), sec. 31. Translation by Robert B. Louden in *Anthropology from a Pragmatic Point of View* (Cambridge, UK: Cambridge University Press, 2006), 78.

96. Ibid., sec. 44 (p. 102 in English edition).

97. See William Marx, *Vie du lettré* (Paris: Éditions de Minuit, 2009), 96–98.

98. Ibid., 23–26.

99. Celsus, *On Medicine* preamble 6. This quotation and those below are taken from an inspiring article by Heinrich von Staden: "The Dangers of Literature and the Need for Literacy: A. Cornelius Celsus on Reading and Writing," in Alfrieda and Jackie Pigeaud, eds., *Les Textes médicaux latins comme littérature* (Nantes: Université de Nantes, 2000), 355–368.

100. Celsus, *On Medicine* 1.2.1.

101. Ibid. preamble 1–5.

102. Ibid. preamble 5.

103. Ibid. 1.7, 1.8.1, 3.18.11, 4.10.1, and esp. 4.13.3. See von Staden, "The Dangers of Literature," 359–361.

Fourth Trial: Society

1. Alexis de Tocqueville, *De la démocratie en Amérique (1835–1840)*, book 2, part 1, chap. 9 ("Comment l'exemple des Américains ne prouve point qu'un peuple démocratique ne saurait avoir de l'aptitude et du goût pour les sciences, la littérature, et les arts"), in *Oeuvres*, Bibliothèque de la Pléiade (Paris: Gallimard, 1992), 2:545–550. Translated as "How the Example of the Americans Does Not Prove That a Democratic People Can Have No Aptitude and Taste for the Sciences, Literature, and the Arts," in *Democracy in America*, trans. and ed. Harvey C. Mansfield and Delba Winthrop (Chicago: University of Chicago Press, 2000).

2. Nicolas Sarkozy, statement to members of the UMP party, Lyon, February 23, 2006, available online at http://discours.vie-publique.fr. On the controversy sparked by this statement and those that followed, see Clarisse Fabre, "Et Nicolas Sarkozy fit la fortune du roman de Mme de La Fayette," *Le Monde,* March 29, 2011; François-Ronan Dubois, "Lire et interpréter *La Princesse de Clèves* dans la France des cités," October 30, 2013, http://contagions.hypotheses.org/469; and the website of the Société internationale pour l'étude des femmes de l'Ancien Régime, http://www.siefar.org/debats.

3. Nicolas Sarkozy, statement to the new members of the UMP, Paris, June 10, 2006, http://discours.vie-publique.fr.

4. Nicolas Sarkozy, statement on the modernization of public policy and reform of the state, Paris, April 4, 2008, http://discours.vie-publique.fr.

5. Nicolas Sarkozy, statement on youth and popular education, Batz-sur-Mer, July 24, 2008, http://www.dailymotion.com/video/x68n3c_nicolas-sarkozy-sen -prend-a-la-prin_news.

6. André Santini, interview with Christophe Barbier on LCI, November 20, 2007, http://discours.vie-publique.fr.

7. André Santini, interview with C. Barbier on LCI, February 19, 2008, http:// discours.vie-publique.fr.

8. André Santini, interview on Radio Classique, June 5, 2008, http://discours .vie-publique.fr.

9. André Santini, interview on LCI, June 10, 2008, http://discours.vie-publique.fr.

10. Corinne Desforges and Jean-Guy de Chalvron, *Rapport de la mission préparatoire au réexamen général du contenu des concours d'accès à la fonction publique de l'État,* Ministère du budget, des comptes publics et de la fonction publique; Secrétariat d'État à la fonction publique; Inspection générale de l'administration, February 2008, 2. In this report, relatively cursory both in content and in form, the question of the pertinence of tests of literary knowledge was only mentioned once, without further comment, on page 17: "Must the administration validate knowledge in history or literature to recruit a reliable civil servant?" Since it does not entirely anticipate the answer, the interrogative form seems to indicate that the authors did not wholeheartedly agree with the opinions forcefully voiced by the president of the republic and the secretary of state in charge of their report. This did not matter much to the secretary of state in question, who constantly cited the report to back up his statements about *The Princesse de Clèves.*

11. I was honored to have participated in one of the media discussions with Charles Dantzig, on France Inter, at the invitation of Guillaume Erner, on June 29, 2009. A public reading was held for an entire day on February 16, 2009, on the Place du Panthéon, in Paris. Among published books, the most memorable was probably the volume by Yves Citton, *Lire, interpréter, actualiser: pourquoi les études littéraires?* preface by François Cusset (Paris: Éditions Amsterdam, 2007), and the most recent is Bruno Clément and Laurence Plazenet, eds., *La Princesse de Clèves: anatomie d'une fascination* (Paris: Gallimard, 2015). For the film adaptation, see *La Belle personne* (2008), by Christophe Honoré. For an edition of the complete works, see *Oeuvres complètes*, ed. Camille Esmein-Sarrazin, Bibliothèque de la Pléiade (Paris: Gallimard, 2014).

12. Ernst Robert Curtius, *The Civilization of France*, trans. Olive Wyon (1932; New York: Vintage Books, 1962), 91. French translation cited by Michel Winock on his blog, December 21, 2009, http://histoire.typepad.fr/france_identite_nationale /2009/12/littérature-encore.html. See also Priscilla Parkhurst Ferguson, *Literary France: The Making of a Culture* (Berkeley: University of California Press, 1987); Pascale Casanova, *La République mondiale des lettres*, Points (1999; Paris: Seuil, 2008), xv; Alain Finkielkraut, "La France doit demeurer une nation littéraire," *Libération*, January 28, 2011.

13. Jean-Marie Rouart, "La Face cachée de Nicolas Sarkozy," *Paris Match* no. 3399, July 10, 2014.

14. Geneviève Fioraso, quoted by Véronique Soulé, "Réforme du supérieur: le projet fade déjà," *Libération*, March 20, 2013.

15. Antoine Compagnon, "Un amour de Madame Fioraso," *Libération*, April 3, 2013.

16. See Casanova, *La République mondiale des lettres*.

17. J. M. G. Le Clézio in 2008 and Patrick Modiano in 2014.

18. Along the same general lines, one could mention the blunder made by the minister of culture (Fleur Pellerin), who, on October 26, 2014, proved unable to name a single title by the recent French Nobel Prize–winner Patrick Modiano and disingenuously confessed that for the previous two years she had no longer had time to read. Let's not be naïve: many political leaders do not read, for lack of time or interest; one has to give the minister credit for her honesty. Nevertheless, when one is responsible for the Ministry of Culture, such an admission, expressed plainly and without false shame, functions as a denial of literature's role in France—or else as an ultimate sign of caution, for the simulation of literary knowledge can turn into a fiasco: one is reminded of the politician

(Frédéric Lefebvre) who on April 2, 2011, sought to present *Zadig* as his favorite book, but confused Voltaire's novel with the well-known ready-to-wear brand Zadig & Voltaire.

19. See William Marx, *L'Adieu à la littérature: histoire d'une dévalorisation (XVIIIᵉ–XXᵉ siècles)* (Paris: Éditions de Minuit, 2005).

20. Émile Zola, "Mes souvenirs sur Gustave Flaubert," *Le Figaro. Supplément littéraire du dimanche*, December 11, 1880, 199.

21. Émile Zola, *Le Roman expérimental* (Paris: Charpentier, 1881), 358–359. Translated by Belle M. Sherman, *The Experimental Novel and Other Essays* (New York: Cassell Publishing Co., 1893), 359–360.

22. Joachim Du Bellay, *Les Regrets* (1558), 11. Translated by David R. Slavitt, *The Regrets* (Evanston, IL: Northwestern University Press, 2004), 37–38. See also sonnets 149 ("Vous dites, courtisans . . ."), 153 ("On donne les degrés . . ."), and 154 ("Si tu m'en crois, Baïf . . .").

23. Simon-Augustin Irail, *Querelles littéraires ou mémoires pour servir à l'histoire des révolutions de la république des lettres, depuis Homère jusqu'à nos jours* (Paris: Durand, 1761), 2:236. The anecdote that follows is taken, nearly verbatim but in a somewhat condensed form, from the same passage. It concerns the philosopher and philologist Johann Georg Wachter (1673–1757), whom, significantly, Irail presents as a poet; Wachter wrote Latin mottos for the king. The source of the anecdote, which Irail repeats nearly word for word, is the conversations of Frederick II with his secretary Henri de Catt (posthumous ed., *Unterhaltungen mit Friedrich dem Großen* [Leipzig, 1884], quoted by Winfried Schröder, *Spinoza in der deutschen Frühaufklärung* [Würzburg: Königshausen & Neumann, 1987], 67). On Wachter's mottos, including the famous *Sapere aude* ("Dare to know!"), borrowed from Horace (*Epistles* 1.2.40), which had such a large influence on the German Enlightenment, see the remarkable book by Martin Mulsow, *Prekäres Wissen: eine andere Ideengeschichte der Frühen Neuzeit* (Berlin: Suhrkamp, 2012), 224–229. All my thanks to Denis Thouard and Martin Mulsow for their help in this research.

24. Louis-Antoine Fauvelet de Bourrienne, *Mémoires sur Napoléon, le Directoire, le Consulat, l'Empire et la Restauration* (Paris: Ladvocat, 1829), 5:93–94.

25. See note 18, above.

26. De Bourrienne, *Mémoires sur Napoléon*, 97.

27. Juste Lipse, *Epistolarum selectarum chilias* (Avignon, 1609), 4:letter 81 (to Janus Lernutius), 920.

28. Joseph-Juste Scaliger, *Scaligeriana, sive excerpta ex ore Josephi Scaligeri* (The Hague: Vlacq, 1666), 313.

29. François de La Mothe Le Vayer, *Doute sceptique si l'étude des belles-lettres est préférable à toute autre occupation* (1667), in *Oeuvres* (Dresden: Groell, 1757), vol. 5, part 2: 352–353.

30. Ibid., 354. The Greeks credited the hero Palamedes with the invention of eleven additional letters of the alphabet; La Mothe Le Mayer is playing on the meaning of the word *letters*. The Latin comic Terence was known for using very pure language.

31. Ibid., 354–355.

32. Michel de Montaigne, *Essais,* ed. Jean Balsamo, Michel Magnien, and Catherine Magnien-Simonin, Bibliothèque de la Pléiade (Paris: Gallimard, 2008), 182 (book 1, chap. 25). My italics. English translation by Donald M. Frame, in *The Complete Works of Montaigne* (Stanford, CA: Stanford University Press, 1958), 131.

33. Montaigne, *Essais,* book 1, chaps. 25, 26, 31, and 55; book 2, chaps. 10 and 17; book 3, chaps. 2, 5, 8, and 9 ("scribbling").

34. See Jean-Marc Chatelain, *La Bibliothèque de l'honnête homme: livres, lecture, et collections en France à l'âge classique* (Paris: Bibliothèque Nationale de France, 2003).

35. Salomon de La Broue, *Le Cavalerice français,* 4th ed. (Paris: Du Mesnil, 1646), preface, 2.

36. Charles Sorel, *Le Berger extravagant, où parmi des fantaisies amoureuses on voit les impertinences des romans et de [la] poésie* (Paris: Du Bray, 1627), 491–492. *L'Anti-roman, ou l'histoire du Berger Lysis* was published in 1633.

37. Francesco Berni, *Dialogo contra i poeti* (Rome: 1526), 21, 12.

38. Ibid., 20. Piovano Arlotto, also known as Arlotto Mainardi, was a famous comedic preacher in the fifteenth century.

39. Ibid.

40. See Vito Avarello, "L'invective dans les *Rime* 'bernesche': poétique du *dileggio* et rhétorique du défi chez Francesco Berni," in Agnès Morini, ed., *L'Invective: histoire, formes, stratégie* (Saint-Étienne: Publications de l'université de Saint-Étienne, 2006), 91–112.

41. See the Third Trial.

42. In the sixteenth and seventeenth centuries, the paradoxical criticism of literature became practically a commonplace of rhetoric. One of the most successful examples can be found in the second letter of the *Philological correspondence*

(*Cartas filológicas,* 1634) by Francisco Cascales, entitled: "Against letters and all the arts and sciences. Jeu d'esprit" (Juan García Soriano, ed. [Madrid: Ediciones de "La Lectura," 1930], 1:81–96).

43. Richard Hoggart, *The Uses of Literacy: Aspects of Working-Class Life, with Special Reference to Publications and Entertainments* (London: Chatto and Windus, 1957).

44. Raymond Williams, *Culture and Society (1780–1950)* (London: Chatto and Windus, 1958).

45. See, most notably, Harold Bloom, *The Western Canon: The Books and School of the Ages* (London: Macmillan, 1995), 519, as well as Marx, *L'Adieu à la littérature,* 169–171.

46. Many of their works dealt with literature and teaching literature: see, for example, Richard Hoggart, *Teaching Literature* (London: National Institute of Adult Education, 1963) and Raymond Williams, *Reading and Criticism* (London: Frederick Muller, 1950).

47. Williams, *Culture and Society,* 321.

48. See the Second Trial.

49. See Marx, *L'Adieu à la littérature.*

50. Jean-Claude Passeron, "Présentation," in Richard Hoggart, *La Culture du pauvre: étude sur le style de vie des classes populaires en Angleterre,* trans. Françoise and Jean-Claude Garcias and Jean-Claude Passeron (Paris: Éditions de Minuit, 1970), 7.

51. Pierre Bourdieu and Jean-Claude Passeron, *La Reproduction: éléments pour une théorie du système d'enseignement* (Paris: Éditions de Minuit, 1970), 143. Translation by Richard Nice, *Reproduction in Education, Society, and Culture* (London: Sage Publications, 1990), 115. This is the translation used throughout the chapter.

52. Bourdieu and Passeron, *Reproduction in Education, Society, and Culture,* 127–128.

53. Ibid., 123, 124.

54. See Pierre Bourdieu, *La Distinction: critique sociale du jugement* (Paris: Éditions de Minuit, 1979). English edition: *Distinction: A Social Critique of the Judgement of Taste,* trans. Richard Nice (London: Routledge, 1984).

55. Pierre Bourdieu, *Ce que parler veut dire: l'économie des échanges linguistiques* (Paris: Fayard, 1982), 47. English translation by Gino Raymond and Matthew Adamson, "The Production and Reproduction of Legitimate Language," in

Language and Symbolic Power, ed. John B. Thompson (Cambridge, MA: Harvard University Press, 1991), 58.

56. See William Marx, *Le Tombeau d'Oedipe. Pour une tragédie sans tragique* (Paris: Éditions de Minuit, 2012), 115–122.

57. Pierre Bourdieu, *Méditations pascaliennes* (Paris: Seuil, 1997), 92, 126–127. English edition: *Pascalian Meditations,* trans. Richard Nice (Stanford, CA: Stanford University Press, 2000).

58. One only has to see how, in his long book on Flaubert, Bourdieu deals with the question of style in a single page, as if it were a mere obligation, and despite the fact that to the novelist it was absolutely central (*Les règles de l'art: genèse et structure du champ littéraire* [Paris: Seuil, 1992], 58–59).

59. See Pierre Bourdieu and Jean-Claude Passeron, *Les Héritiers: les étudiants et la culture* (Paris: Éditions de Minuit, 1964), 114. English edition: *The Inheritors: French Students and their Relation to Culture,* trans. Richard Nice (Chicago: University of Chicago Press, 1980).

60. Plato, *The Republic* 3.392c–398b.

61. Ibid. 10.600c–e.

Conclusion

1. See Georges Didi-Huberman, *L'image survivante: histoire de l'art et temps des fantômes selon Aby Warburg* (Paris: Éditions de Minuit, 2002). It is important not to give up on periodizations, however partial and fragmentary. By allowing one to avoid the constraints of strict chronological succession, these at least have a heuristic value. Michel Chion discussed this in his lecture, "'En dépit des angles morts': pour une chronologie périodisée du cinéma de fiction comme forme audio-logo-visuelle," Wissenschaftskolleg zu Berlin, March 17, 2015.

2. See Hans Ulrich Gumbrecht, "Beginn von 'Literatur' / Abschied vom Körper?" in Gisela Smolka-Koerdt, Peter M. Spangenberg, and Dagmar Rillmann-Bartylla, eds., *Der Ursprung von Literatur: Medien, Rollen, Kommunikationssituationen zwischen 1450 und 1650* (Munich: Wilhelm Fink, 1988), 15–50; Rainer Rosenberg, "Eine verworrene Geschichte: Vorüberlegungen zu einer Biographie der Literaturbegriffs," *Zeitschrift für Literaturwissenschaft und Linguistik,* no. 77 (1990): 36–65.

3. See Antoine Compagnon, *La littérature pour quoi faire?* (Paris: Collège de France / Fayard, 2007), 76–77.

4. Aristotle, *Poetics* 1447b.8–19, 1451b.1–3.

5. See William Marx, *Naissance de la critique moderne: la littérature selon Eliot et Valéry (1889–1945)* (Arras: Artois Presses Université, 2002); Marx, "Brève histoire de la forme en littérature," *Les Temps modernes* no. 676 (November–December 2013): 35–47.

6. See Christian Jouhaud, *Les Pouvoirs de la littérature: histoire d'un paradoxe* (Paris: Gallimard, 2000), 367–373.

Acknowledgments

THE WRITING OF THIS BOOK greatly benefited from my residency as a fellow of the Wissenschaftskolleg zu Berlin in 2014–2015.

I would like to thank the entire staff of the Wissenschaftskolleg, particularly the library staff and the other fellows, as well as the rector, Luca Giuliani, and Thomas Pavel, without whom my stay would not have been possible.

I would like to warmly thank all those who have contributed their knowledge to the writing of this book: in particular, Claude Calame, Michel Chion, Antoine Compagnon, Florence Dupont, François Lavocat, Hugues Marchal, Jean-Charles Monferran, Martin Mulsow, Antoine Pietrobelli, Anne-Elisabeth Spica, Malika Temmar, and Denis Thouard; and also, as ever, Gilles Philippe.

This American edition of *The Hatred of Literature,* published by Harvard University Press, would not have seen the light of day without the support and trust of my editor, John Kulka, who undoubtedly does not hate literature, nor without the meticulous copyediting of Louise Robbins. But this book would certainly not be what it is without its admirable translator, Nicholas Elliott, in whom I have had the rare luck of finding something like the American doppelgänger of my French writing self.

Index